The Leader's Guide to Standards

Douglas B. Reeves

The Leader's Guide to Standards

A Blueprint for
Educational Equity and Excellence

JOSSEY-BASS
A Wiley Imprint
www.josseybass.com

Published by Jossey-Bass
A Wiley Imprint
989 Market Street, San Francisco, CA 94103-1741   www.josseybass.com

Jossey-Bass books and products are available through most bookstores. To contact Jossey-Bass directly call our Customer Care Department within the U.S. at 800-956-7739, outside the U.S. at 317-572-3986 or fax 317-572-4002.

Jossey-Bass also publishes its books in a variety of electronic formats. Some content that appears in print may not be available in electronic books.

Library of Congress Cataloging-in-Publication Data

Reeves, Douglas B., 1953–
  The leader's guide to standards : a blueprint for educational equity and excellence / Douglas B. Reeves. — 1st ed.
     p.   cm. — (The Jossey-Bass education series)
Includes bibliographical references and index.
  ISBN 0–7879–6402–6 (alk. paper)
     1. Education — Standards — United States. 2. Educational leadership — United States. I. Title. II. Series.
  LB3060.83 .R45   2002
  379.1'58'0973—dc21   2002011846

Printed in the United States of America
FIRST EDITION
HB Printing   10 9 8 7 6 5 4 3 2 1

To Andrew Reeves, whose vision and generosity has helped children
in his neighborhood and around the world

Contents

List of Tables, Figures, and Exhibits

Preface
Why Standards?

With passage of the most sweeping federal education legislation in thirty years, academic standards are now a part of every public school in the nation. Over the past decade, an increasing number of private schools in the United States and throughout the world have transformed their approach to assessing student performance from the tradition of comparing students to one another to comparing students to academic standards. Nevertheless, my travels of more than a million miles in the past several years to schools, faculty meetings, parent gatherings, administrator conferences, school board meetings, and academic seminars makes one conclusion abundantly clear: standards are not implemented with legislation or resolutions. The ultimate success of academic standards depends on effective educational leaders who grasp the difference between a fad and a value. This book is based on the value of fairness. Fads come and go, but values endure. Standards do endure not through legislative mandates or administrative cheerleading, but because they are the fairest way to assess student performance.

The case for standards is not obvious. There is an active and virulent antistandards movement, and to be sure there have been plenty of missteps in the first decade of state and local academic standards. Some standards have been excessively vague, others hyperspecific (Marzano, Kendall, and Cicchinelli, 1998). Almost all of the state standards documents are too long, requiring more time than is available in the school calendar. Moreover, for many teachers, parents, and students, standards have become inextricably linked to standardized tests. If they dislike the latter, they blame the former (Kohn, 1999). Thus it is relatively easy to become dissatisfied with standards if we accept the superficial notion that we can eliminate what we dislike without considering what fills the void.

Every educational leader must consider this question: If we do not use standards as the way of evaluating student performance, what is the alternative? There are two choices: we can compare the quality of student work either to an objective standard or to the work of other students. In the absence of standards, there is only the second choice. The most obvious manifestation of the comparison of students to one another is the bell curve and, more appropriately, the normal distribution. The reference point is typically the average of student performance. Indeed, many report cards today continue to refer to a grade of C as average. There are two problems with using the bell curve or any other evaluation system that compares student performance to the average: it is inaccurate, and it is unfair.

Comparison evaluation systems are inaccurate because they purport to tell students, parents, future employers, and the community that a student is proficient, when the only truthful statement that can be made is that the student is similar to other students or not. Saying a student is an "average writer" does not tell us if the student writes well. Saying a student is an "above average mathematician" does not allow us to know if the student is capable of more advanced work. Comparable evaluation is unfair because it denies opportunity to a student who has earned it. If a student has met every requirement for academic proficiency but is nevertheless "below average" because other students have performed at a higher level, it is unfair to deny the student an opportunity associated with academic proficiency.

Using academic standards eliminates the fiction of claiming that the student who has performed better than 51 percent of her colleagues is successful while the student who has performed better than 49 percent of her colleagues is unsuccessful. When we use standards rather than comparisons, it is possible that both of those students are proficient, or that neither is. We will not lie to students and tell them that they are proficient merely because they beat other students. We will not remove opportunities from students merely because other students have higher scores. The point of assessing student performance is accurate assessment of proficiency, not meaningless comparison and competition.

Leaders cannot eliminate opposition to standards, but they can change the focus of the discussion. If the case for standards rests on a foundation of a legal mandate, then the leader mutters with resignation, "It's the law, so like it or not, we have to do it." If, however, the case for standards rests on a foundation of the fundamental value of fairness, then the professional conversation surrounding standards can be far more productive. We can acknowledge the flaws in standards without sacrificing the value of fairness. We can accept legitimate criticism of standardized tests without abandoning commitment to the values inherent in standards. We can, in sum, agree to disagree about the evolving means of implementing standards while we share a bond created by our common values.

At the end of a very long and frustrating day, even the best educational leader may question his role in the profession. During these inevitable challenges, he does not seek renewal through just the right policy, the perfect technique, the latest nostrum, or contemporary prescription. Accolades from colleagues or popularity with subordinates is not enough to sustain us in the rough times. Even improved student results do not offer the resilience that we need in those darkest moments of self-doubt. Rather, the perseverance, resilience, and renewal that every leader needs results from our understanding of our values. The leader who implements academic standards can say, "I helped to make this school a place of fairness, mutual respect, and unlimited opportunities for success." May that confidence sustain you the reader in your challenging days as an educational leader.

Although this book can be used a text by reading its chapters in sequential order, the practitioner who already has extensive familiarity with the case for academic standards may find it useful to focus on Part Three, Leadership Roles for Educational Standards. Here you will find details on applying data to decision making, leadership issues surrounding standards-based assessment, alternative models of educational accountability, and ideas for developing the next generation of educational leaders.

There is a natural temptation on the part of the leader to dispense with the preliminaries and take action. However, please consider a more patient approach, with reason preceding action. With millions of new educators and school leaders entering our profession in the next several years, many of whom were nurtured on the bell curve, the case for academic standards is not obvious. Before you leap into implementation plans, take time to lay the groundwork carefully, explaining *why* before you list the steps for *what* and *how*. At the end of the day, it is not a list of procedures that creates effective standards implementation, but rather the values and fundamental rationale for standards-based professional practice. This must be self-sustaining, not dependent upon daily administration and supervision but inculcated in the value system of every educator and leader.

Acknowledgments

Building managers sometimes label the floor above the twelfth level the "penthouse" to avoid dealing with superstitious aversion to the thirteenth floor. In completing my thirteenth book, I should first acknowledge all those who love black cats, regularly walk under ladders, step on cracks in the sidewalk, and otherwise are deliberately indifferent to superstition. We need more such people in positions of educational leadership, where the "fact-free" debate is sometimes more obvious than a rational dialogue based on evidence. I have been fortunate to be associated with rational and thoughtful people in producing this volume who offer encouragement and criticism, but never old husband's tales.

My colleagues at the Center for Performance Assessment are a continuing source of challenge and wisdom. In particular, our senior staff (including Larry Ainsworth, the "intellectual godfather") is one of the nation's most thoughtful advocates of connecting leadership theory to classroom practice. Our executive director, Anne Fenske, is a living model of leadership by example. Special thanks go to Michele LePatner, Nan Woodson, and Eileen Allison for thoughtful contributions to the leadership tools in the Appendix. My thanks also go to Chris Benavides, Audrey Blackwell, Nan Caldwell, Cheryl Dunkle, Tony Flach, Bette Frazier, Paul Kane, Jill Lewis, Janelle Miller, Stacy Scott, Devon Sheldon, Mike White, Katherine Woodson, and other colleagues at the center and with other organizations, who offer their careers as testimony to their single-minded commitment to the principle that leadership and learning are inextricably linked.

I have been fortunate to learn from some of the nation's best educational leaders and thinkers: William Burns, Lucy Calkins, Bill Habermehl, Jeff Howard, Larry Lezotte, Tom Lockamy, Vickie Markavitch, Robert Marzano, Betty McNally, Dennis Peterson, Millie Pierce, Mike Schmoker, Ray Simon, John Simpson, Don Thompson, Terry Thompson, Grant Wiggins, Paul Williams, Harry Wong, Chris Wright, Karen Young, and others in the forty-nine states and five continents where I have observed educational leaders in action.

This volume marks my first collaboration with Esmond Harmsworth, of the Zachary Shuster Harmsworth literary agency in Boston and New York. I owe to him another new association, that with Jossey-Bass, whose acquisition editor, Lesley Iura, played an instrumental role in shaping this book into two volumes, with this book focusing on standards for building and local educational leaders, and the next book focusing on the strategic leadership needs of district, state, and national leaders. Thanks to Lesley, you are not holding an unfocused five-hundred-page monster. Pamela Berkman's management of the project was superb. Tom Finnegan's editing was exceptional.

My thinking was inevitably shaped by a heritage of leaders and learners, among them a grandmother, Laura Anderson Johnson, who served as a school superintendent in the early days of the twentieth century; a father, Jean Brooks Reeves, who served as a combat leader in the Second World War and was surely as much a teacher then as he was in his last days as a professor; and a brother, U.S. Army General Stephen Reeves, whose career has included teaching and now, at a time of urgent need, a leadership role in the nation's chemical and biological warfare defense efforts. My other brother, Andrew, is a volunteer coach who shares his time and resources with children, who relish his thoughtful balance of enthusiasm and fair play.

Pioneers and everyday heroes in my genealogical backyard help give me a perspective with a simultaneous sense of humility and urgency. Our work can, at times, seem mundane compared to the exigencies of international affairs. Nevertheless, the decades ahead will require diligent students, committed educators, and extraordinary leaders. Only an educational system based on equity, shared values, and unremitting commitment to excellence will cause an intersection between the interests of educational leaders and the needs of our world.

My shortcomings are obvious enough, but if I ever need help articulating them, I need only listen more than talk during a family dinner. There James, Julia, Alex, and Shelley will conduct such an analysis, confident that I love them even more. Brooks, now at college, still makes time for long letters and extended conversation. His enthusiasm for learning, his resilience in the face of disappointment, and his relentless pursuit of his dreams make me eternally grateful I was a brief part of his journey to manhood.

Douglas B. Reeves
Swampscott, Massachusetts
August 2002

The Author

Douglas B. Reeves is the chairman and founder of the Center for Performance Assessment and one of the nation's leading authorities on academic standards, performance assessment, and accountability. He is the author of fifteen books, including *Making Standards Work* (3rd edition); *Accountability in Action; Reason to Write; 101 Questions and Answers About Standards, Assessment, and Accountability; 20-Minute Learning Connection; Holistic Accountability;* and *The Daily Disciplines of Leadership* (Jossey-Bass, 2002). He delivers more than eighty keynote addresses each year to education, business, and government groups throughout the world; his research and current activities can be accessed through the Center's Website (www.makingstandardswork.com). In addition to his work at the Center, Reeves is active in programs sponsored by the Harvard Graduate School of Education, including the Leadership and Policy Forum. He lives with his wife, Shelley Sackett, and four children in Swampscott, Massachusetts.

Books for Parents, Educators, and School Leaders by Douglas Reeves

101 Questions and Answers About Standards, Assessment, and Accountability (Denver: Advanced Learning Press, 2000)

20-Minute Learning Connection: A Practical Guide for Parents Who Want to Help Their Children Succeed in School (New York: Simon & Schuster, 2001)

Accountability in Action: A Blueprint for Learning Organizations (Denver: Advanced Learning Press, 2000)

Crusade in the Classroom: How George W. Bush's Education Reforms Will Affect Your Children, Our Schools (New York: Simon & Schuster, 2001)

The Daily Disciplines of Leadership (San Francisco: Jossey-Bass, 2002)

Holistic Accountability: Serving Students, Schools, and Community (Thousand Oaks, Calif.: Corwin, 2002)

Making Standards Work: How to Implement Standards-Based Performance Assessments in the Classroom, School, and District (3rd edition) (Denver: Advanced Learning Press, 2002)

Reason to Write: Help Your Child Succeed in School and in Life Through Deeper Thinking, Better Reasoning, and Clearer Communication (New York: Simon & Schuster, 2002)

The Reason to Write Student Workbook (New York: Simon & Schuster, 2002)

The Leader's Guide to Standards

Part One

The Standards Imperative

Chapter One

The Case for Standards

Leadership Keys

The case for standards is not obvious

Leaders must make the case for standards

Rejecting standards requires retreating to comparative evaluation

Standards are fair

Standards are effective

Every educational leader must make the case for standards. It is not obvious to your staff, students, and stakeholders. Although every public school in the nation has a curriculum that is theoretically governed by state academic content standards, the reality is considerably more complex. In most schools, a significant number of faculty members have heard of standards, but an equal or greater number regard standards as an administrative imperative rather than a reflection of the school's fundamental values and educational principles. In a growing number of schools, there is organized opposition to standards, with the aggravation teachers and students feel toward standardized tests directed toward the entire standards movement. As a result, the leaders must continuously make the case for standards, just as an effective leader in any organization never stops articulating the fundamental beliefs, values, and mission.

The Only Two Ways to Assess Human Performance

The key to understanding the case for standards is to recognize that there are fundamentally only two ways to assess human achievement, whether it is in the classroom, the executive suite, the performance stage, or the board room. Irrespective of the context, we can either compare the performance to other performances we have observed, or we can compare it to an objective standard.

In many realms of human endeavor, we make the former choice, comparing the time of one runner to another in the Olympic one-hundred-meter run. In that context, we award gold, bronze, and silver medals whether or not the gold medalist completed the event in a time that the judges thought was as fast as an appropriate Olympic standard. The fastest runner gets the gold and the runner who finishes even a thousandth of a second later is awarded the silver medal. We don't know if either runner meets a standard, because a consistent standard does not exist.

Records, as the athletes say, are made to be broken. On fields ranging from Olympic competition to the admissions office at Swarthmore, the decision system rests on the premise that there are only a very few winners, and the job of the judges is to separate—if even by a fraction of a second, grade point, or test score—the winners from the losers. This method of evaluation is so common that some people accept it as universal practice. The presumption deserves a challenge.

Consider other fields, such as licensing drivers, brain surgeons, and jet pilots, where merely beating competitors is scant assurance of safety for passengers or patients. If every pilot in a class of one hundred meets the standards for navigation, weather, and air traffic control, we do not object to calling all of them proficient. If none of those hundred pilots is proficient, we insist that the truth be told and nonproficient pilots not receive their wings. This system is fair to the public, and to the student pilots. We do not tell the public that someone is proficient merely because she is competitive; she must be a proficient pilot. We do not tell a prospective pilot that she is unsuccessful because another pilot had a higher score on the air traffic control test; both are proficient if they have achieved the standard.

Comparison of human performance to a standard is the only appropriate way to evaluate student achievement—and, I would argue, the performance of educators and leaders as well. If there is great risk to the public and to individuals should we make an error, then the standards-based approach is what we use. There is less risk to the public in recognizing a nonproficient Little League champion than a nonproficient pilot. There is less risk of unfairness to the individual who needs a wheelchair ramp at the office if we have objective standards that require ramps for everyone in a wheelchair. We do not rank all those in a wheelchair and offer ramps to some of them, but use a clear and consistent criterion whether there is one person or a dozen who meet it. Thus whether our perspective is protecting the rights of the public or protecting the rights of the individual, a standards-based approach is society's preferred method of operation.

The dichotomy between these two methods of assessing human performance is stark and mutually exclusive. Either we evaluate students compared to a clear objective standard or we compare them to one another; there is no third alternative. My article "If You Hate Standards, Learn to Love the Bell Curve," published in *Education Week* in the summer of 2001 (Reeves, 2001b), produced a torrent of letters to the editor that lasted for weeks. The vast majority of the letters were negative, and many of them were angry. Writers detested standards and, as a careful reading of their letters indicated, particularly hated the standards in their state; most of all they found fault with the tests associated with those standards.

Although the debate among letter writers continued throughout the summer, not a single one offered a third alternative for evaluating student performance. We do not have to like standards, but we must recognize that our alternatives are limited. Rejecting standards as the method for student evaluation leaves us with an evaluation system based on comparison of one student to another, a system that is inconsistent, unfair, and ineffective.

Are Standards Really New?

Although critics have attempted to label the educational standards movement a passing fad, standards are in fact about as old as Socrates. In the Lyceum, the issue was not merely whether Glaucon got the better of his opponents in an argument, but whether any argument met the teacher's challenges on the basis of logic and truth. At the dawn of the Enlightenment, scholars argued that the scientific method was a better way to test a hypothesis than a popularity contest among medieval superstitions. Galileo did not ask, "Is the theory a little bit better than the others?" but instead "Does the theory conform to observable facts?" In other words, use of educational standards is not a passing fad, or even a particularly new development.

Although critics have compared standards to "new math," "whole language," or any other reform that they disliked, applying clear and objective expectations for student performance is hardly a novel idea. As historian Diane Ravitch (2000) has extensively documented in her studies of more than a century of self-proclaimed educational reforms, there is little new under the sun. In particular, the assertion that the standards movement has directly resulted in extraordinary and unprecedented demands upon children is a claim unsupported by the evidence. An article titled "A Crime Against Children: The Scourge of Homework in Our Schools" was not a product of the antistandards movement of the twenty-first century, but a lead in the *Ladies Home Journal* at the dawn of the twentieth century. Indeed, there was probably a Cro-Magnon adolescent complaining about homework, a Neanderthal parent complaining about excessive testing, and a fresh-faced *Homo erectus* school administrator who despaired of the lack of time to accomplish all the demands in the school day. The leaders of our present era must not be taken in by superficial disparagement of the new or dismissive contempt for the old. The only qualities on which the matter of educational standards should be judged are fairness and effectiveness, and on that basis they stand the test of time.

Standards Are Fair

Standards: The Rules of a Fair Game

Fairness may at first seem to be an elusive concept. After all, one person's fair play may be another person's rigged game. We need not engage in an appeal to the esoteric in order to judge the issue. Most practitioners reading this book have performed playground duty and know how frequently the cry "That's not fair!" punctuates the minutes of recess. Children have an innate sense of what is fair and what is not, and we should heed their counsel. Fairness is best ensured when the rules of an activity are clear and precise. Listen to children explain a game and you hear the language of exact specification (you can go *here*, but you can't go *there*; you can do *this*, but you can't do *that*). Guesswork is not required. In those instances in which ambiguity replaces specificity, chaos reigns. If the rules of the game are made up as we go along, then defiant and angry charges of unfairness are certain to follow.

Some readers may be surprised at the use of a playground game to illustrate such an important principle. The choice is a deliberate one. When a leader makes the case for academic standards with parents and students, the mandates of state law and federal legislation are less important than a simple appeal to fairness. Moreover, parents and children tend to take games quite seriously (Reeves, 2001b). The context of the playground does not diminish the importance of the central concept of fairness; rather, it makes clear how pervasive a standards-based approach to life is, from the play of kindergartners to certification of pilots.

The Language of Fair Standards

For standards to meet the test of fairness, they must be consistent. Here some states fall far short of the mark, particularly when they use the vocabulary of standards to describe a comparative expectation. The requirement that "students will read a fourth grade level text, compare it to another text on a similar topic, and accurately recall details, similarities, and differences in the two texts" is a standard. The requirement that "students will score at or above the 51st percentile" is not a standard. The imprimatur of *standard* on the cover of a document containing such a statement does not transform a comparative statement such as a percentile rank into a standard. The language of comparison—with its percentiles, quartiles, stanines, and averages—inevitably implies a statement of student proficiency on the basis of standards. The leader should take scant comfort in a report that student achievement is "above average" when the essential question is whether the performance is proficient.

Adding Value to Standards. Just as in a game, clarity in articulating academic content standards is preferable to ambiguity. Unfortunately, the political process by which standards were established in many states rendered the documents full of equivocation, imprecise words, and a mysterious threshold for success. School leaders cannot fix any political process at the state level that is inherently ambiguous, but school leaders can add value to standards by taking the state documents and recreating them with greater precision, focus, and prioritization. In Chapter Four, we consider the concept of "power standards" and identify a process for school leaders who must add value to the standards they have been given.

Rather than going on the defensive over a flawed set of state standards, the school leader can honestly admit that every set of state standards and the tests accompanying them have some flaws. In some cases, there are too many standards; in others the standards are vague, or hyperspecific, or inappropriate. Because perfection is not an option in creating standards and because defense of inadequate standards looks silly, school leaders should not attempt to defend the indefensible but rather articulate a set of alternatives. We do not need to argue that standards represent educational perfection, but we must consider what we should do in response to imperfection. One alternative is to reject standards and return to a comparative method of student evaluation. With such a choice, we forfeit the fairness that a standards-based approach to education offers students and the public. The other alternative is to add value to standards with focus and prioritization, collaborating with educators and school leaders to get the most out of standards rather than retreating to an alternative that is unfair.

Fairness to the Public. The final issue to consider in this discussion of standards and fairness is our obligation to look beyond the boundaries of the classroom. Although there is clearly an obligation for a school to be fair to the individual student, standards represent the best way to provide feedback on student performance that is clear, consistent, and fair. The leader also has an obligation for fairness beyond the classroom. This includes fairness to teachers in future grades, administrators in future schools, and above all to the communities in which students live. If we say that a student "meets standards" in reading or mathematics, we have an obligation to say so with integrity. Our failure to be accurate in this statement leads to frustration on the part of students, parents, and future teachers and misallocation of resources thanks to rescheduling and course failures. Just as our students have the right to expect fair treatment in assessment of their work, so also our community of parents, employers, and educators in other schools have the right to expect accuracy in our description of student achievement.

A significant part of the continuing crisis in confidence in public education can be attributed to the difference between what educators say a student can do, as documented with report cards and diplomas, and what students can actually do, as observed at work and in the home. The choice is not whether to be fair and accurate in our assessment comparing students to a standard, but rather the timing of this assessment. We can find problems proactively, gently identifying needs and implementing interventions; or we can find problems passively, reacting only after a child has faced severe academic trauma.

Standards Are Effective

Research on Standards Implementation

Researchers from quite different educational, theoretical, and political perspectives have determined a common element to their findings: academic standards are effective. Documenting dramatic improvement in schools around the nation, Schmoker (2001) found that one consistent prerequisite for success was a focus on specific academic areas and identification with absolute clarity of what successful performance looks like. This is consistent with other authors who have studied schools containing students from a spectrum of demographic backgrounds (Haycock, 1998; Reeves, 2000a).

Although critics take issue with his choice of subjects and his term "cultural literacy," E. D. Hirsch, Jr., has made a significant contribution (1996) to the standards debate by reminding us of long-term observations in Europe in which schools with defined curriculum objectives significantly outperformed schools without them. In particular, he notes that the impact of clear curriculum definition affords not only educational excellence but also equity of opportunity. Economically deprived immigrant children, he reported, fared far better in schools in which expectations are absolutely clear and consistent from one school to the next. His findings are consistent with researchers on this side of the Atlantic.

There should be nothing surprising about research that indicates that when students and teachers focus more on an objective, they are more successful than when they do not. Nor should it be surprising that standards alone are a framework for focus, while a comparative system simply encourages teachers to try harder and beat the other schools.

Implementation: The Key to Effectiveness

Of course, the mere existence of a standards document achieves nothing. It is the diligence with which teachers and school leaders implement standards that is of greater importance. The Appendix includes several practical checklists for a leader to use in bridging the gap between the good intentions of standards and the actual results that occur only from a consistent and rigorous pattern of professional practice and leadership behavior.

One telling method of evaluating the extent to which a school has implemented academic standards is to evaluate student work. Ask several teachers of the same grade to bring an assignment in a particular subject that they regard as proficient. You are not asking for the best assignment nor one that is exceptional, but merely what most students should be achieving after instruction, hard work, feedback, and final performance. In the vast majority of cases in which I have conducted such a review, the results are astonishing. What one teacher regards as proficient is unacceptable by the standards of another teacher, while a third participant in the forum finds that quality of work beyond the ability of most students. When teachers are asked to explain their reasoning for regarding the work as proficient, the language of comparison dominates the discussion. "It's the best she could do," they explain. "He tried very hard, and this represents exceptional effort," they continue, not recognizing that as important as effort and perception of ability may be, they are far afield of the only question on the table: Is the work proficient when compared to an objective standard?

Measuring Effectiveness

In considering the effectiveness of your standards implementation effort, there are three essential considerations: student performance, teaching practice, and leadership behavior. The most important statistic in evaluating student performance is the percentage of students who are performing at the proficient level or higher. In exceptional cases, you might serve students of whom a large proportion are already meeting standards at the proficient level. If this is the case, then it may be more appropriate to measure the percentage of students who are performing above the proficient level. In any case, it is essential that you select a single metric and then measure it consistently. Although teaching variables are rarely evaluated, it is quite possible to measure them with fairness and accuracy.

The key to effective measurement of the professional practices of teachers is consistency and precision. We cannot measure earnestness or attitude, but we can certainly measure the frequency with which a teacher uses standards-based assessments in the classroom. We can also measure the degree to which teachers collaborate with one another, and the percentage of their agreement in evaluating the same piece of student work. Leadership behavior is also subject to measurement, provided that we first define what the standards of successful leadership behavior are. For example, a principal can measure the frequency with which faculty meetings focus on issues surrounding student achievement; the principal can track the frequency with which teacher excellence in implementation of standards is recognized.

If this sounds like a lot of measurement, then we must remember a cardinal principle of quality: it is more important to measure a few things frequently than to measure a lot of things infrequently. Annual standards assessment is little more effective than a colorful wall chart emblazoned with state standards that are ignored by students and teachers. Effective standards implementation requires leaders to identify a few variables, measure them frequently, and make instructional and leadership decisions on a reliable basis that reflect the results of those measurements. Chapter Six, on data-driven decision making, offers specific guidance on measurement of achievement, teaching, and leadership variables.

Chapter Two

Standards and Norms

What's the Difference?

Leadership Keys

Standards are fundamentally different from norms

Standards are fair and focused on proficiency

Norms represent constantly changing rules of the game

Standards are more rigorous than norms

The leader must make the case for standards to a skeptical public

Nine out of ten U.S. senators support academic standards, as do a similar proportion of members of the House of Representatives. The legislatures of forty-nine of the fifty states have endorsed statewide academic standards; the fiftieth, Iowa, requires standards for every district. If standards are so widespread and common, then why is it necessary for the educational leader to make the case for them? Aren't the benefits of standards obvious? Can't support for standards be assumed in most communities?

In a word, no. In my travels throughout the United States and abroad and in conversation with thousands of teachers, parents, and community leaders, the difference between standards and norms is unclear. Moreover, association of academic standards with standardized tests diverts conversation about the merit of the former to the defects of the latter. Finally, the imperfect and inconsistent manner in which standards have been implemented at the classroom and local school district levels in the past decade has caused a backlash against the entire notion of academic standards.

Therefore educational leaders cannot begin to implement standards without first making the fundamental case for the superiority of this method of assessing student performance.

The fundamental comparison to be made in this chapter is that of standards to norms. Student work must be compared either to an objective performance criteria—a standard—or to the average work of other students—a norm. The advantages of standards over norms are overwhelming, but the superiority is not obvious. This is why the leader must understand the difference and make the argument cogently and consistently.

Standards Are Fixed; Norms Move

As was suggested in Chapter One, any reader who has spent some time on the playground has heard the plaintive cry "That's not fair!" If the circumstances are sufficiently aggravating, the complaint can quickly give way to tears and fights. At the very least, children involved in a game that they know is unfair are unlikely to play it in the future.

The most typical reason for unfairness in any game is that the rules change in the middle of it. Children on the playground have an innate sense of fairness, and educational leaders should listen to the wisdom of those children. Students, along with their teachers and school leaders, remain engaged in a task if the goal is clear and they perceive that their individual efforts help them move toward that goal. Good academic standards produce clear and unambiguous goals. By contrast, the goal established by a norm-referenced test is to be "above average"—a goal that changes with each administration of the test.

Pursuing the moving average creates two problems for the educational leader. First, it fails to recognize progress that is made by struggling students and exceptionally challenged schools. If a student in the sixth grade, for example, progresses from a third grade reading level to a fifth grade reading level in a single year, the leader must recognize and celebrate that progress, at the same time recognizing that the child has not yet achieved the sixth grade standard. The most effective models of standards implementation recognize a continuum of performance, ranging from failure to meet the standard to progressing toward standards, then to proficiency, then to exemplary performance. The student can be recognized as "progressing" even as we are completely honest about his failure to read on the sixth grade level. If we report only that the student failed to meet the average of other sixth graders, we have neither an appropriate celebration nor a necessary challenge, but only the unhelpful comment that the child is not above average.

Consider the case of a student who is already above average and in fact has entered every grade reading above that grade level. Using norm-referenced tests is a prescription for complacency for this child, providing only bland confirmation of what he already knows. A standards-based assessment, by contrast, acknowledges that this student has achieved proficiency and at the same time challenges him to reach the next level of performance. Merely beating other students is not a standard; achieving a specific level of exemplary performance is a meaningful challenge for the student and the teacher. Even this high-achieving student, however, loses motivation if the definition of success is constantly changing. Exemplary performance, like proficiency in the standard itself, is not a mystery; nor is it a function of the performance of other students. It is a clear and challenging goal to which every student can aspire. The variable is the hard work of students and teachers, not successful guesswork or the defeat of other hard-working students.

Standards Are Cooperative; Norms Are Competitive

The effectiveness of cooperative learning strategies is a matter of settled research (Walters, 2000). Nevertheless, there is a prevailing ethic that we live in a competitive world and that for children to succeed they must learn competition in the classroom. This is a notion that deserves a second look. Standards actually promote successful competition, but not by pitting one student against the other. Rather, standards promote success by building teamwork and successful reinforcement among members of a learning team. Listen to the most competitive employers in your community and throughout the world. Their most frequent request is for employees who are literate and able to work cooperatively in a team. In other words, using cooperative learning is not antithetical to competition; indeed, cooperative teamwork is essential for successful competition. The challenge, however, is to use competition in the right context.

The Real Sources of Success

If students believe that success in the classroom is a function of who they beat rather than the standard that they achieve, they lurch between the aspiration of mediocrity and disappointment even when successful. If the same students work in a standards-based classroom, they know that it is possible for every student to succeed. With diligence and focus, with cooperation and mutually reinforced learning, all students can achieve a standard. This is the only way the best athletic coaches and orchestra leaders get a group of people with divergent abilities to succeed together.

Winning athletic teams do not succeed because the running back beat his teammate, the quarterback, or because the forward was superior to her teammate, the center. Similarly, students are most successful not when they relax knowing that their efforts, though falling short of a standard, are sufficient to beat the other students in the room. Nor do students succeed if they believe that no matter how hard they work, their efforts are never quite good enough to beat another student in the class. Students succeed academically when they know that their success is a direct result of their hard work. Moreover, the success that they most celebrate is the success of the entire class. Thus the standards-based classroom has incentives for group success, for students who help one another, and for students who are willing to be vulnerable enough to ask one another for assistance.

The Implications of Cooperation on Grouping and Tracking

The necessity of cooperation among students often leads to discussion of grouping and tracking. Educational leaders perceive themselves as caught in the dilemma expressed in this challenge: "You say that you believe in cooperation, but how can you have a student who cannot read working with an independent reader?" This challenge is followed closely by the assertion that if you truly believe in cooperation, then you must never separate students into different groups.

As is frequently the case with extreme positions, both are wrong. Through flexible grouping, the educational leader and classroom teacher group students of similar ability when they are building common skills, just as a choral director uses a sectional rehearsal and an athletic coach groups team members to focus on skills most needed by those students. Before rehearsal and practice session have been completed, however, the entire ensemble can sing together, just as the entire team can play together. In the context of academic classes, students can work together in small groups of similar skill level when they need to develop a common skill, such as learning multiplication or phonics. The same students, however, can work with an entire class or a group of students with differing abilities when the discussion turns to prediction, evaluation, or comparison.

A similarly balanced approach can be applied to discussion of tracking. If the ultimate goal is to reduce tracking in high school, where some students are given an opportunity for college while other students are systematically assigned to courses that are inconsistent with postsecondary educational opportunity, then it is necessary to recognize academic needs in middle school and elementary grades and address deficiencies. For example, if I wish a student to have an opportunity in ninth grade for academic rigor and no tracking, it may be necessary for me to give this same student additional intensive literacy instruction in eighth grade. The eighth grade grouping of students who need literacy skill is necessary, therefore, to "de-track" students in the ninth grade. If we refuse to group students in the eighth grade, the result is likely to be segregation of students not only in the ninth grade but throughout the remainder of their academic and employment careers.

The discussion of academic standards must not be sidetracked by the partisans or opponents of grouping. The leader of a standards-based school finds times when it is necessary to group students according to their ability and other times when it is strategic to group students of differing ability. The common element of a leadership strategy is neither its label nor its popularity, but rather the extent to which it advances the leader's goal of academic achievement. By focusing on the goal and embracing a flexible strategy, the effective leader can take maximum advantage of the effectiveness offered by a cooperative learning strategy and not succumb to the false assurance of norm-based test results. Ultimately the leader does not need to know who beat whom, but only the percentage of students who meet or exceed standards.

Standards Measure Proficiency; Norms Measure Speed

Just as coaches and musicians know that students of different ability can work well together, they also know that in perfecting any skill, proficiency precedes speed. This is an essential difference in assessing standards compared to assessing norms. Consider the example of state writing requirements, in which students are expected to prepare a multiple-paragraph persuasive, analytical, or expository essay. The performance standards are clear: the paper must adhere to the conventions of English grammar, spelling, and punctuation; be well-organized; include appropriate topic sentences and transitions; and have supporting illustrations and evidence that are linked to a clear central theme. Not a single state writing standard, however, expresses the requirement that the writing be performed quickly. Indeed, there is no differentiation between accomplishing these standards on the first draft or the third draft.

The only issue is the assessment of the standards. In norm-referenced tests, by contrast, the typical requirement for standardized test conditions includes a common constraint on time. Therefore the norm-referenced test assesses student proficiency but also the speed with which the student processes the information. Perhaps there are tasks in which speed is important, and where that is the case one should expect a standards document to make such a specification. A technology standard might, for example, specify that a student be able to keyboard at forty words per minute with 98 percent accuracy. I have not seen, however, a standard that requires students to "solve the quadratic equation quickly" or "complete the writing process expeditiously." A true standards-based test focuses on proficiency, not speed.

The typical objection to deemphasis of speed is the fear that students will abuse freedom, as well as the expectation that the real world requires speed. Let us consider each of these concerns, first the fear that if a student has no time limit she could take all day or all week to complete the assignment. No thoughtful person is suggesting that time stands still in a school while a student takes an infinite number of minutes to complete an assessment. Rather, if most students complete a writing assignment in forty-five minutes, then a reasonable time limit in a standards-based test might be ninety minutes. In this way, students who needed only an extra ten or twenty minutes are able to become proficient and the test data do not inaccurately label them as nonproficient. For those students who are unable to complete the task in ninety minutes, the problem is probably far deeper than the task at hand, perhaps involving inability to read the assessment or to address the task at all. These students require intensive intervention and additional instruction, not merely more time for the task.

The argument that in the real world tasks are timed deserves scrutiny. The quality model in the world's most advanced enterprises is rarely one that is characterized by the worker who says, "Here it is, boss; it's the best I can do, so take it or leave it." Rather, the quality model asks workers, engineers, attorneys, or executives to submit work, get feedback, and then improve it. This cycle of feedback and improvement is what leads to quality, not the expectation that work is completed once irrespective of quality and then the worker proceeds to the next task. A successful enterprise begins with a demand for quality rather than speed, confident that as quality improves, speed will be achieved in due course. However, the enterprise fully understands that speed without quality is not a prescription for success.

Standards Are Challenging; Norms Are Dumbed Down

The use of the average, the staple of norm-referenced tests, is a formula for mediocrity. It allows students who fail to meet standards to become inappropriately complacent by claiming that they are above average whether or not they meet the standard. There are a number of states, such as Virginia and New York, that were initially alarmed when a large number of their students did not fare well on standards-based tests. Indeed, a chorus of critics announced that if 80 percent of students failed to achieve proficiency in a standard, it must be the test or the standard that is at fault. The logic of this allegation rests with the false presumption that 50 percent of students—those above average—should automatically be successful. In fact, it does not surprise classroom teachers to read a standard that is rarely applied and infrequently tested and discover that 80 percent of students do not meet it.

If educational leaders are committed to the principle of student achievement, however, the answer is neither to shoot the messenger nor to subvert the message. In fact, the first reaction to the news that 70 percent of students do not meet standards should be a positive one, as it offers clear evidence that the standard is more rigorous than the norm. In a system that blindly applauds the above-average student, 20 percent of the students—those between the 50th and 70th percentiles—would be complacent in their apparent victory over their below-average colleagues, while failing to notice that these above-average students were not proficient. This is precisely what happens when honor roll students in middle school, comfortable in their relative merit when compared to other students, run into trouble in high school because the expectations are dramatically different from what the middle school students had expected.

The rigor of standards compared to the mediocrity of norms is played out in a number of ways every day in schools. Teachers can examine the scores of any class and find a student who is in the 55th percentile on a test of verbal ability, and then examine the written work of the student and fail to find an expository essay that meets the state standard. Similarly, teachers can find students who achieve a 60th percentile score in a norm-referenced math test but fail to find evidence that the student is able to apply that mathematical knowledge to the typical requirements of social studies and science standards to interpret data. In brief, the existence of standards makes it clear that being above average is not as important as meeting a standard.

Leaders must also consider the impact of academic rigor in standards when considering measurement of improvement. The most important metric for the school leader in a standards-based system is the percentage of students who meet or exceed standards—that is, the percentage who, on a specific performance task, score at or above the proficient level of performance. The move of the average score from the 55th to the 60th percentile may or may not imply an improvement in the percentage of students who are proficient. Conversely, percentile scores can be stagnant, yet the percentage of students who are proficient can rise. Schools will, as a matter of statistical fact, never have more than 50 percent of any distribution above average, but it is possible for all students to meet a standard. Thus at the same time that standards represent a more rigorous level of achievement than norms, standards also open the door of success to far more students than do norm-referenced tests.

Standards Are Complicated; Norms Are Simple

Many people like norms because they appear to encapsulate, in a single number, the achievement of a student. A single composite score is used to represent the ability of a student, his rank among other students, and perhaps his potential as well. Achievement of standards, by contrast, is not amenable to description with a single number.

In fact, standards invite complexity. School leaders in a standards-based environment may report that 82 percent of students are proficient readers, but only 42 percent are proficient in writing; 93 percent are proficient in math computation, but only 55 percent are proficient in mathematical analysis and problem solving. This is, to be sure, much more complicated than saying that the average fourth grade score places a group of students in the 52nd percentile nationally.

We must ask, however, what the fundamental purpose of assessment and accountability is. If it is, as I believe, to improve teaching and learning, then announcing a rank is not very helpful. Teachers and school leaders require the complexity of a standards-based report to know that, in this example, they need to focus more on problem solving. Indeed, the success in math computation perhaps suggests some teaching techniques that can be applied to the area that is deficient. Similarly, the teachers in that school can discover that reading well is not enough, and that they need to expand their literacy emphasis to include writing as well as reading. A single norm-referenced score would never provide such helpful insight. The leader must create a delicate balance here, as test data can be notoriously complex. Teachers and school leaders need enough data to modify instruction, but not so much information that it is overwhelming.

The acid test of data relevance is this question: Do the people who must make decisions that improve performance understand how they personally influence the next data report? For example, if a teacher does not perceive that his instructional decisions influence student achievement, then test data will not influence that teacher's decisions. This is particularly true if the data are not related to the teacher's decisions. For example, if the teacher says "The students who fail never show up to school," then it is necessary to analyze the data by attendance, producing a list of students who have 90 percent or greater attendance but are nevertheless failing. If the teacher says "The students who fail are all learning-disabled," then it is necessary to analyze the data by showing students who are not learning-disabled and still failing. If the teacher says "The students who are failing are all in someone else's class," then it is necessary to analyze the data individually by teacher. Each increment of data analysis, in other words, is a step toward personal responsibility. Without it, the data are abstract and irrelevant to the daily decisions of the teacher and leader. Chapter Six has more detail on the leadership and practice of data-driven decision making.

Standards Address Causes; Norms Display Effects

Consider a teenage student happily reporting, "I just lost twenty-five pounds!" Before we join the celebration, we must ask a few questions. Our reaction to the news of the weight loss depends on whether the cause is associated with prudent diet and appropriate exercise, or a combination of anorexia and drug use. In other words, the report of the score—in this case, the score reported by the scale—is not enough to allow us to make a sound decision on the data. We need to understand causes, not merely effects.

Because standards address a range of student achievement and behavior, in using them the educational leader can better understand the relationship between cause and effect. For example, whenever I ask teachers and school leaders to identify the most important standards—that is, the "power standards" (Reeves, 2000a)—they intelligently list a combination of the academic requirements and the behaviors that reflect the components of student success.

By analyzing the achievement of these students, a leader can understand if the cause for poor science achievement is a lack of science content knowledge by the student, misalignment of curriculum between the science class and the assessment taken by the student, the inability of the student to write a lab report properly, or failure of the student to have the time management and organizational skills associated with being a successful student in any class. Whereas a science score on a norm-referenced test merely announces a result and a rank, the report of the student's achievement of various standards illuminates the entire picture of student achievement. The leaders can make decisions, coach teachers, guide parents, and ultimately improve learning only if they have an understanding of which standards the student has and has not achieved.

The Impulse Toward Ranking

If the case for standards is so clear-cut, then why is there so much institutional and individual resistance to applying academic standards? Why do parents in particular have difficulty with the notion achieving a standard rather than ranking students against one another? First, we must acknowledge that for a large number of parents (including those most likely to be active in school affairs) the bell curve has been their friend. Using norm-referenced comparative data validates them as parents and announces to the world that their child is a success, at least compared to the child in the norming group. Moreover, because the traditional purpose of testing has been merely to announce a result rather than to improve learning, there is little or nothing to be gained from any test that yields bad news.

Therefore, confronted with the choice between a norm-referenced test that is encouraging and within the parental comfort zone and a standards-based test that suggests all is not well, parents understandably prefer the former. Moreover, successful parents have themselves defined success by ranking. A's are not enough;

their child must aspire to be valedictorian. Challenging grades are not enough; their child must have quality points to allow the possibility of a 7.5 average on a 4-point scale. From an early age, children witness their parents ask not "Is my child proficient?" but rather "Is she the best in the class?"

The Appeal of Ranking and Norms

The impulse toward ranking happens not only among affluent and competitive parents. Children themselves quickly sort out the world into those on top, those in the middle, and those left behind. The way we post scores and rank students confirms this early predisposition. There is a fundamental problem, however, that must be confronted. Ranking is not an accurate measure of student achievement; achievement of standards is far superior.

Consider the case of the aspiring valedictorian. The premise of chasing the graduating class microphone is that the student who receives a 7.458 grade-point average is superior to the student who receives a 7.457 grade-point average. This is the classic error of a distinction without a difference. If both students are exemplary performers—that is, not merely the best in the school, but capable of demonstrating performance that meets not just academic standards but explicit standards for exemplary performance as well—then both deserve recognition as exemplary. If, by contrast, both are at the top of the class but neither of them completed a research paper with the appropriate research citation that state standards required, then the valedictorian's victory is hollow. The trophy should read "superior but not proficient," a truth that will elude proud parents but become evident soon enough during the first year of college.

Breaking the Cycle: The Value of Standards for Parents Who Love Ranking

Educational leaders have an obligation not merely to set policy but to communicate the values, vision, and ideals on which policy is based. In the case of standards, the leader must address the question that parents, teachers, and students always have: "What's in it for me?"

For parents and students, the answer lies in constructive use of assessment. The first principle of assessment is that the purpose of testing is not to rate, rank, sort, and humiliate students or parents, but rather to improve teaching and learning. The role of the school is not to announce a judgment but to coach improvement. This is one reason frequent measurement of a few standards is so important. Parents do not embrace the value of standards on the basis of an annual report. Rather, they and their children must see, every time they cross the threshold of the school door, evidence that each month students are getting better and better. The percentage of students achieving a rigorous standard in writing, reading comprehension, mathematical problem solving, or other academic area of particular interest to the school is growing higher and higher each month.

Changing Grading Patterns in the Standards-Based School

Before addressing any change in something so tradition-bound and emotionally sensitive as grading, the leader must first address what does not change. Parents and community members must first receive assurance that, at least at the secondary level, using letter grades and high school transcripts remains intact. Any documentation of student performance with respect to academic standards is an addition to, not a replacement of, the traditional transcript. In the culture of some communities, you may need to offer the same reassurance to elementary school parents. This reassurance of stability is not because I have concluded that letter grades are a splendid concept and the ideal way to assess student performance. Rather, I have gauged the culture wars in our nation and decided that standards are too important to be caught in the cross-fire over letter grades. If the culture of your community is such that letter grades are part of the *Magna Carta*, Bill of Rights, and the state constitution, then accept it. Use letter grades, even though many observers recognize that they are utterly unrelated to student achievement. The key for the standards-based leader is not to fight a losing battle over letter grades, but instead to supplement the letter grades with a report that is meaningful, fair, and consistent. The Standards Achievement Report (Reeves, 2000b, 2002c) allows teachers to amplify and explain the meaning of a letter grade.

In addition to making the evidentiary case for standards, the leader must address the particular concerns of competitive parents of a high-achieving student. These parents need to know that there is value in unpleasant truth. If we are to state that their child does not meet a standard, then we must be able to state at the same time that the child can meet the standard with additional work, and that the grading system in place rewards and recognizes accomplishment of the standard, not the rate at which it is achieved. In practical terms, this means abolishing the average as a means of determining a grade in a standards-based school.

The penalty for failing to achieve a standard, in other words, is not a low grade, disappointment of parents, and the thin envelope rather than the thick package from Harvard. Rather, the consequence for failing to achieve a standard is the opportunity for detailed feedback, more work, and ultimate success. This is precisely the model that coaches and musicians use. The performance we hear at a spring concert is not, thank goodness, the average of the rehearsals held throughout the year. It is the pinnacle of quality, a representation of what the students are able to do at the end of the year. Similarly, the grade in a standards-based school is not the average of work done throughout the semester, but an accurate representation of the performance of the student at the end. Track coaches admonish their students that "It's not how you start that counts, but how you finish." Every academic teacher can apply that lesson.

The average is a fixture in most grading systems, and many secondary schools have even institutionalized it, using computer programs that require use of the arithmetic mean, or average, of grades throughout each quarter, semester, and year. This is strange in a standards-based school, particularly since every middle school mathematics standard in the nation requires sixth and seventh grade students to understand that the mean is not always the best measurement of central tendency. This is why they must learn about the median and mode; the average does not always represent the data accurately. The teachers of these students and the leaders of their schools must meet the same standard.

Consider two students, Stewart and Maria. Stewart comes to school fresh from summer camp and complacently strolls through the semester with these weekly scores: 85, 85, 85, 85, 85, 85, 85, 85, 85. The average is not difficult to calculate, and Stewart happily settles for his "gentleman's B." Maria struggles for everything she has learned and turns in this performance: 50, 60, 65, 70, 80, 85, 90, 90, 90. Maria's average of a little over 75 will, depending on the grading scale, allow her to take home a C or D on her report card if the teacher is slavishly devoted to the average, even though any fair observer would note that she is a better mathematician and a more responsive student than Stewart.

This is not a subjective judgment or an expression of sympathy. It is a statistically rigorous examination of a set of data in which the average fails to explain the results accurately. If we look at the data objectively and evaluate Maria's proficiency, she will receive either the same grade as Stewart (a B) or—preferably, in the mind of many teachers—the average of her last three assessments (an A). Should we commit such heresy, you can expect to see Stewart's parents at the next school board meeting. "Our son," they will indignantly declare, "was proficient all semester long, while THAT GIRL [pointing to Maria] was only proficient for the last few weeks." They conclude with the wounded expression of playground anger, "That's not fair!"

How shall we respond? Embracing standards and consequently abandoning the average entails some risk, and the leader must give teachers a clear and unambiguous response for use with such a challenge. My rejoinder would be: "We are a standards-based school in a standards-based district in a standards-based state. This means that we compare student work to a standard, and that we do not compare student work to that of other students. I will happily devote as much time as necessary to discussing Stewart's work relative to our standards. I cannot, however, devote an instant to comparing Stewart's work to Maria's or that of any other student. That is not the way we evaluate student work here."

It is that clear, blunt, and simple. The leader cannot equivocate on this point. Either we compare student work to standards or we compare it to that of other students; we cannot have it both ways. Ultimately, how an effective leader makes the case for academic standards to a skeptical public is a twofold appeal on the basis of fairness and rigor. I do not, however, promise that universal acceptance and popularity will follow, no matter how effective and eloquent the argument. Some parents always prefer ranking to standards, just as some teachers always prefer grading as an exercise in mysterious judgment to an objective achievement of standards.

The role of the leader is not to achieve popularity or universal acceptance, but to articulate the values that represent the core beliefs of stakeholders. There is a core belief statement, rarely inscribed in documents but frequently carried out in practice, that states, "Some kids get it and some kids don't, and we're here to validate the social hierarchy that existed long before these kids came to our school."

The core belief statement that guides the standards-based leader, however, is quite different. It contains certain immutable principles. To begin with, student success is not the result of luck, genetic determinism, or discovery of a mystery known only to a select few. Success in this school is the result of achieving standards through honest evaluation, diligent work, and exceptional effort. Our standards are never a secret; successful accomplishment of those standards can be achieved by every single student. When you leave this school, we will not announce who beat whom; rather, we will celebrate your accomplishments and those of every student who attained and surpassed our clear and unchanging standards.

Chapter Three

Standards-Based Performance Assessment

The Key to Standards Implementation

Leadership Keys

Assessment is the key to influencing every other element of classroom performance

Performance assessment is the best way to assess student proficiency

The leader must be the architect of collaboration in assessment design and evaluation

The leader must focus professional development on assessment quality

State standards include expectations ranging from factual recall and declarative knowledge through complex requirements that entail demonstration of student proficiency in ways that a typical multiple-choice test cannot possibly address (Marzano, Kendall, and Cicchinelli, 1998; Wiggins, 1995, 1997). Although state tests may evaluate student performance on a few state standards, comprehensive and meaningful assessment of academic standards can only take place in the classroom. It is therefore essential that classroom assessment be clearly linked to the standards, in content and complexity. I have reviewed thousands of classroom assessments over the years, and it is clear to me that the vast majority of schools require significant improvement in the quality of classroom assessment. Neither educational leaders nor teachers can offer a compelling alternative to the flaws of standardized testing if the assessments used in the classroom, school, and district do not generate valid and reliable alternative assessments that are clearly related to the academic requirements of the state standards.

Performance Assessment: The Key to Standards Implementation

However persuasive the case for academic content standards may be, there is a strong core of resistance to standards. Much of it is based on associating standards with standardized testing (Leeman, 1999). Other scholars have taken issue not so much with the tests themselves but with how test data are misinterpreted and misused (Popham, 2000; Wiggins, 1997). Educational leaders have a responsibility to listen carefully to the opposition to standards on the part of their faculty and among other stakeholders.

Listening, however, is not capitulation. The leader can acknowledge that standards have flaws, that many tests associated with standards have flaws, and that there are uses to which test information is put that is also deeply flawed. The remedy for these concerns, however, is not to reject standards or glumly accept standardized tests. The leader must build recognition among faculty, parents, and students that classroom-level and building-level assessment can be fair, effective, and related to academic standards. Whereas large-scale state tests may be limited in scope and provide untimely feedback to students, the best way to address these concerns is with effective performance assessment in the classroom.

Performance assessment has some distinctive characteristics that large-scale state tests almost never have. First, as the name implies, performance assessment requires the student to demonstrate performance of a standard, not merely to answer questions about a standard. The performance might be an essay; laboratory demonstration; application of mathematical knowledge; or analysis of a combination of maps, historical letters, and treaties. The thinking and analysis required in these performance tasks is far more rigorous than the guesswork entailed in many typical multiple-choice tests. More important, the results of these performances are immediately available to the teacher and student and thus can be used to improve student performance.

The Structure of Standards-Based Performance Assessment

Although there are many activities that bear the label "performance assessment" and that claim the appellation "standards-based," the best standards-based performance assessments follow a consistent format that includes, at a minimum, standard, scenario, performance tasks, and a scoring guide (rubric) for each task.

Relationship to Standards

Because of the proliferation of standards, many curriculum and assessment documents make the bald claim that they are standards-based. The simple question, "To which specific state standards does this activity relate?" is frequently met with stony silence by the purveyors of these documents. When teachers are planning curriculum and when the school leader is examining curriculum and assessments, the first question is, "To which specific state standards does this activity relate?"

However obvious the question may be, the answers are not equally obvious. In fact, activities accumulate in the classroom as much from tradition and popularity as from their relationship to academic requirements. As standards are used in an increasing number of schools, some traditional activities persist, and a leap of imagination and logic is required to relate those activities to standards. In other cases, traditional activities unrelated to standards and new standards-based activities have been piled on top of one another, guaranteeing only heavier backpacks for children and greater superficiality in the classroom, but failing to produce a set of coherent tasks that are directly related to state standards.

Once the question of standards has been addressed, the second issue that must be considered is whether the standards addressed by this task are the most important ones. Because standards are so voluminous and broad in most states, it is possible to find some standard that relates, however remotely, to virtually any activity. A simple relationship to a standard, therefore, is not a sufficient justification for any classroom activity. Rather, the educational leader must consider whether the activity under review is related to the power standards, those that the school leader and faculty have determined are most essential because they possess the qualities of endurance, leverage, and readiness for the next level of instruction (see Chapter Four for a thorough discussion of power standards).

Assessment Scenario

The scenario is the real-world context within which a performance task takes place. Like adults, students prefer to do meaningful work. The scenario creates meaning and conveys great respect to students who otherwise might regard tasks as busywork or utterly unrelated to their lives.

A scenario addresses the questions, "Why is this important?" and "How might I really use this knowledge in the years to come?" We learn about the Constitution, for example, not merely because this requirement appears in the social studies standards but because each student has rights that deserve protection. We can only assert and protect the rights we understand. We learn about geometry because we can use it to design gardens, rooms, houses, and schools. We learn about science because we can use the same hypothesis-testing procedures of the laboratory to challenge popular but inaccurate wisdom on matters ranging from personal health to social issues.

Developing a scenario for performance tasks helps to engage students in the assessment and also to improve the thinking of teachers. After years of addressing an academic subject as a set of abstract skills, the intellectual discipline required to ask and answer the question "Why in the world do we do this anyway?" is valuable.

Application of an academic skill to realistic circumstances promotes deep understanding not only for the students but also for the teacher who designs and administers the assessment as well.

Performance Tasks

Standards-based performance assessments include a range of performance tasks, from those that must be completed prior to approaching the standard to others directly related to a demonstration of proficiency in the standard, through tasks that are designed solely for enrichment and that allow students to demonstrate proficiency far beyond the standard. There is a great deal of emphasis in many schools on the concept of differentiated instruction. This reflects the reality of many a classroom, in which two dozen students representing quite a range of skills (from those two or three grade levels below the current class to those several grade levels above it). Properly applied, differentiated instruction maintains the same standard of performance but allows variation in time and instructional strategy.

However meritorious differentiated instruction may be, however, it rings hollow to most teachers and students if we do not also differentiate assessment. Differentiated assessment does not mean that less is expected of students who start at a lower level or who process information more slowly. Rather, differentiated assessment means that the same accomplishment for some students may be several incremental steps toward a single task rather than completion of one task. A good rule of thumb is that each standards-based performance assessment should have a minimum of four tasks. Depending on the level of differentiation required in your school, more than four tasks may be required.

Scoring Guides (Rubrics) for Each Task

There is some debate in the assessment community over whether performance assessment should receive a single score (holistic scoring) or whether each task or each dimension of an assessment should receive a separate score (analytical scoring). To resolve this argument, let us return to first principles. What is the most important purpose of assessment? Improvement of teaching and learning. If we wish to use the results of assessment to improve teaching and learning, then we must have feedback that is as specific as possible. Moreover, the feedback should commend the students on areas of proficient or exemplary work and simultaneously point the student and teacher toward those areas that require improvement. Only an analytical scoring guide, with a separate score awarded to the student after task, can do that. In this way, one student might blaze through the first three tasks of a performance assessment and finally slow down on the fourth task, where the challenge is greater and the work more difficult; another student might repeat the first task three times before proceeding to the second task.

The chaos that this creates in the classroom is constructive chaos, students working on various tasks because they are focusing on their area of greatest need. Avoiding this type of chaos is a false hope that only substitutes one kind of chaos for another. When we fail to differentiate assessment, insisting that students all proceed through the same tasks at the same pace and engaging in the fantasy that whole-group instruction assesses uniform needs for all students, we gain the external appearance of order in exchange for the internal chaos of students who are either bored because the pace is too slow or paralyzed with fear because they do not have the opportunity to perfect the skills necessary to proceed to the next task. By creating a scoring guide for each performance task and offering students feedback immediately after each task rather than after completing the entire assessment, the teacher automatically differentiates instruction and assessment in the manner most appropriate for the students.

The Leader's Role: Creating a Collaborative Environment

Many educational leaders fear that their role in standards-based performance assessment must be limited because administrators cannot possibly have the depth of subject-matter knowledge for each grade level that the classroom teacher possesses. It is true that school leaders do not need to have expertise on everything from the Pyramids to Pythagoras, but leaders have to be expert at two qualities that must pervade every school: fairness and collaboration.

The Fairness Imperative

Expertise in the principle of fairness implies that the leader knows the relationship between fairness and consistency of assessment. "I don't know much about calculus or European history," the leader might begin, "but I do know that every student studying those subjects deserves as a matter of simple fairness to have the same expectations. Therefore, I would like to ensure that the people teaching those classes collaborate with each other to ensure consistency of assessment and that they collaborate with teachers in the lower grades to ensure consistent expectations for the students who are entering those classes in the future."

At the other end of the spectrum of grades, the leader might say, "It's been a while since I taught third grade, but I do know that every third grade student in this school deserves to achieve the same academic standards. Therefore, even though we may differ about timing, pace, scenarios, and emphasis on curriculum areas, we must have absolutely common agreement on what we expect all third-grade students to know and be able to do. Therefore, we will have common, collaboratively scored assessments in reading, writing, and mathematics at the end of each quarter. The classroom activities leading up to those assessments might differ. The need to administer the same assessment at the end of each quarter will not differ."

Effective Classroom Observation: Assessment, Not Just Teacher Talk

When school leaders conduct observation, they must do more than listen to what teachers say. One of the most important, and frequently overlooked, parts of any effective observation of a classroom by an educational leader is an assessment review. Specifically, the leader should ask the teacher to share three examples of assessment that the teacher has created and three examples of student work that the teacher regards as proficient.

This is not necessarily the most exemplary student response, but rather the type of student work for which the teacher routinely awards credit because in the judgment of that teacher the quality of student work meets the standard. A fifteen-minute review of teacher-created assessment and real student work that the teacher regards as proficient tells a school leader a great deal more about the real expectations of a teacher and implementation of standards in a classroom than an hour of observation of the teacher talking to students. Form A-21 in the Appendix offers some guidelines for conducting an assessment observation.

Collaboration in Faculty Meetings and Professional Development

Even after a faculty has created performance assessments and is routinely using academic standards to guide classroom instruction, the leader's job is far from finished. Collaboration is a continuous journey that requires the leader's direct personal intervention. An important thing the leader can do is change how faculty meetings and professional development time is used by focusing exclusively on collaborative scoring of student work.

For example, the leader might dispense with announcements in writing at the beginning of a faculty meeting, and then announce:

> Ladies and gentlemen: Here is a piece of student work. I have taken the name off to protect the privacy of this student. Here is a draft of our school's scoring guide, adapted from the state standards in this subject and the state model rubrics. Please take five minutes alone and evaluate this piece of student work. Then please take five minutes with a colleague to evaluate the work.

After those ten minutes have elapsed, we will come back together for large-group collaboration. I will ask who believes that the first sample of student work is exemplary, who believes that it is proficient, who regards the work as progressing, and who considers the work as failing to meet our standards.

If we achieve 80 percent agreement on this, then the scoring guide is in final form and our work on that particular project is complete. If, however, we have fewer than 80 percent of our faculty members agree on the proficiency level of this sample of student work, then let's work together to improve the quality and specificity of the scoring guide. Remember, if we disagree, the enemy is not one another; the enemy is ambiguity. Now, let's go to work. . . .

I have engaged in such exercises with faculty members and, as Figure 3.1 indicates, had less-than-stellar results during my first outing. A very low level of agreement indicated that our first draft of the scoring guide was ambiguous and subject to many interpretations. But as we went along, the scoring guide improved, as did the ability of the faculty to collaborate.

With the same people on the faculty and the same students in the classroom, the level of agreement increased over the course of the year. This took practice, as collaboration is not something that comes naturally. Sharing student work and explaining to one's

Figure 3.1. Collaboration Improves Over Time

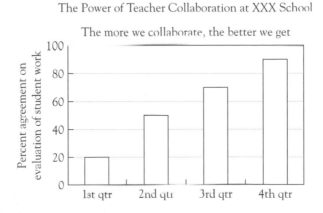

colleagues the rationale behind what has in the past been a personal and sometimes mysterious decision—the evaluation of student work—is an unusual and vulnerable activity for most faculty members.

Let us be clear about the role of the school leader under these circumstances. It is not his job to be a universal expert in all curriculum areas and to arbitrate dispute on subtle matters of academic proficiency. Rather, he should take a stance of deliberate naiveté: "If I can't understand the method for scoring this assignment, then it's pretty unlikely that our students and parents will be able to understand it. Let's review the scoring guide again and see if we can make it clearer so that almost all of us, including me, can understand how a score was awarded." The leader need not be an expert in the subject, but he must be expert, as well as relentlessly persistent, in pursuing fairness and collaboration.

Figure 3.1 demonstrates that with practice and effort over time, the quality of teacher assessment of student work improves. The quality measure used in this case is the degree of consistency with which teachers assess the work. Any scoring guide, no matter how professionally developed, is only as good as the ability of teachers to use it consistently. After a rough start in the first quarter, the group of teachers represented in Figure 3.1 became more consistent in their fairness and, as a result, fairer. In addition, the more the teachers practiced collaborative scoring, the more efficient they became, in the fourth quarter of the year completing the same task of collaboratively scoring student work in a fraction of the time that was required in the first quarter (Figure 3.2).

As the two figures make clear, successful collaboration is not the instant result of the leader's announcement of a "collaboration initiative." Collaboration requires time and persistence. With the support of a leader who understands that fundamental fairness is at stake, collaboration can succeed not only in improving the consistency of assessment but also in reducing the time required for scoring assessments.

Figure 3.2. Practice in Collaboration Saves Time

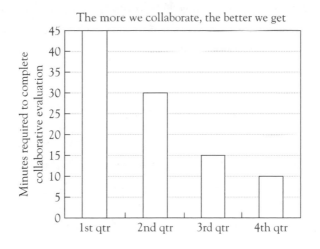

The more we collaborate, the better we get

Ten Steps to Creating Standards-Based Performance Assessment

Although the educational leader need not create standards-based performance assessment nor lead the professional development effort to create these classroom tools, it is imperative that the leader understand the process required for creating effective assessment. This is not something that happens as a result of a half-day workshop. The ten steps that follow are essential if assessment is to be transformed from an abstract concept into practical application in the classroom. These steps have been adapted from *Making Standards Work: How to Implement Standards-Based Performance Assessments in the Classroom, School, and District* (Reeves, 2002c).

Step One: Pull the Weeds Before Planting the Flowers

Before any new initiative, the leader is obliged to consider the fixed number of hours in the school day. Because creating and evaluating performance assessment is so time-consuming, the leader cannot add it as a new initiative. First he must identify some units, activities, chapters, or curriculum that can be terminated. Performance assessment will never happen without time for classroom teachers, and a leader's first obligation is deciding what not to do. Ordering a new initiative without removing some old ones is a prescription for angry and demoralized staff members and ultimately failure of the new initiative.

Step Two: Identify the Primary Standard

Use of power standards, described in Chapter Four, helps the leader focus on those standards that are most important. There is not enough time to create an assessment for every single standard, and as a cardinal principle of measurement it is more important to address a few standards frequently than to attempt to measure every standard once a year.

Step Three: Develop an Engaging Scenario

The scenario allows the assessment designer to understand a task from the student's point of view. If the student asks, "Why do we have to learn this?" the teacher has a compelling answer with a scenario that is realistic and important.

Step Four: Develop Performance Tasks

A performance task is not merely recitation of acquired knowledge. The creator of an assessment must consider the difference between true performance assessment and mere test taking. Traditional multiple-choice tests allow and sometimes even reward guesswork, but performance assessment requires real-world application along with a demonstration of what students can do. I recommend a minimum of four separate performance tasks for each assessment.

Step Five: Develop Scoring Guides (Rubrics)

For each task, we must have a separate scoring guide. The scoring guide specifically describes a range of student performance, from failing to meet the standard at all, through performance that is progressing toward the standard, to demonstration of proficiency in the standard, to that exceptional level of performance that the teacher regards as exemplary. This four-point scoring guide allows the teacher to differentiate between students who understand the standard and task but have not yet accomplished it (progressing) and those requiring extensive remediation merely to approach the tasks (not meeting standards). Moreover, those students who are already proficient have a chance to enrich challenges through pursuit of exemplary performance.

Step Six: Create an Exemplary Assignment

One difficult and unusual part of assessment design is creating an exemplary response. Teachers are sometimes reluctant to do this, and so I ask them to consider exchanging assignments with one another. One would think that two college-educated people should have no difficulty responding to a standards-based performance assessment designed for an elementary or secondary school child. Yet invariably when this happens, the adult playing the role of the student has an understanding of at least some instruction or some element of a scoring guide that differs from what the creator of the assessment intended. This gentle feedback is much easier to accept coming from a professional colleague than hearing the complaint "I don't get it!" from a student.

Once a model of great performance has been created, it gives the teacher a wonderful tool to explain expectations to students. Eventually, the teacher has authentic examples of student work that can be shared with future students so that the requirements of the performance task and scoring guide are not theoretical, but real. To model this expectation in the context of this chapter, I have made available samples of completed performance assessments (www.makingstandardswork.com). They can be downloaded free of charge so that leaders and educators have working examples of complete standards-based performance assessment.

Step Seven: Get Feedback

The first draft of an assignment is never the last one. Colleagues and students misunderstand directions. The task that we assumed was a single requirement is, in fact, two or three discrete tasks that must be separated in the next draft of the assessment. The scoring rubric that seemed so clear in its inception is interpreted differently by several colleagues. There is no substitute for field testing a performance assessment and then getting feedback prior to finally publishing it.

Step Eight: Clarify and Enrich the Assessment

One satisfying step in creating a performance assessment is to recognize how many standards can be applied to a single assessment. As a task grows in scope and complexity, more time is required for students to complete it and for the teacher to evaluate it. The assessment also requires the leader to allow more time for collaboration. The more standards there are related to an assessment, the more time teachers and the school leader can allow for administration and evaluation of the assessment.

Step Nine: The Acid Test—Student Understanding and Use

A frustrating issue the educational leader must face is the gap between intention and action in implementing new techniques in instruction, curriculum, and assessment. When teachers attend a conference or seminar in performance assessment, the leader has the right to expect to see tangible evidence of the learning in the classroom. This is why the leader can reasonably ask teachers to share examples of standards-based performance assessments that they have created. If there are no such assessments, then the money and time invested in a seminar on that subject has been of dubious value.

An example of superior performance in this regard is the assessments accumulated over four years by the Waukesha school district and several companion districts in the southern Wisconsin area. Working with Larry Ainsworth of the Center for Performance Assessment and several faculty members from Alverno College in Milwaukee, the participants in their summer seminars create a solid connection between the theory of performance assessment and the reality of the classroom. They accumulate their work products, post them on the Internet, and share them widely with new and veteran faculty members.

Step Ten: Sharing with Colleagues

Creating an actual assessment is an essential step—and one rarely followed. Even rarer in the Wisconsin seminars as well as a few others around the nation, among them the California International Studies Project, the Norfolk public schools, the Orange County Office of Education, and the Montgomery County Education Services Center, is the action of the participants of systematic sharing of finished performance assessments. The work required to create a performance assessment is so difficult and time-consuming that it is imperative that the leader make systematic means of sharing this work available. Each year, the leader should create a book titled something like "Best Practices in Student Assessment," with the names of teachers who have taken the initiative to create these assessments emblazoned on the front.

In many school systems, there is an ethic that prevents this sort of sharing. In some cases, this is due to modesty; in many other cases, however, teachers fear that recognition of their work may imply disrespect for other colleagues. Excellent work is thereby rarely shared. The leader must address this cultural issue; the best way to do so is with systematic and consistent documentation of superior professional practices. Moreover, the most effective recognition is highly specific, to offer models of superior teacher-created assessment.

Chapter Four

Power Standards

How Leaders Add Value to State and National Standards

Leadership Keys

Add value to your state standards

Apply the criteria for power standards: endurance, leverage, and readiness for the next grade

Unmask the illusion of coverage

The leader does not micromanage the classroom

The leader knows how students perform on power standards

State standards are typically created through a collaborative process. People of goodwill gather together to craft statements representing what students should know and be able to do. As a result of listening to a variety of viewpoints, the group that drafts standards seeks to ensure that the document is balanced and comprehensive. In most cases, the states have achieved those objectives. Unfortunately, the one objective states did not achieve or even consider was brevity. The number of days in the school year has remained fixed, but the quantity of curriculum has expanded.

This leaves school leaders with two choices. The first option is that they can encourage teachers to engage in coverage of curriculum that is increasingly superficial. If teachers must divide a larger quantity of standards and curriculum into a fixed number of school days, then either rapid speech or curricular superficiality becomes a mathematical certainty. The second option is for the leader and educators to add value to state standards through a process of prioritization. The result of this process is a set of power standards, a small subset of state standards that represent the most important elements of the curriculum. By carefully developing and applying power standards, leaders recognize that the question to be asked at the end of every year is not merely what teachers covered, but rather what students learned.

Value-Added Standards: Focus, Discernment, and Prioritization

There is a great deal of talk about the ideal of instructional leadership among school leaders. Typically, however, the ideal soon devolves to the reality of a laundry list imposed on teachers. An effective leader is not simply defined by what he does, but also by what he chooses not to do. By helping teachers identify systematically and carefully those standards that they will abandon and those that require extra emphasis, the leader does more than merely deliver standards from the state capital to the classroom. These decisions require exceptional discernment, the ability to perceive the subtleties of state standards that are not always obvious on the surface, and insight into connections among standards that are not always evident to the groups that create standards.

By leading a process of inquiry marked by discernment, the leader can articulate what every reader knows to be the truth: some standards are more important than others. In fact, some standards are absolutely essential if students are to enter the next grade with success and confidence, while others are little more than a political addition to a laundry list of requirements. I have never heard a fifth grade teacher remark, for example, that the student would have been more successful "if only he had learned a little more about Jamestown and the Articles of Confederation in the fourth grade." But I have heard many fifth grade teachers lament that students would have been more successful had they learned to read and comprehend grade-level material and write coherent paragraphs.

The same is true with respect to high school content area teachers. Few science and social studies educators at the high school level despair over the lack of content in science and social studies in middle school, but a great many high school teachers in those disciplines know that students who leave middle school unable to read high school textbooks have few opportunities for success in the science and social studies classes that await them. The key to narrowing the focus of standards and thereby adding value to them lies in developing power standards.

The Criteria for Power Standards

Establishing power standards is a building and district function. Many school leaders wish that the state would give them standards in prioritized order, but the function of the state in creating academic standards is collaboration and accumulation. Only in the classroom and building can we separate the essential from the peripheral. Some commentators have suggested that this process can be quickly accomplished by a vote. They quickly rank various requirements, publish the results, and voilà: the essential skills. I dissent. Educational leaders have as a primary calling the ability to distinguish between what is popular and what is effective. Listing what everyone wants to teach or what other groups think is most important is a popularity contest, not a means of adding value to curriculum and standards. A better way is careful application of three criteria to every standard: endurance, leverage, and readiness for the next level of instruction.

Endurance

Standards that meet the criterion of endurance give students skills or knowledge that remains with them long after a test is completed. Standards on research skills, reading comprehension, writing, map reading, and hypothesis testing are all examples of enduring knowledge. Teachers can look years into the future of a student now in elementary school and see how each of those standards will be used again and again. By contrast, there are other requirements, particularly those associated with specific events and people, that may be an important part of the cultural literacy of the citizens of a state but are not more important than learning to read. Moreover, there are classroom activities that have become part of the tradition of many a school and that consume many hours of learning time but do not give students enduring knowledge. This criterion, as with the others that lead to power standards, can be applied not only to state documents but to professional and leadership practices at the classroom and building levels as well.

Leverage

The criterion of leverage helps the leader and teachers identify those standards applicable to many academic disciplines. Two examples that one can find in every set of academic standards are nonfiction writing and interpretation of tables, charts, and graphs. The evidence is quite clear that if students engage in more frequent nonfiction writing, their performance in other academic disciplines improves (Reeves, 2000b). Therefore, the power standard of nonfiction writing, accompanied by editing, revision, and rewriting, is worth far more than a single line in a state standards document.

In fact, writing deserves a full hour of emphasis every day in elementary schools, in addition to the sixty to ninety minutes typically provided for reading. If devoting 2.5 hours each day to literacy implies reducing time available for clay models of a Roman amphitheater or perfecting a performance that features a handful of students, then the priority is clear: literacy is more important. Creating and interpreting tables, charts, and graphs is another example of a standard with leverage. These requirements are in every state math standards document, but a careful look at the other academic disciplines reveals that the necessity of mastering the creation and interpretation of tables, charts, and graphs is also present in the social studies, science, and language arts standards as well. If standards possess leverage, they give students skills that have broad applicability and build confidence in essential skills throughout the curriculum.

The principle of leverage also helps teachers in curriculum planning, particularly when a team of teachers is working to create integrated thematic units of instruction. Thus creating a pie chart in math displays population distribution in a geography class; a timeline can be applied to a progression of events in a novel in a literature class, to a sequence of events in a history class, and to the change in a chemical substance in a science lab.

Readiness for the Next Level of Learning

The criteria of leverage and endurance would be sufficient if we were readily introspective, examined our own curriculum, removed some elements, and expanded others that are more important. Unfortunately, it is easy for any of us to fall in love with particular instructional practices. A leader does not have the time or expertise to individually dissect and analyze every single classroom practice. She can, however, facilitate a process in which teachers collaborate not only in systematically reflecting on their own classroom curricula but also in working together across grade levels to apply the criterion of readiness for the next level of learning. The best way to apply this criterion is a role play exercise in which the leader asks teachers to engage in a scenario the leader introduces with these words: "I'm a new teacher in this building, and in fact I'm new to the profession. I need your advice. I'm teaching in the next grade lower than you; if you're teaching fourth grade, I'm teaching third grade, and if you're teaching seventh grade, I'm teaching sixth grade. Here's what I need you to do. For each subject for which you are responsible, write down the knowledge and skills that I must give to my students this year so that they can enter your class next year with success and confidence."

I have done this exercise with several hundred teachers, and their responses are remarkable. Not once has a teacher ever said, "If your students are to enter my class next year with confidence and success, then this year you must cover every single state standard." Rather, the teachers create a list that is balanced and brief. The list is balanced because it includes information in the content area and also requirements for literacy and behavior. For example, an eighth grade social studies teacher may include some content requirements, such as map-reading skills or basic historical knowledge. Then, after listing four or five content-specific standards, the teachers invariably say, "The students must be able to read an eighth grade social studies textbook." After a few moments of reflection, they add the requirement that "The students must be able to keep an assignment notebook, turn work in on time, and cooperate on a team with other students." All requirements together, including content, literacy, and behavior, rarely exceed a dozen in number. This list, balanced and brief, forms the final threshold for power standards.

In one Midwestern district, I observed fourth grade teachers collaborate with their colleagues in the upper elementary and secondary grades. Their initial quandary was the set of more than two hundred requirements for knowledge and skills of fourth grade students in the subjects of language arts, science, math, and social studies. In half a day of work applying these three criteria—endurance, leverage, and readiness for the next grade—they narrowed the list to twenty power standards. In California, I have observed ninth and tenth grade teachers narrow the math and language arts requirements from more than sixty requirements to fewer than fifteen.

Potential Dangers in Power Standards

The inevitable objections come from those who note that a standard that does not appear in the final list of power standards might be on the state test. This is true. Selecting power standards does not imply universal coverage of every conceivable test item. In fact, the use of power standards virtually guarantees that teachers will omit some items that might be on the state test.

The choice the leader and teachers face is not perfection, but rather these two alternatives. Through use of power standards, we can give our students proficiency with those standards that address 80–90 percent of the content of the state test, and also give them the reading, writing, and reasoning skills to help them on any state test question. On the other hand, we can reject power standards and embrace coverage, in which case students will be exposed to 100 percent of the potential content of the state test, and they might master 50 percent of those skills. Both choices entail risk, but the risk of power standards is a far wiser risk for an instructional leader or educator to take.

The Illusion of Coverage

The inevitable rejoinder from curriculum directors, teachers, and principals is: "The state standards require that we cover everything. If we fail to do so, we are short-changing students by failing to give them the information they need for the test." This statement is seductive. Who would want to short-change children? However, it depends upon a dangerous illusion: the notion that with just the right mix of perfect schedules, the absence of unforeseen events, cooperative students, and rapid speech by the teachers, a teacher of mythical capabilities can cover all the standards. Conversation with teachers at the end of every academic year reveals the fantasy that lies behind this illusion. Teachers invariably talk about the curriculum areas that they didn't get to, how the year went by so quickly, and how next year will be different. The end of each academic year reveals that what we have is not universal coverage but "coverage by default"—curriculum areas addressed on the basis of an accidental confluence of calendar, student readiness, and teacher plans.

A superior alternative to coverage by default is curriculum by design. In this model, teachers and the leader decide at the beginning of each school year and periodically throughout the year the most important standards to address. They know that as the year progresses, their obligation is to have all students proficient in power standards—not to have a few students proficient in everything, or most students proficient in only a fraction of the standards—but all students exposed to as many standards as the teacher can cover. Leaders must acknowledge this truth: perfect curriculum coverage never happens. There are only two choices left: coverage by default or by design. Power standards help the leader make the wise choice.

Practical Implications for the Leader

Employing power standards is not a theoretical enterprise but a practical approach to leadership and learning. The first and most important practical implication is that the leader must make time for teachers to collaborate within and among grade levels to identify the power standards. Perhaps your school already has regularly scheduled collaboration time for teachers. A growing number of schools have forty-five minutes to an hour for teachers every single day for collaborative work. More than half of this time is typically governed by administrative discretion rather than left for unstructured teacher work time. In the vast majority of school systems, however, time for collaboration is limited and planning time in the daily schedule is already used by teachers for parent communication and evaluation of student work. Therefore, leaders must look at the time they can control and consider how to use those hours wisely.

The two sources of time most frequently misused in a school are faculty meetings and professional development. A growing number of schools where I work have committed themselves to a "zero announcement" policy for faculty meetings. Principals print the announcements on paper or distribute them by e-mail, and faculty members entering a meeting sign a document that simply says, "I have received and read the announcements." The entire meeting is therefore focused on student achievement in which the faculty works independently, in small groups, or as a large group to collaboratively evaluate student work, create power standards, or do other work that is essential for improving professional practice and student learning. Similarly, the model of professional development in many schools is changing from a catalogue of courses offered by outside vendors to blocks of time used by teachers and leaders for collaborative work on assessments, curriculum, and standards that have an immediate and positive impact on the teaching and learning in that school.

By using faculty meetings and professional development wisely, the leader defeats the traditional excuse of "I'd like to develop power standards, but we just don't have the time." This is a fundamentally inaccurate statement, as the clocks in every school in the world are based on the same twenty-four-hour day. The truth is that we have the time, but we have historically chosen to employ the hours available in diverse, frequently nonproductive ways. We must ask, "What is the risk of not making announcements in faculty meetings? The risk that someone may not understand the announcement or may not comply with it?"

This is, of course, precisely the same risk that we have when verbal announcements are made in a faculty meeting. Using faculty meetings to focus on student achievement carries no additional risk and significant additional rewards in curriculum and assessment. What is the risk of diverting professional development time to teacher-led collaboration on curriculum and assessment? The risk that the professional development lessons that might have been delivered would not be applied in the classroom?

This risk prevails even if we continue the traditional series of disjointed workshops and seminars that dominate most professional development in schools. As Guskey (2000) and the National Staff Development Council (2001) have argued persuasively, the most effective professional development is not that characterized by grandiloquent speeches or clever seminars; it is application in the classroom in such a way that there is a measurable impact on student achievement.

Leadership Frameworks: An Alternative to Micromanagement

For many teachers and administrators, the term *instructional leadership* represents a fantasy, dependent on the magical administrator being present in every classroom all the time to observe, coach, and lead instruction. Teachers resent the specter of micromanagement, while leaders endure the crush of longer days in which they are expected to devote themselves to instructional leadership in the classroom while simultaneously being available in the office for parent communication and student discipline, and at the same time being at every important meeting called by the central office at which principal attendance is mandatory.

In fact, no leader in any organization can lead through direct instruction. We know that the most effective teachers do not cast themselves as the sole source of feedback and instruction in the classroom; instead they make their expectations so clear and their standards of performance so transparent that students regularly evaluate their own work, make appropriate corrections, and proceed to the next level of achievement.

In great standards-based classrooms, I have seen students approach the teacher's desk, apparently ready to hand in a completed assignment. Then the student sees the standard, along with the teacher's clear explanation in student-accessible language boldly printed on a large poster near the teacher's desk. The student stops, turns around, and returns to her seat, making the correction before the teacher has begun to read the student's paper. The best leaders emulate this model of teaching. They know that they cannot and should not dictate every move of the classroom teacher. Rather, they collaboratively create a framework that includes the most important standards along with a clearly agreed definition of what proficient work really means. The framework establishes clear boundaries; within that framework, teacher creativity is encouraged and valued. Neither the leader nor the teacher needs to engage in guesswork about expectations or boundaries. During evaluation, the leader does not need a diary of every activity in the classroom but instead can focus on the framework.

This approach saves the leader time and grants respect to teachers. The question at the end of the first quarter is not "Can I see your lesson plans and the documentary evidence that you covered the standards?" but rather "What percentage of your students are proficient or higher in the three power standards that we agreed on for the first quarter?" This brief report, along with two or three examples of student work that is proficient, allows the leader to know what is being assessed and how the students are performing; the leader then considers midcourse corrections to improve professional practice and student learning.

After identifying the power standards, the leader can take the next step toward leading implementation of standards-based performance assessment. Later, we explore standards-based assessment as the key to effective implementation of standards. This kind of assessment represents the difference between standards as conceived in an abstract document and standards as a vital presence in every classroom.

Chapter Five

Instructional Leadership

Leadership Keys

Teaching is the most important job of every leader

The essential message: standards, not standardization

Know the hallmarks of a standards-based classroom

Instructional leadership for new teachers

Leading experienced teachers

Dealing with a divisive faculty

Instructional leadership is an elusive concept. It appears to be more than management and administration, yet every veteran leader knows that management and administration are vital functions in a school. The phrase emphasizes instruction; this appears to convey that the leader has a role in curriculum and teaching, yet most veteran leaders have confronted a wall of opposition whenever they attempt to impose their will on the classroom. Many give up in frustration, knowing that once the door to the classroom is closed, the influence of the leader is greatly diminished. In this chapter, we consider the extraordinary challenges that face the educational leader and how she or he must address the divergent needs of new and veteran faculty members.

The Leader's Most Important Job: Teaching

In his landmark studies on leadership, University of Michigan Professor Noel Tichy (1997) studied leaders in business, government, and education. Among his most important findings were the connection between leadership and teaching. Successful leaders were clearly focused on a mission; they knew that an extremely important job was to focus the entire organization constantly on the mission, values, and principles that will sustain the organization through any challenges in the future. Peter Senge (1990; Senge and others, 1999) has made a similar argument, saying that the imperative for the mental discipline of systems thinking is as important in education as it is in the business world. Researchers as diverse as Barth (1990) and Benfari (1999), who approached the challenges of leaders from entirely different perspectives, came to remarkably similar conclusions about the role of teaching and communication in the daily practice of the successful leader.

Because a school is such a complex and diverse place, many leaders may find the notion that they can be an effective teacher to people in numerous disciplines, with differing skills, with diverse interests, and with a vast range of learning styles and needs to be absurd. Who could possibly handle a task this complex? The answer, of course, is teachers, and we expect them to do so every day. Kindergarten teachers across the land must confront a classroom in which a child reading a *Harry Potter* book is sitting next to a child who does not recognize letters, who is sitting next to a child who recognizes Cantonese characters perfectly but knows nothing of the English alphabet. From the skill of teachers who deal with complexity daily, the educational leader can learn several things about the role of leader-educator.

Values Transcend Learning Style

However differentiated instruction may be in the kindergarten class described in the preceding paragraph, there are some classroom values that transcend culture, language, and learning background. Every child is expected to respect others, take turns, share toys, and listen attentively to one another. Every child is expected to have information of value to which the teacher will listen respectfully, just as every child is expected to understand that the teacher has information of value to which the students will listen respectfully. These values and principles are often codified in the "class rules," which are posted in language everyone can understand and which are almost invariably limited to a single page of very large print.

Students even at an early age also understand that a balance is struck every day between those activities and times that are constrained by teacher prerogative and those in which students can exercise independent judgment (provided that this independent judgment is not abused). Even in the most unstructured of time, for example, students are not permitted to use hate speech or to trample on the rights of another member of the class. The kindergarten teacher, in brief, recognizes that there are some clear and consistent values that everyone in the classroom understands and accepts. There are also times at which everyone in the classroom makes independent judgments, so long as they are within the boundaries established by the teacher.

The leader can take a page from the wisdom of the kindergarten teacher. The values and principles that form the foundation of the teaching message must be as clear as the class rules, expressed in language that is accessible to every stakeholder. Rather than say "We adhere to the standards mandated by the state and use rubrics for student assessment," the leader could say: "We believe in fairness. Because we believe being fair to students, teachers, and the community is so important, the only way that we assess student work is by comparing it to a set of expectations that is so clear that everybody—students, parents, teachers, and community members—understands what is expected. When you hear people talk about standards, that's what we mean: just simple fairness, so that everyone knows what is expected."

Turning Values into Action

If the leader is to express more than platitudes, she must make clear the implications of the values and principles that she espouses. What does *fairness* mean? To many students and adults, the claim

"That's not fair!" might apply not just to decisions that are genuinely unfair but also to those that are merely unpopular. Thus she must be an advocate simultaneously for the fundamental value of fairness and for communicating precisely what that value means in terms of the daily activity of the student, the teacher, and the leader herself. The fundamental reason, after all, to change from traditional instruction to standards-based teaching is not a state mandate or a wave of popular calls for standards. The one and only reason to change to standards-based teaching is that it conforms to the foundational values of the leader, the community, and the educational system serving the community.

As political trends ebb and flow and fads grow and wither, values remain. If people are not committed to the organization's core values, they may continue to work there but they will not be happy. If people are engaging in practices that are antithetical to the organization's core values, they must leave. A bank doesn't continue to employ people who think that counting money is unimportant. A hospital doesn't continue to employ people who think that patient care is a bother. A school must not continue to employ people who think that fairness is a passing fad and not worthy of their attention. Hospitals, banks, and schools might all have unionized employees, but the existence of a union is no obstacle to consistent establishment of values and, of equal importance, to professional practices that put those values into action.

The professional practices associated with a standards-based classroom are objective and clear. Just as we expect teachers to articulate clearly their expectations for students, so also must the school leader state without ambiguity his or her expectations for professional practice. A good start might be the material in the subsections that follow, which is recorded in a shorter checklist format as A-19, A-20, and A-21 in the Appendix.

Standards Are Highly Visible in the Classroom. Visibility need not imply every standard related to that grade level or subject, but it certainly must include the standards that are being addressed in the class during the current week. Students have a right to understand the expectations they are to meet, and teachers have a right to understand the parameters within which their instruction takes place. This serves to focus students and teachers and is also an antidote to administrators and policy makers who are sometimes tempted to suggest extras for the classroom.

To put a fine point on it, a school leader must think twice before taking a good idea such as character education and transforming it into an additional curriculum in the school day. Teachers can reasonably ask, "Which standard on this wall shall I take down to make room for the new requirements?" The same is true for myriad curriculum requirements that, by themselves, seem innocent but taken together form a mountain of time requirements for classroom instruction that inevitably compete with academic content standards. Examples I have heard are not simply the obvious ones of character education and drug or alcohol or tobacco education, but also newly established mandatory curricula: sensitivity training; bully-proofing; diversity training; free enterprise education; sexual orientation tolerance training; and a host of other items requiring curriculum documents, assemblies, and even assessments.

If these ideas are implemented as part of a curriculum in critical thinking, social studies, or health education, that's one thing. If they have the practical impact of reducing the amount of reading and writing in a classroom and overall reducing the focus on achieving academic standards, then the leader must confront the divergence between principles based on the value of fairness and the practice of standards-based education on the one hand and, on the other, the reality of a fragmented day in which some students succeed, some fail, and teachers frantically bounce from one curriculum area to another like a pinball in a poorly leveled machine.

The Standards Are Expressed in Student-Accessible Language. A few states, such as Illinois, have taken the time to express some of their standards in language that makes sense to students, and for that matter to parents not immersed in the jargon of standards. The work of most states, however, can be charitably described as the result of efforts of a very earnest committee. Membership in the committee typically excludes fourth graders, and as a result the wording of the standard eludes our students and strikes their parents as obscure.

The remedy for this problem is not complaining about standards, but adding value to the standards by restating them in language that is clear and accessible to all students. There is ample precedent for this. Teachers do not put the state's criminal statutes on a poster at the front of the room; nor do they display the local board of education disciplinary code. Instead, they display the class rules, using language that students, parents, and teachers alike can understand. This should be the model for expressing standards and expectations for student academic proficiency.

Examples of Proficient and Exemplary Student Work Are Displayed Throughout the Classroom. In some schools, this display is called the "wall of fame," on which the work of present and former students is displayed. Some schools even use the trophy case for this purpose, making it clear to parents and visitors that student achievement is valued and that students in this school have already demonstrated that success is possible. Some displays do not include student names. The purpose is not to elevate one student over another, but rather to give a model to all students of what successful writing, mathematics, science, or social studies work looks like.

Success in these schools is never a mystery. Displaying student work clearly links the standards to real student work. These displays have the added advantage of allowing school leaders to check that each classroom has the same level of quality expectations, and that expectations for student proficiency are always linked to the standard rather than to idiosyncratic judgment about students.

Expectations of Proficiency Are Known in Advance. For every assignment, the teacher publishes in advance the explicit expectations for proficient student work. Although a full scoring guide may not always be necessary, it is absolutely essential that students enter every academic activity knowing in advance what success means. They need not guess, nor must students merely attempt to beat other students. They know precisely what is expected, whether through a rubric, a checklist, or another document that clearly establishes the rules of the assignment.

Student Evaluation Is by Standards, Not on the Curve. Student evaluation is always done according to the standards and scoring guide, and never on the curve. When I ask students, "How did you get that grade?" I frequently hear the honest reply, "I don't know." In a standards-based classroom, this is never the case. The rationale for grading is not the mysterious judgment of the teacher, but a reflection of a scoring guide that is based upon a clear set of standards.

Teachers Know the Expectations and Can Explain Them. The teacher can explain to any parents or other stakeholder the specific expectations of students for the year. Parents must be able to ask, "What does my child need to know and be able to do in order to be successful this year?" They should receive an answer that is consistent and coherent. Although the initial impulse to reply "Work hard and follow directions" may be tempting, parents and students deserve more detail. In any activity outside of school, parents would expect a clear definition of success, and they deserve the same within the school. Leaders can profitably devote the first few faculty meetings of the year to role play in which the leader poses as a parent and asks the question. Teachers and the leader can collaborate in crafting the best response to the query regarding what students must know and be able to do to succeed. The time to answer the question is at the beginning of the year, not after controversy arises about a grade or curriculum decision.

The Teacher Has Flexibility. The teacher has the flexibility to vary the length and quantity of curriculum content daily to ensure that students receive sufficient time on the most essential subjects.

This criterion is counterintuitive to many teachers and leaders, particularly if they have assumed that implementing academic standards implies standardizing teaching practice. In fact, an integral part of successful standards implementation is greater flexibility for the teacher. Because student needs vary from one classroom to the next, the greatest need is flexibility in timing and emphasis, so long as it does not lead to flexibility in expectations. Therefore, administrators should devote attention to classroom assessment and teacher expectations instead of debating whether each teacher is delivering the same lesson at the same time on the same day.

Students Can Spontaneously Explain What Proficiency Means for Any Assignment. Larry Lezotte asks the question well when he inquires, "What are you learning about today, and how do you know if you are learning it?" If students are unsure or hesitant, it may be time to allow them to play a greater role in restating standards and creating a scoring guide. My experience suggests that if students have a chance to create expectations, the requirements end up clearer and more rigorous than when the job of articulating requirements is left exclusively in the hands of adults.

Commonly Used Standards, Such as Those for Written Expression, Are Reinforced in Every Subject. Spelling, capitalization, and grammar always count. When teaching mathematics, whether to elementary students or graduate students, I begin the semester by explaining: "Mathematics is about describing the universe using numbers, symbols, and words. We will use all three this semester, and all three are important enough that we will express them correctly." Symbols, including inequalities, exponential notation, periods, or commas, are important. Words and letters, whether in an algebraic equation or an English sentence, are important. The same emphasis on clarity of expression applies to science, social studies, physical education, and music. There is, in other words, no class in any school in the United States in which

English expression is unimportant or in which thinking, reasoning, and communication are extraneous.

Teachers Create Performance Assessments Frequently. The teacher should create at least one standards-based performance assessment each month. Training teachers in standards and standards-based assessment is not enough. The real question is whether the training is being used in the classroom. With respect to the issue of determining if standards are really in use, the question is not whether the teacher likes standards or had a good attitude about the last training session. The only relevant question is whether an assessment the teacher creates and uses in the classroom is related to a state academic standard.

Teachers Evaluate Collaboratively with Colleagues. A teacher should exchange student work with a colleague for review and collaborative evaluation at least once every two weeks. Collaboration is the hallmark of effective implementation of standards. In fact, standards have never been implemented by virtue of a colorful wall chart from the state department of education. Standards have only been implemented successfully when professional educators and school leaders agree, through intensive and consistent collaborative efforts, on what the word *proficient* really means.

The Teacher Gives Feedback on the Standards. The teacher should provide feedback to students and parents about the quality of student work—compared to the standards and not to the work of other students. School leaders are called to deal with this criterion when aggrieved parents notice that their child received the same score as another child but the other child had to submit the assignment several times to be deemed proficient. "That's not fair," the parents assert. "Our child got the problem right the first time, and that child only got the problem right after working hard, respecting teacher feedback, meeting the standard, and resubmitting the work. That just can't be fair!"

The leader must support teachers as they give two clear rejoinders to this complaint. First, in a standards-based school, teachers never compare the work of one student to that of another student. "I'll devote an entire hour to comparing your child's work to a standard," the teacher might say, "but I will not spend a single moment comparing your child's work to that of another child. That sort of discussion is out of bounds, and I won't do it." Second, the teacher might note: "I'm quite familiar with the academic standards of this state, and not a single one of them requires that our students complete proficiency quickly. In fact, not a single standard refers to speed, but all of them refer to the quality of work. Therefore, I evaluate student work on the basis of the standards and the quality of work, never on a comparison of one student to another."

The Teacher Builds Consensus. The teacher should help to build community consensus in the classroom and with other stakeholders for standards and high expectations of all students. National polling data make clear that teachers are trusted purveyors of information, particularly about educational policy. Voters trust teachers more than they trust board members, state policy makers, or school administrators. Therefore teachers bear particular responsibility for carrying the message of the fairness and effectiveness of academic standards. The effective leader gives teachers the tools, time, and opportunity to practice effective communication with the community at large. Role-playing dialogue with skeptical community stakeholders is excellent practice for a faculty meeting or professional development seminar.

There Are a Variety of Assessment Techniques. The teacher should use a variety of assessment techniques, including extended written response, in all disciplines. Although I believe in performance assessment, I am not a zealot on the subject. In fact, there is a time and place for multiple-choice items, short answers, extended response, demonstrations, and projects. Effective teachers use all of these assessment techniques.

Special Needs of the New Teacher

Take a moment, if you dare, and reflect on your first few hours, your first few days, as a teacher. Now magnify those feelings of apprehension manyfold for today's new educator, who must not only satisfy a local principal and deliver a textbook-based curriculum but also thoroughly understand the standards, assessments, and curriculum and mesh all three of those elements into a coherent classroom learning environment. Harry Wong (Wong and Wong, 2001) identifies some of the most compelling anxieties faced by the new professional. To his excellent list I would add three criteria for the school leader: focus, power standards, and assessment. By *focus*, I mean that the school leader must help new educators understand what they can safely ignore. The sheer quantity of curricular requirements can be overwhelming, and every single element of those requirements feels like a mandate. Help the new teacher understand what can be dropped. *Power standards* are an essential concept, empowering the teacher to collaborate with colleagues to identify the most important standards. *Assessment* is an emphasis that the new teacher may not expect. The best of the lot may be prepared with lesson plans and curriculum. At the end of the day, however, the leader cannot observe or check lesson plans for every curriculum area at every grade. The leader can, however, examine teacher-created assessments. This reveals the link to standards, the level of expectation, and the clarity of a teacher's communication with students and parents.

Special Needs of the Veteran Teacher

"Do you mean to tell me," the veteran teacher asks, "that everything I've been doing for twenty-eight years is wrong?" Before the leader offers impulsive reassurance, let us stop and consider these questions. Do we expect a pilot in the twenty-first century to know more about weather, air traffic control, and passenger safety than we expected of a pilot in the 1970s and 1980s? Do we expect a physician to make decisions and use tools today different from what we expected twenty-eight years ago? Do we expect our barber or hairdresser to have learned new information and make different decisions today than three decades ago?

For everything from personal appearance to health to personal safety, we expect professionals to change. This expectation of change implies no disrespect to hairdressers, doctors, or airline pilots. If educational leaders and teachers do not accept such a minimal requirement—that we accept change nondefensively and expect to change professional practices accordingly—then we place ourselves far lower on the professional ladder than those professions that are willing to use new knowledge to change professional practice. When we appeal to veteran teachers, we are seeking to appeal to them as professionals. We ask them to regard the value of their work in the same light as those professionals who regularly receive new information and react to it by changing professional practice.

Note well that we do not ask that these changes be popular, only that they be effective. It is difficult to imagine that any professional development specialist or organizational leader ever asks a physician, "How do you feel about that new antibiotic?" or inquires of an airline pilot, "Do the new air traffic control patterns adversely affect your self-esteem?" No, on matters of health and safety we only inquire about effectiveness, not popularity. At some point, leaders must stop giving veto power over their commitment to fairness to any stakeholder, including teachers, students, and parents, who do not like the idea of fairness. The issue is not what they like, but what is effective.

We come inevitably to what I have called the "hygiene and vaccination" standard. Think about how you would respond if the school cafeteria staff insisted: "These new hygiene requirements just don't work for us. After all, we've been doing this for twenty-eight years and we know what we're doing, so don't bother us with talk of bacteria and diseases." Consider your response to the school nurse who says: "These vaccination records are just impossible. Some kids won't cooperate and many parents don't like them. I've decided to let the vaccination records go this year."

Health and safety criteria make our decision an easy one. Neither personal opinion nor a characterization of public opinion stands in the way of the health and safety of the children you serve. Thus the only question is whether school success rises to the hygiene-and-vaccination standard: Does the quality of our work in literacy and school success affect the health and safety of students? Most secondary school counselors insist that the answer is clear: school success is as important as hygiene and vaccinations, or more so because the absence of school success leads to student behaviors that expose them and others to significant health risk.

Thus even if the school nurse or cafeteria manager has been working in her position for many years, we do not let her assertion of experience deter us from our commitment to health and safety. So it must be with regard to the leader's reaction to anyone in the system who inhibits our commitment to the intellectual, emotional, or physical health of students.

Dealing with a Divisive Faculty

Without doubt, the most common question I hear in traveling to schools across the nation is, "How do I get buy-in from reluctant faculty members?" The premise of such a question is that if we have just the right speech, just the right incentive, just the right explanation, then the opposition will slam their fists to their foreheads and collectively exclaim, "Now I get it!" With this great revelation, all opposition to new initiatives is withdrawn and faculty members retreat to their rooms, enlightened by their new knowledge and adorning the walls with colorful charts from the state department of education. When pigs fly (Madonna, 1999).*

The most important concept to bear in mind in dealing with a divisive faculty is that behavior precedes attitude. Leaders cannot wait for attitudes to become adjusted, as the delay of

---

*Special note to sticklers for detail: this is a joke.

implementation until buy-in by all faculty members grants to the most recalcitrant member of any faculty veto power over progress. In the end, the leader's question is not "Was a good time had by all?" but rather "Was this innovation effective in improving student achievement?"

Collaboration is not universally popular, but it is effective. Increased nonfiction writing, with editing and rewriting, is not universally popular, but it is effective. The leader is not called on to get everyone to agree, but to implement the most effective possible professional practices. If new practices deliver results, then they become popular. Behavior, in sum, precedes attitude. This is not unlike our experience with students who will thank us many years hence for today's challenges. Faculty members do not universally respond with enthusiasm to the principle of fairness and the imperative of collaboration. The issue is not popularity, but effectiveness.

Nurturing Champions

A fundamental principle of leadership is that it is faster and easier to build on strength than to compensate for weakness. In their groundbreaking research based on more than one million interviews and multidimensional indices of organizational success, Buckingham and Coffman (2001) established what veteran leaders have learned through difficult experience: leadership by argument doesn't work. The most effective strategy that the leader can employ is to systematically identify the strengths of each team member and then capitalize on those strengths.

At the Center for Performance Assessment, we created a "strength map" that plotted the key strengths of each person. Using Buckingham and Coffman's thirty-three strength indicators as a starting point, we initially discovered that despite superficial similarities no two people had identical strength profiles. Many people had strengths that were totally different from others, with not a single one of their five predominant strengths being the same as for a coworker. This helped to explain some differences in working and learning style. When differences are understood as strength, however, a new strategy ensues. The leader's job is no longer to plead, "Why can't the rest of you be more like me?" Rather, the leader's task is to work with individuals and groups, ensure that each group has the core strengths that are required for its work requirements, and help each team recognize and use the strengths it has. At Elkhart Elementary School in Aurora, Colorado, for example, the dynamic and effective principal, Laura Nachazel, compiled a book of the best practices of her faculty. Even in an environment in which poverty and second language challenges are prevalent, the leadership focus remains on developing, recognizing, and capitalizing on the strengths of the faculty.

Schmoker (1996, 2001), Anderson (2001), Reeves (2000a), and Haycock and others (1999) have documented case after case of extraordinary success by educational leaders. A common theme of these case studies is not that the schools were merely lucky with respect to exceptional personnel who landed at the right place at the right time. Indeed, the very ordinariness of the buildings, staff, and resources of these exceptional schools was something that stands out from the research. As one faculty member interviewed for case study research of successful schools indicated, very few people volunteer to come to a troubled school; most faculty members are simply assigned there. Their success occurs because the leader finds strengths in people that they don't know they have.

Documentation of success, development of success, recognition of success, and systematic application of success . . . these are the hallmarks of the learning leader. Even when student achievement is low, the effective leader conducts a relentless search for the variables that are most related to student achievement to understand and apply the antecedents of excellence and thus ride the resilience continuum described in Chapter Nine. Unfortunately, most educational leaders spend a disproportionate amount of time not on their champions or in discovering strength but in an endless battle with weakness and belligerence.

Conduct your own calendar study for a week. Compare the amount of time spent responding to, arguing with, and listening to the complaints of the most antagonistic opponents of academic standards. Compare this to the time allocated to nurturing the champions, who not only accept the fundamental case for standards but also create their own standards-based performance assessments and share them willingly with other professionals.

The leader's primary task is to catch colleagues doing things right. We do not have the time to catch people doing something right if our entire energy is focused on dealing with those who are in error. Build on strength. It is the only way you as a leader can sustain your most effective efforts.

Chapter Six

Standards and Community Leadership

Communicating with Parents, Politicians, and Community Members

Leadership Keys

What parents want from schools

How the leader can listen to parents

How parents can learn from the school leader

Making the case to policy makers and community activists

In November 2001, I had the opportunity to address the Leadership and Policy Forum at the Harvard Graduate School of Education. The director of the Principal's Center, Mildred Pierce, began the day by asking the assembled school leaders, policy makers, board members, union leaders, researchers, and scholars to answer the question, "What are your wants and needs for public education?" The results did not seem surprising at first. Most of the responses said that students needed to respect one another and enjoy learning. With the tragedies of September 11 fresh in everyone's mind, responses spoke of valuing democracy, respecting different points of view, and tolerating other cultures. There were a few offerings regarding the need to study and understand great world religions, improve knowledge of geography, and understand the foundations of civil liberties. I listened as each table reported its results, and I quickly tabulated the sense of the group as shown in Figure 6.1.

My methodology was not scientific, nor was the sample of people reporting in Cambridge that day anywhere close to a

Figure 6.1 Informal Survey of Harvard Seminar Participants for Their "Wants and Needs for Public Education"

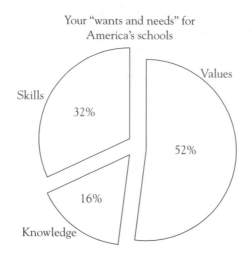

representative sample of the population. In fact, that is precisely the point. Before I began my remarks, I posted the hastily constructed chart in front of the audience. Fewer than one-third of the items referred to student skills; I asked the assembled group, "If we had a group of parents in this room, how would they have described their wants and needs for public schools?" I know that as a father of four I have a strong desire that my kids learn to read and gain the academic skills necessary to succeed at the next level of instruction, whether advancing in an elementary school or entering Harvard.

The dichotomy between the opinions of the participants in the Leadership and Policy Forum and the communities that we serve is not unusual. Educational journals are full of self-congratulation and indignant rejoinders to any national study that indicates dissatisfaction with public education. Talk radio, meanwhile, is dominated by the presumption that public education is an irredeemable failure. School leaders will not close the gap between the idealism of academic gatherings and the cynicism of many in our communities by scoring debating points. Moreover, leaders do not advance their cause by implying that every point of view is equally valid and that if we just work hard enough, everyone will be happy. Students are not customers; even if that analogy is foisted upon us, the customer is not always right. The leader must recognize the difference between an agenda in the community and the agenda of the school, and either reconcile them if it is appropriate or else explain and defend an unpopular decision if that is necessary.

Parents are, however, enraged by what they regard as the patronizing we-know-better-than-you-do attitude that pervades many schools. Accountability reports are hard to find, test scores are undecipherable, curriculum documents are protected. The theme that runs through many schools is that parents who want to learn more about their school and become actively involved in their child's education are unwelcome, and their motives and values are subject to suspicion. Although every school claims to be a parent-friendly place where parent inquiries are welcome, the reality is that a parental inquiry on a substantive matter can be greeted with outright hostility. In a nonpartisan analysis of the new federal education legislation (Reeves, 2001a), I offered some checklists for parents that would allow them to learn more about the choices that the school offered, including the presence of charters schools or school vouchers. Among the six questions on the checklist were these two items: "Is my child required to attend the school nearest to me?" "Is there a report that will provide detailed information about the enrollment, teaching staff, and academic programs of each school in the district?"

One reviewer, reflecting an attitude that is not uncommon among educators and university faculty who train future teachers, regarded these questions as "adversarial." When school leaders presume that the reason for an inquiry is negative and that parents equipped with "too much" information might either misuse it or fail to understand it with the depth and sophistication of the experts, the chasm between community and public education system grows wider. If the leader is to build understanding and eventually create support, she must be committed to the words of Isaiah, "Come, let us reason together." Specifically, the leader must understand what information parents want and provide it consistently and proactively. In addition, she must listen to parents, collaborating where possible but never capitulating on core values.

What Every Parent Needs to Know

Parents require straight answers to questions in three areas: the performance of their own child, the performance of the entire school, and the availability of choices that parents can exercise.

Individual Student Performance

"How is my kid doing?" Report cards rarely give a clear response to this question, as there are a number of students who have high grades but are not proficient. One remarkably honest principal of a Midwestern middle school recently discovered that more than 60 percent of students who failed to achieve a score of at least "proficient" on the state test in reading, writing, and mathematics had received grades of A, B, or C in those subjects. Thus when leaders address the question "How is my kid doing?" they must do more than send the parents a copy of the transcript.

A holistic view of student achievement includes, at a minimum, the report card, test information, and (most important) a clear and unequivocal statement about the standards that students can and cannot meet. Guskey and Bailey (1999) published a splendid set of examples for how parents can receive superior information from teachers and schools without imposing an excessive burden on teachers.

One model that I have advocated (Reeves, 2000b, 2002c) giving parents excellent information and saving teachers time is the Standards Achievement Report. As the example in Exhibit 6.1 indicates, the teacher can keep student records in a one-page-per-student format, and then copy the report and send it to parents at the end of the quarter. In this way, parents know precisely what has and has not been achieved. In the example of Exhibit 6.1, the parents can understand that even though Alex is generally a splendid science student, his work is not always submitted on time. Teacher Sackett may still have to award a traditional letter grade, but the Rosemans need not guess what the grade really means.

When this parent asks, "How's my kid doing?" it is necessary to extract information from a grade book or create a narrative explanation. Alex's parents know that he's a fine student and proficient in almost all of the science standards, but they also know he doesn't turn work in on time.

Conversely, another student might consistently submit work on time that reflects a pre-Newtonian understanding of science. Both students might have a C on their report card. But with the Standards Achievement Report, parents, students, and teachers understand that the letter grade represents two quite differing levels of proficiency in different standards.

School Performance

The second question that parents ask is, "How is the school doing?" In fact, they want to know how all the schools are doing. Schools that make this information difficult to get do not deter parents from asking the question; they only ensure that the source of information will be a collection of rumors, newspaper stories, and the musings of real estate agents. If educational leaders believe that they have a compelling story to tell, then they must communicate this to parents proactively. This is not easy to do in a time of test scores that may not reflect the actual success of schools.

Terry Thompson, one of the most innovative and dynamic school leaders in the nation, was recently dismayed when the newspapers reported flat test scores in his school system. He serves a rapidly growing area in which hundreds of new students enter the high school each year; one elementary school has seen enrollment balloon from about six hundred to more than one thousand

Exhibit 6.1. Standards Achievement Report (Example)

Grade 7 Science   Teacher: Sackett

Student: Roseman, Alexander   Year: 2002–03

Note to students and parents: this report summarizes the achievement of a student on five key academic standards for this class (S1–S5), as well as student performance in three additional standards that the teacher has determined are particularly important for student success (S6–S8). These records are updated every week. Please call the teacher at any time to review the progress of this student.

Code:

E = exemplary; P = proficient; IP = progressing, not proficient; N = not meeting standards

	S1– Scientific Method	S2– Structure of Matter	S3– Chemical Reactions	S4– Understanding Scientific Reports	S5– Designing Experiments	S6– Lab Safety	S7– Submits Work on Time	S8– Cooperates with Other Students
Lab	P		IP			P		P
Essay		E					N	
Quiz			IP					
Lab	P				IP	P		P
Quiz		P						

	S1- Scientific Method	S2- Structure of Matter	S3- Chemical Reactions	S4- Understanding Scientific Reports	S5- Designing Experiments	S6- Lab Safety	S7- Submits Work on Time	S8- Cooperates with Other Students
Test		E						
Lab	P		P		P	P		
Essay			E				IP	
Quiz					P			
Research paper				P	P		IP	P
Lab	P		E		E	?		
Lab	E		P		E	P		P
Quiz				P				
Test			E	P				

students. When new students enter the school without a background in the academic curriculum that he has emphasized, their performance on state tests does not reflect the impact of Thompson's leadership.

When, however, the same cohort of students was analyzed for the past two and three years, he discovered double-digit gains in several academic areas. The same sort of analysis can reflect growth that the typical newspaper story fails to notice. If a school can demonstrate that the longer a student remains, the better student achievement becomes, then it can make a strikingly positive case to parents and community members. Average test scores never tell the entire story. By carefully analyzing data and sharing with the community the full story, leaders such as Thompson do not engage in the traditional response to unpleasant test scores (critiquing the media or the test) but rather analyze the data in such a way that the public receives the most accurate and comprehensive picture possible.

Parental Choices

The third question to which parents demand an answer is, "What choices do I have?" Some public educators, along with their leaders and advocates, have created a false dichotomy between the advocates of school choice, referring to charter schools and publicly funded school vouchers on the one hand and public schools on the other. Creating such an inappropriate division suggests that a school is against choice and that if parents are in favor of choice, then they must resort to vouchers or charters. Public school leaders should embrace choice, as it is one of the most motivating factors in decision making by students and parents.

In Milwaukee, the "first choice" program allows more than 90 percent of parents to receive their first choice of public school. In Riverview Gardens, Missouri, Chris Wright's innovative use of a number of career academies within the high school allows a similarly large percentage of students to have their first choice of curriculum program. Within an individual school, the leader and teachers can collaborate to create parental choice in curriculum emphasis, reading materials, and extracurricular activities. Each time parents make a choice, they are placing a bet on the success of their child. The judgment of the parents suggests that the child will do well if a particular choice is made, and they become invested in seeing the wisdom of that judgment confirmed. Finally, the attitudes that underlie choice are inevitably transmitted from parent to child. Rather than surrendering to school mandates, parents are exercising choice, happily taking their children to school, inquiring about their success, and reinforcing the message of teachers and school leaders.

Communicating with Political Leaders and Policy Makers

When we think of educational policy makers, the first office holders in the mind of many educational leaders are the members of the local board of education. In most school systems, there is a formal protocol governing communication between board members and school system employees. Specifically, board members make information requests only through the superintendent, and the superintendent then identifies the most appropriate source of that information. If your board does not already have such a policy, then this is an excellent opportunity for the board to announce that part of the district's commitment to standards is that the board will set some standards for itself.

The Norfolk, Virginia, board of education, for example, is a national model in focusing its goals (actually they have only one, dealing with student achievement), and holding itself accountable for its agendas, activities, and information requests. Many other boards have created standards for the civility of their decorum, even in the midst of contentious and hotly contested political issues. By making it clear that standards are to be applied to the adults in the school system, including those in the most senior positions, the board sends a powerful message of leadership by example.

In addition to communication with the local school board, educational leaders have the chance to communicate with (and inevitably advocate positions before) a variety of political, community, and policy leaders. These include legislators, analysts, state department of education officials, grant providers, city and county officials responsible for making budgetary decisions that include schools, and a variety of other community and political leaders. These officials are frequently overwhelmed with information; there is rarely a shortage of opinion related to every issue they must consider. There is frequently, however, a shortage of objective and factual information. School leaders who wish to have the greatest influence on public policy follow four guidelines in presentation and communication: accuracy, compelling illustrations, zealous protection of individual privacy, and a hypothesis-testing approach to every issue.

The Accuracy Imperative

The most effective lobbyists, whether operating in the halls of Congress, a state legislature, or a local county commission, know that their greatest advantage is not necessarily silver-tongued advocacy but factual information. Lobbyists with information that is invariably accurate—even when that information does not favor the lobbyist's cause—are known as a credible source of data. In a contest of competing analysis and facts, the more credible advocate carries the day.

School leaders have an ethical obligation to offer information that is accurate. Fortunately, ethics and effectiveness coincide. The leader who has a clear-cut accountability system; consistent measurement of student achievement information; and believable analysis of teacher, leadership, and curriculum practices can explain a point of view with clarity and conviction. A leader who lacks information, relies exclusively on external sources, or appears to accompany each data source with an excuse or an attack will not long enjoy an audience of policy makers who need facts, not opinions, on which to render their judgment.

Compelling Illustrations

School leaders can do more than report the numbers. As good sports writers do every day, they can report the story behind the numbers. Consider these examples. The headline may be that college admission test scores, such as those reported on the SAT or ACT, are down. The story behind the numbers, however, could be a dramatic increase in the number of students taking the test as a result of the commitment of counselors, teachers, and school leaders to improve equity of opportunity for all high school students. Thus if the small number of academically elite students who traditionally take college entrance examinations are joined by a large number of students who, for the first time, regarded themselves as potential college students, equity improves but average scores decline. The teachers deserve praise, not opprobrium.

Another principal was facing budget cuts, particularly when people noticed that the school had many more extracurricular activities than other schools did. The story behind the headline is that the school faced a serious problem with truancy, tardiness, and absenteeism. The leaders and teachers sought to replace adult pressure with positive peer pressure, creating new extracurricular activities that involved every student in the school. This was expensive, tripling the number of extracurricular activities and increasing by half the amount of resources devoted to these apparently nonacademic areas. Within a year of the increase in extracurricular activity, however, student tardiness and absenteeism was reduced by 22 percent. Naturally, as attendance improved, student achievement improved as well. Given this chain of events, one should hesitate before calling the extracurricular activities in that school nonacademic. If a leader offers compelling examples and illustrations to make his point, he gives life to statistics and helps policy makers communicate complex ideas to their constituencies.

Privacy Issues

Leaders have an ethical and legal obligation to zealously guard the privacy of students and adults in the school. This becomes problematic when data are broken down into small groups so that the identity of a student can be easily inferred from the data alone. If the principal announces reading scores by ethnicity, and the school has only one American Indian student and two of Asian descent, then listing test scores or disciplinary incidents disaggregated by ethnicity makes it too easy for the casual observer to have knowledge of individual test scores or behavioral problems. Policy makers have a legitimate interest in trends and descriptive statistics for a group of students, but they do not have a right to private information on an individual student or employee unless there is a specific policy-level action (such as an expulsion or termination) that warrants their attention. Outside of the school system, public officials rarely if ever have a legitimate interest in the details of an individual student's records, and school leaders have an obligation to maintain the privacy of those records.

Hypothesis Testing

In communicating with community leaders and policy makers, it is tempting for school leaders to immediately seize the opportunity to advocate their own point of view. I have seen principals, superintendents, central office administrators, and other school leaders pointlessly cross swords with school board members, legislators, and other officials, seeking only to express an opinion that the audience already knew was strongly held by the speaker.

An unusual but far more effective tactic is the hypothesis-testing approach. Using this technique, the leader expresses a typical hypothesis about the matter at hand: "The board appears to be convinced that the following hypothesis is true: if all ninth grade students take the same algebra class, then student achievement in mathematics will improve. Before I go any further, may I please confirm that this is the hypothesis before us?"

This approach of stating the hypothesis and confirming that it represents the predominant view is essential for mutual understanding. After confirming that the majority of the board embraces this hypothesis, the leader should continue: "If this hypothesis is true, then the data should look like the following chart . . ." and explain the relationship between the data and the hypothesis. Staying with the example of all students taking the same class, the hypothetical chart might look like that in Figure 6.2.

The leader can then proceed with the results of two experiments, one of which directly tests the hypothesis while the other is an alternative for the policy makers to consider. (These figures are adapted from the actual pilot programs and data from the eighth and ninth grade math scores of a large urban district.) Figure 6.3 indicates that when all students are forced to take the same algebra class, regardless of their preparation, the scores decline significantly. The number of failures jumps dramatically, and these students are now a year behind their peers.

Another pilot program was also attempted in which students challenged in mathematics were given the chance to take the same algebra class over two years rather than one year; we called it

Figure 6.2. Hypothesis: Identical Algebra Classes Will Improve Student Achievement

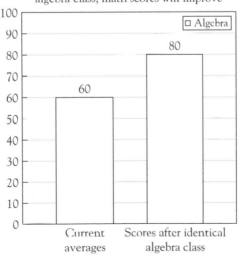

Figure 6.3. Actual Data to Test Hypothesis

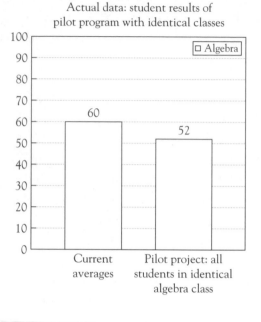

Actual data: student results of
pilot program with identical classes

"stretch algebra." We then gave all students an identical final exam. As Figure 6.4 indicates, the students who devoted two years to the class—students who were markedly deficient in mathematics preparation and who very likely would have failed the standard algebra class—had scores almost identical to those of students who took the one-year class. In other words, the hypothesis that requiring every student to do the same thing does not appear to be supported by the evidence. Rather, we can have the same academic requirements, without instituting the same class and time requirements for each student. By maintaining our standards but varying our time and instructional strategies, we have the best of both worlds: high achievement without a large number of failures.

Using these principles of advocacy—accuracy, compelling illustrations, zealous protection of privacy, and hypothesis testing—the school leader can gain credibility with policy makers, be an effective advocate for a point of view, and promote the esteem in which educational leaders are held.

Figure 6.4. Pilot Program Data: Impact of "Stretch Algebra" Classes

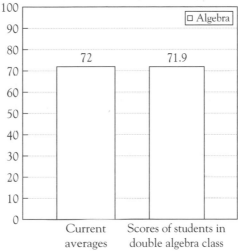

Hypothesis: if all students take the same algebra class, math scores will improve

☐ Algebra

Current averages: 72

Scores of students in double algebra class: 71.9

Dealing with Community Opposition

Opposition to standards is widespread and well organized. Moreover, many of the leading opponents of standards are intelligent people of goodwill. Some of them bring to the debate decades of experience as classroom educators, and others are keen observers of educational research. Thus it is particularly important that educational leaders who wish to support standards differentiate between those who oppose academic standards out of personal conviction or serious research concerns on the one hand and from rumor, innuendo, and plain falsehood on the other. All of these points of view might be represented in a roomful of angry people who have only one thing in common: antagonism toward academic standards. Here are some common allegations I have heard about standards:

- Standards were created by big businesses to create a workforce for them.
- Standards destroy creativity in the classroom.

- Standards are based on fuzzy-headed educational theories such as whole language and new math.

- Standards are nothing but outcomes-based education recycled, and just like Outcomes-Based-Education (OBE) they are an invasion of parental rights.

- Standards are created in Washington, D.C., and are an imposition on local control of schools.

- Standards are inappropriate for students, forcing elementary kids to do work far beyond what is developmentally appropriate for them.

In dealing with community opposition to standards, the leader should begin with a search for common ground. I sincerely believe that the opponents of standards, including those who have launched personal attacks on the advocates of standards, have this in common with me and with educational leaders everywhere: they love kids and want the best for them. Thus it does not advance the cause of reason for the advocates of standards to take the bait of some standards opponents who presume that an advocate of standards is a co-conspirator with tobacco companies and entertainment conglomerates and has not the slightest interest in the well-being of children. Rather, even in the face of provocation, standards advocates should assume the best motives of their opponents and seek common ground. Your best course of action is to refrain from responding to personal attacks and challenges to your own motives. Focus on the central issue of the conversation: a mutual search for the best way to promote fairness and success for every student in every school.

In addition to presuming good motives and searching for common ground, an educational leader must remain focused on the facts. In one incident that remains quite clear in my mind, a group that was violently opposed to educational standards distributed a fax to every school in the state, asserting, among other things, that the state standards relied upon whole language to the exclusion of phonics and endorsed new math to the exclusion of the basics.

Other allegations, including almost comical misquotations from my own writings, accompanied the vitriolic attack on standards. The cause of reason is not served, however, by a response in kind to people who are neither nice nor willing to carefully read the documents available to them.

The best response is a factual one. "On page 12 of the standards," I began, "there is a clear requirement for students to learn phonics. On page 31," I continued, "there are explicit requirements for students to add, subtract, multiply, and divide, with and without a calculator. These requirements appear to be precisely what the opponents of the document would like to see. When they insist that the standards of this state lack an emphasis on phonics or the basics of math, it is possible that they did not notice these pages in the standards." When confronted with people who impugn your motives and call you names, you are tempted to respond in kind. Focus on the facts, and take your frustration to the gym.

When introducing an audience to the leadership issues surrounding educational standards, I invite the inevitable opposition to become transparent. "Please tell me," I begin, "all of the reasons that standards will not work, will particularly not work here, and why standards are doomed to ineffectiveness in your particular school." For about fifteen minutes, the floodgates open, and I quietly write down each objection and allegation. When the flood slows to a trickle, I inquire several times, "Anything else?" We should then have the definitive list of the reasons that standards are doomed in a school or district.

The challenge is to take each of those arguments seriously, and equip every leader, educator, and community member with the facts necessary to respond to each allegation. For example, let us consider the allegations noted earlier and show how an educational leader might respond to them:

- *Standards were created by big businesses to create a workforce for them.* Actually, our standards were created by teams of teachers, parents, and community members from this state.

Of course, the business community was a part of, but not the dominant force in, this discussion. I think that we want our kids to have opportunities for economic success after they leave school, and that includes having the skills to get a job. Are there specific standards that appear to be related to job opportunities that you think are a bad idea?

- *Standards destroy creativity in the classroom.* I've visited a lot of schools; in fact, I traveled more than three hundred thousand miles last year and listened to a lot of teachers, parents, and school leaders. What impresses me is that some of the most creative and innovative teachers I have ever seen are in standards-based classrooms. They use the academic standards as the basis for their instruction, but they develop amazingly creative ways to help their students achieve these standards. I am particularly impressed by their creative use of assessments to challenge their children, foster rigor in the classroom, and help students understand the real-world relevance of their academic activities. On the other hand, I've seen some classrooms that studiously avoid academic standards, and the instruction is bound by textbooks and tradition-bound activities. In other words, some creative teachers use standards, and some very uncreative teachers avoid standards. My actual observation of real teachers just doesn't support the theory that standards and creativity are mutually exclusive.

- *Standards are based on fuzzy-headed educational theories such as whole language and new math.* This may have been true in other states, or in early versions of standards. But if you take a quick look at the actual words of our state standards, you find exceptional rigor. In fact, some people complain that the standards are too rigorous. You can understand how it is difficult for me to accept a criticism that a standard is simultaneously too easy and unchallenging, and a few minutes later hear the criticism that the same standard is so hard that it is inappropriate for a child.

- *Standards are nothing but outcomes-based education recycled, and just like OBE they are an invasion of parental rights.* It is difficult to know what your negative experiences were with outcomes-based education, but most of the opposition to OBE had to do with the fact that a few schools ventured into psychological expectations that some parents viewed as an inappropriate incursion into the right of the family to discuss questions of value and religion without public schools injecting a different point of view. Other challenges to OBE came from those who viewed some of the assessments as intrusive and inappropriate. Others opposed OBE because the report card and letter grades with which parents were most familiar were replaced by a statement of objectives. Let me reassure you that the academic content standards that we use are just that: academic. There is not a single syllable about psychology, attitudes, political beliefs, religion, or values. The only conceivable exception to this is that we expect students to respect themselves and one another and to be honest in their dealings. For example, our standards of ethical behavior do not allow students to copy the work of other students or to use library resources on a research paper without appropriate attribution of information to the source.

- *Standards are created in Washington, D.C., and are an imposition on local control of schools.* There are no national or federal standards. A few professional organizations, such as the National Council of Teachers of English, have offered some suggestions, but our actual standards were developed right here, in this state, by teachers, parents, and community members.

- *Standards are inappropriate for students, forcing elementary kids to do work far beyond what is developmentally appropriate for them.* It is possible that some standards are, in fact, inappropriate. As time goes along and we assess students on standards, we will learn more about this. But before you presume that because a child has not met a standard in the past it is automatically inappropriate, we should look at the facts. Many elementary students in other states are writing research papers in the fifth and sixth grade. Many eighth grade students are achieving proficiency in algebra. Many high school students are successfully integrating technology into every subject and are able to leave school with a good understanding of word processors, spreadsheets, databases, and graphics. If students in other states can succeed using these standards, it doesn't seem very likely that those requirements are developmentally inappropriate only for the children of our state.

These controversies are hardly new. As New York University history professor Diane Ravitch (2000) reminds us, many of the controversies in education that rage today are decades, even centuries, old. The task of the leader is not to eliminate opposition with withering criticism or to cower opponents with superior argumentative skill. Rather, we must engage every element of the community, search for shared values, and ultimately address each controversy with the facts.

Critical thinking standards in almost every state require a child in the earliest grades of elementary school to distinguish fact from opinion and fantasy from reality. Adults engaged in debate over educational standards would do well to commit themselves to this same standard of intellectual achievement.

Chapter Seven

Data-Driven Decision Making

Leadership Keys

Distinguish popularity from effectiveness

Seven steps to data-driven decision making

Examine test data and professional practices; accountability
is more than test scores

Measure the antecedents of excellence

Analyze and learn from mistakes

The title of this chapter comes close to being a cliché. After all,
using data to inform decisions seems to be so obvious that only
a leader belligerently indifferent to fact and reason would make a
decision without supporting data. Nevertheless, an astonishing
number of educational leaders make critical decisions about curriculum, instruction, assessment, and placement on the basis of
information that is inadequate, misunderstood, misrepresented, or
simply absent.

Even when information is abundant and clear, I have witnessed
leaders who are sincere and decent people stare directly at the information available to them, and then blithely ignore it. Consider
these examples, encountered in the past twelve months:

"We have examined our data and now have a list of all the students
who are two or more grade levels below their current grade in reading ability," the principal explained proudly. The superintendent

wanted data, and he had data. So how, I asked, would the curriculum, schedule, and instruction for those students be different now that we knew they faced a profound risk of future failure unless there were immediate and drastic changes in their schooling? "We just haven't gotten that far yet," the principal explained. The information was clear, but the principal failed to use it.

"I heard what you said about writing," the principal explained, "but our kids are really doing just fine in that area. Most of them get 4's or higher [on a 6-point scale]." That was quite impressive, I replied, but it seemed a bit unusual. Generally, when students have excellent writing skills, they also perform well in other academic areas, and though this group of students appeared to be writing very well they were performing badly in other areas. Was the principal quite certain about the data? "Oh yes," she explained, "I've looked at the data." Within minutes, a cursory review of the data revealed that more than 60 percent of the students in that school scored below a 4 in writing. The information was available, but the principal either didn't see it or refused to believe it.

"We have a great intervention program for our sixth grade students," the principal explained. "We tracked the progress of the students who participated, and many more of them succeeded than those who did not have the benefit of this intervention." I then asked how such a wonderfully successful program would be expanded, on the basis of this sound analysis of its effectiveness. "Actually," the principal explained, "we have discontinued the program. The teachers just didn't like it very much." The information was obvious, but the principal chose to ignore it.

These vignettes are not unusual. Although school systems have devoted enormous resources to developing data resources, the number of educational leaders who use them to influence their decisions remains small. Legions of administrators are sentenced to a day of professional development in a seminar called Data-Driven

Decision Making or something similar, but application of data to real decisions remains the exception rather than the rule. Consider this multiple-choice question:

The school nurse reports that 44 percent of students do not have their required vaccinations. What is the appropriate leadership decision?

(A) Fire the nurse.

(B) Conduct a five-year study of the vaccination program.

(C) Call the newspaper so that they can publish an embarrassing story about the vaccination program.

(D) Hide the results so that the district is not embarrassed by the failure of the vaccination program.

(E) Do whatever is required to get the kids vaccinated.

The essence of data-driven decision making is the final choice, the decision to act decisively and appropriately. Unfortunately, if we change the subject of the scenario from vaccinations to reading or mathematics, we find that choices (A) through (D) are all too common. Leaders already have the data they need; the issue is how they use it. This chapter is a blueprint for action that is based on fact and analysis.

Distinguishing Popularity from Effectiveness

"They absolutely loved it," the staff development director gushed. "We have the highest evaluations of any program all year long!" The superintendent reviewed the evaluations and concurred that the program was indeed quite popular. She then asked if there was any reason to believe that the participants had used the information that they received in the classroom. "They are so enthusiastic that they will obviously use it," the staff developer explained.

It isn't obvious. Tom Guskey (2000) carefully distinguishes between evaluating professional development on the basis of popularity and evaluating on the basis of student learning, and it is clear that the former is pervasive while the latter is rare. Consider the last professional development conference you attended. When were the evaluations completed? Invariably they fill the interval after the presentation and before application in the classroom, making it impossible for student performance and professional practice to play a role in the evaluative process.

The distinction between popularity and effectiveness must be made not only in evaluating professional development programs but also with respect to every curriculum intervention and educational program. Telling an eighth grade student that he needs three hours a day of literacy and that, as a result, he will have no electives in his final year of middle school is imparting a difficult message. Parents are enraged, students are angry, teachers complain that the school is becoming a boot camp. Equally unpopular is the administrator who must tell a fourth grade teacher that the traditional holiday program can continue, but rehearsals that seem to predominantly benefit two or three students are not permitted to interfere with sacrosanct reading time. A near riot may ensue when the educational leader suggests that the time devoted to the clay models of the Greek amphitheater in second grade, clay models of the Egyptian pyramids in third grade, and clay models of the Spanish missions in fourth grade are all activities less important than learning to read and write.

These decisions are not a matter of personal preference or idiosyncratic judgment. School leaders have evidence before them of effective practice. "In the classrooms that devoted three hours a day to literacy," the principal might observe, "we appear to have better student achievement in reading and writing than in those classes that have a sixty-minute literacy block. Therefore, I must compare the risk of students proceeding to the next grade without sufficient literacy skills to the risk of unpopularity just because we have a twenty-year tradition of amphitheaters, pyramids, and missions. I think I will take the second risk."

This is the essence of data-driven decision making. It is not finding perfection, and it is certainly not finding the optimal combination of a decision that is both effective and universally popular. It is, rather, about finding the decision that is most likely to improve student achievement, produce the best result for the most students, and promote the school's long-term goals of equity and excellence. It is, in brief, a deliberate trade-off in which the leader accepts some risks (say, unpopularity) to avoid other risks (illiterate students). A risk-free decision is never a choice; the only choice is the nature and degree of risk.

Accountability Is More Than Test Scores

When educational leaders analyze data, the first place to which they turn is the obvious source of data, the results from state and district tests. Although these results can offer some insight into student achievement, they never tell the whole story of the interrelationship between student achievement results and curriculum strategies, teaching practices, and leadership decisions. In fact, accountability, when properly applied, is not merely about announcing an evaluation of schools, but rather about deep analysis of cause-and-effect variables. Typically, we only analyze effect variables, such as test scores, attendance, and student safety. The cause variables, which include professional practices, curriculum availability, and leadership decisions, are also an integral component to understanding educational achievement.

Appendix forms 24 through 31 are reproducible materials that allow a leader to guide faculty members and school administrators through a reflective process considering not just test scores but also the professional practices associated with those scores. As the leader uses data to inform decisions, he can go beyond the typical analysis of test scores by considering three data analysis imperatives. First, he must avoid using the average, or arithmetic mean, in understanding test scores. Second, he must rigorously measure the antecedents of excellence, including teaching and leadership practices. Third, he must consider qualitative as well as quantitative information in analyzing student achievement.

The Average Is Not Your Friend

The mathematics standards in most states require that seventh grade students understand the difference among measures of central tendency: mean, median, and mode. The reason we expect preadolescents to understand this concept is that we know that in many cases across numerous disciplines (science, social studies, mathematics, education) the average, or arithmetic mean, is not the best measure of central tendency. It is therefore astonishing that the most frequent measurement of student achievement in accountability systems remains the average test score. The mean is a distorted measurement.

Although the average score is not particularly illuminating, some test data can reveal important information about teaching and learning. In particular, the subscales of a test reveal significant differences not among children but about curriculum. For example, if a group of students has a high score in place value and shapes and a low score in measurement, the difference cannot be explained by demographic characteristics, as the very same children in the same families perform well in one area and not so well in another. Whenever I explore this issues with teachers and leaders, the explanation is obvious: "We've been doing place value since first grade and shapes since kindergarten, but we didn't get around to measurement until after the test was already over."

By using test score data to evaluate curriculum emphasis and teaching strategies, we can turn what might have been a futile exercise in explaining, excusing, or blaming children and families into constructive means of understanding the strengths of teachers and students. We can then build on those strengths to address weaknesses. In the previous example, if the strengths in place value and shapes are explained as a result of a multiyear emphasis, obviously including attention to math classes but also to art classes, then the weaknesses in measurement can be addressed by a multiyear emphasis and commitment to addressing measurement learning needs in math class and in other areas, such as physical education and art.

The Seven *Continuous* Steps of Data-Driven Decision Making

In one of my more disheartening conversations of the past few years, a staff development director explained that "We did data-driven decision making last year" and thus did not require any more work in that area. I could not have been more dumbfounded had the director of food service explained that, despite an abundance of vermin and bacteria in the cafeteria, "We did hygiene last year" and thus did not require any more work in that area. Properly applied, data-driven decision making is a continuous process, requiring data gathering, analysis, and correction to decision making on a regular basis. The ten steps given here and the reproducible forms in the Appendix support this process.

Step One: Treasure Hunt (Appendix A-25)

Veteran educational leaders have described the treasure hunt process as "the best staff development I've had in thirty years" and "the first time I really understood my own data." The key to an effective treasure hunt is at least two hours of totally uninterrupted time. In many cases, Saturday morning has been the most effective time for this, as it gives administrators and lead teachers the only relief in their week from the interruptions of cell phones, announcements, and other demands on their time and attention. In some cases, the data may already be arranged for you in a convenient computer-spreadsheet format. Usually, though, the data are in a variety of paper reports, so the treasure hunt process allows the leadership team to gather the data and arrange it coherently and understandably.

Step Two: Data Analysis and Strength Finder (A-26)

Gathering the data in step one is a beginning; unfortunately, many leaders stop there. Charting data and announcing results is not analysis. Analysis occurs only when the leader digs into the data to find strengths and discover challenges. As the reproducible forms in A-26 indicate, analysis of subscale data is absolutely essential to gain understanding of the challenges and successes of the district and individual schools.

Step Three: Needs Analysis (A-27)

Successful data-driven decision making depends upon prioritization. If the result of data analysis is a list of twenty-five focus areas, then it has been a waste of time. The question that the leader must consider is this: Given the many data points that could be considered in planning curriculum and instruction, what are the greatest needs of this particular group of students?

There are two levels of analysis that the leader must consider. First are the needs of the individual students within a group. If low reading performance is not representative of an entire class but a reflection of the exceptional needs of a small group of students, then the challenge is planning interventions for that small group. In addition to considering the needs of individual students, however, the leader must also ask what the data suggest about the need for curriculum and teaching strategy. If the same strengths and challenges continue over the course of two or three years, then it obviously reflects not a problem with just one group of students but the impact of teaching and curriculum on any child who happens to come to that school.

Step Four: Goal Setting and Goal Revision (A-28)

Virtually every educational leader claims to have goals. A closer look at the statements that we label goals, however, reveals that there is frequently a mixture of generality, intention, task, and true goal. To be worthy of the name, a goal must meet several criteria, known by the acronym SMART, which has been used by many authorities in time management, leadership, and goal-setting and is decades old. Thus any contemporary claim to have invented either the acronym or the criteria is not justified.

The criteria associated here with the SMART acronym reflect the collective thinking of my colleagues at the Center for Performance Assessment. First, a goal must be *specific*. Thus "Improve student achievement" is not a goal, while "Increase the number of students who are proficient or higher in reading comprehension from 70 percent to 85 percent" is a goal. Second, a goal must be *measurable*. Thus "Apply interdisciplinary instruction" or "Use performance assessments" does not represent an adequate goal, but "Increase the number of classroom assessments that include student performances in more than one academic subject from 5 percent to 20 percent" does represent a measurable goal.

Third, the goal must be *achievable*. The most frequent debate regarding this criterion is the typical "100 percent" argument, which goal setters regard as imperative and teachers and principals regard as unrealistic. There is a middle ground here. Rather than expressing a goal such as "One hundred percent of students will meet all academic standards," the leader can consider a goal that strikes teachers and school leaders as challenging, fair, realistic, and achievable:

- One hundred percent of students with an individualized education plan (IEP) will achieve 90 percent or more of the IEP goals for the current school year.
- One hundred percent of students identified with reading comprehension one or more grade levels below their current grade will receive reading intervention assistance.
- One hundred percent of students will receive writing assessments, with appropriate adaptation and accommodation where required, every month.

- One hundred percent of teachers will participate in collaborative scoring conferences at least nine times during the year.
- One hundred percent of students will achieve a score of proficient or higher on a math problem-solving assessment, given multiple opportunities for success and appropriate adaptation and accommodation where required.
- One hundred percent of students will achieve a score of proficient or higher on a nonfiction writing assessment, given multiple opportunities for success and appropriate adaptation and accommodation where required.

The fourth criterion for effective goal setting is that the goal must be *relevant*. Specifically, it must be relevant to the people responsible for it. Teachers, for example, are most responsible for goals over which they have immediate and direct control (classroom assessment, collaborative practices, creating multiple opportunities for student success). Parents are responsible for goals over which they have immediate and direct control (participation with their student in direct support activity before, during, or after school). School leaders are responsible for goals over which they have immediate and direct control (teacher recognition, documentation of best practices, appropriate use of faculty meeting and professional development time).

Although it is commonplace to hear it asserted that "Everyone is accountable for student results," the fact is that people are most accountable for those specific actions and decisions that are under their direct control. Therefore it is the responsibility of the leader to ensure that these decisions are related to student achievement.

The final criterion for effective goal setting is that the goal be *timely*. A large goal is sometimes used to create a vision for an organization—the most famous one being President Kennedy's challenge in the early 1960s to put an American on the moon by the end of the decade—but the educational leader must also articulate goals that can be monitored frequently. Again, as a cardinal principle of leadership it is more important to measure a few things frequently than to measure many things once a year. If students, faculty, and parents all see a few goals that receive monthly measurement, that receive frequent leadership attention, and that result in regular feedback and reinforcement, then the entire educational organization is likely to focus on accomplishing those goals. In general, the results of state test scores are too late and infrequent to meet the standard of timeliness, and therefore the leader must create other intermediate goals that reinforce or allow midcourse correction.

Worksheet A-28 allows the leader to help the faculty differentiate between effective and ineffective goals and select goals on the basis of the specific needs analysis, data analysis, and treasure hunt that has been conducted.

Step Five: Identify Specific Strategies to Achieve Goals (A-29)

Educational effects have many causes. Using the forms in A-29, a leader can help faculty members identify multiple causes for each area of performance related to the goals identified in step four. Many of those causes may be beyond the influence of the educator or school leader. The key is to identify those variables that can be influenced by teaching practice, curriculum strategy, and effective leadership.

Step Six: Determine Results Indicators for Targeted Strategies (A-30)

The educational world is awash in things labeled *strategy* that are poorly defined and rarely measured. This essential step moves strategy from the abstract to the real by identifying specific practices that can be tracked, measured, and improved. There should be at least a one-to-one relationship between strategies and goals. In fact, there may be several strategies associated with a single academic goal. This is absolutely essential to link the goal-setting process to the Leadership and Learning Matrix. The goals of student results cannot be adequately understood and pursued unless there are also measurable strategies that describe the action of teachers and school leaders.

Step Seven: Action Plan, Schedule, and Review (A-31)

The action plan and schedule allows the goal setting process to take on a personal quality, with individual team members responsible for specific tasks at a particular time. Perhaps the most important part of this step is periodic review, which allows the leader and team members to evaluate progress throughout the year and make appropriate modifications in the goals. During the course of periodic revision, which should take place at least quarterly, the leader should address these specific questions:

- Can we improve the indicators we have selected?
- Can we improve how we measure these indicators?
- Can we select additional effect variables?
- Can we improve the measurement of effect variables, particularly leading indicators such as classroom- and building-level student achievement?
- Can we measure the relationship of cause variables to effect variables?
- Can we revise or discard indicators that are not working well?

Data-driven decision making is a continuous process. I know of schools that have dramatically changed their traditional opening-of-school routine, rejecting the familiar motivational speaker and frantic assembly of bulletin boards, and devoting two or three days instead to analysis of data; setting of goals; and focusing on specific needs in student achievement, teaching practice, curriculum strategy, and leadership.

Myths of Data-Driven Decision Making

The first myth of data-driven decision making is that test statistics and psychometrics are technical fields requiring experts for analysis.

It is true that a great deal of the information from test authorities at the state and district level is complicated, but complexity is an invitation for clarity, not an impediment to teacher and leader analysis of assessment data. The notion that test data should be left to the experts creates a gulf between data and decision makers that is unhelpful and potentially dangerous.

Educational reforms have been littered with methods and procedures that opt not to respond to the essential question "Why?" Parents ask, "Why should we trust this reform as applicable to the needs of our children?" Teachers ask, "Why should we abandon the practices of the past that are within our comfort zone?" Leaders ask, "How do the recommended practices relate to the specific needs of this school?"

No matter how complex the data may be in format and content, it is imperative that a leader translate the data into clear and understandable statements. Rather than "The mean scale score for our students is 573.6, with a standard deviation of 47.6," the leader must be able to say: "Forty percent of our students need assistance in reading; specifically, they need help in drawing inferences from nonfiction text. Therefore, we are going to focus in English, social studies, and science classes on text segments, followed by questions, summaries, and drawing inferences from the text. We have created our own classroom-based assessment for reading comprehension and will report every month our progress in improving the percentage of students who are proficient or better on that assessment."

Myth number two is that the central office is responsible for data analysis.

For any district consisting of more than one school, the central office departments of curriculum, assessment, research, and statistics can provide data, but they cannot provide analysis, strategy, or deep understanding of the needs of students and the practice of teachers at an individual school. There is no substitute for classroom-by-classroom, school-by-school analysis.

The third myth is that we don't have the time for this!

Without question, the most frequent objection I hear regarding any educational initiative, but particularly data-driven decision making, is the lack of available time. This complaint, however frequent, is fundamentally inaccurate. Time is available, but how we choose to spend time has been established by tradition and habit.

What is most astonishing is that there is invariably time for teaching and curriculum practices that are not supported by data but that are supported by tradition and habit. Each region of the country has its favorite activity that consumes scores of hours of classroom time, few of which have been rigorously linked to improvement in student achievement. The essential advantage of data-driven decision making is that new strategies can be tested, and where appropriate discarded. Similarly, existing strategies can be related to student achievement and, where appropriate, expanded or discarded. Only in this way do tradition and habit give way to rigorous analysis of data.

A Case Study in Data-Driven Decision Making

Here are notes taken from an actual data-driven decision-making seminar, a collaboration of a group of teachers and school leaders. These professionals have come up with a good balance of intermediate and annual indicators. Moreover, their strategies allow teachers to have immediate feedback on their progress; they need not wait until the end of the year to observe measurable progress in their efforts and the achievement of their students. Finally, the results indicators chosen by this group are balanced between student achievement and specific actions by teachers and school leaders. In brief, they understand the relationship between student results and the antecedents of excellence.

Needs Analysis

Thirty-seven percent of regular education grade one students lack basic reading skills at the conclusion of the first semester, and it is predicted that without reading intervention they will not be prepared to enter grade two with the proper skills to be successful.

Goal Statement

By the end of grade one, 80 percent of regular education students will be reading on grade level as identified by using the Gates-McGinity Reading Comprehension, Decoding and Vocabulary Assessment as well as the Terra Nova Reading Comprehension Assessment. Both assessments will be administered between April 25 and May 25.

Strategies

Between January and June of this school year, grade one students identified as reading more than two months below grade level as determined by a body of evidence, including the Houghton-Mifflin Reading Assessment and Running Records, will receive specific support through a comprehensive reading intervention program. This program is a strategy that we believe will benefit those students reading more than two months below grade level. The intervention program will include specific materials intended for reading intervention and be taught by specifically trained reading intervention teachers using specific reading intervention strategies.

Action Steps

To meet our stated goal of 80 percent of grade one students reading on grade level by June, the following actions will take place:

1. Identify and order specific reading assessments.

2. Identify and order specific reading intervention materials if not currently available at building site.

3. Identify and train reading intervention teachers.

4. Determine testing dates for all regular education grade one students.

5. Administer reading assessments.

6. Score and analyze reading data.

7. Specify those students reading more than two months below grade level.

8. Confer with the current reading teacher of the identified students.

9. Inform parents through letter and conference about the reading intervention program and the purpose of special support.

10. Establish an Excel spreadsheet on each student, showing current grade level equivalent reading comprehension score, grade level vocabulary score, and/or current grade level decoding score.

11. Establish dates of ongoing (monthly) assessments that will take place to monitor continuous student achievement.

12. Establish collaboration meetings with reading intervention teachers and grade one classroom teachers.

13. Review specific reading strategies that could or should be used in the reading intervention instruction as well as during regular reading instruction for additional support.

14. Meet every six weeks with parents of identified reading intervention students, giving them viable and useful steps and actions they can do at home to support reading intervention at school. These meetings also will be used to distribute up-to-date information as to the level of progress students are making.

15. Assess students during the end-of-year testing window.

16. Score assessments; analyze data.

17. Identify and highlight (in yellow) students listed on the spreadsheet who have reached or surpassed the goal of reading level of 1.9 *and* a Reading Recovery level of 18.

18. Determine the percentage of grade one regular education students who are reading on a grade one end-of-year level.

19. Determine plans for those students who are not at the expected reading level: summer school, summer at-home packets, conference with parents, tutor suggestions, etc.

Results Indicators

Evidence that action steps have been completed:

- Number of students assessed
- Number of identified students for the reading intervention program
- Spreadsheet created; alpha order with necessary, current assessment data
- Number of parents who were contacted and showed up for initial intervention conferences
- Number of teachers receiving intervention training
- Number of bimonthly collaboration meetings with regular ed teachers and reading intervention staff
- Assessments ordered, inventoried, and used with students
- Reading intervention materials ordered, inventoried, and checked out to intervention teachers
- Final analysis of the percentage of students in June who are reading on grade level

Part Two

Strategic Leadership for Educational Standards

Chapter Eight

Creating Ownership and Support for Standards

Leadership Keys

Create ownership

Require congruence among policies, practices, and the mission

Encourage experimentation

Nurture success

Focus

Leaders and board of education members have difficult jobs. Their tenure is notoriously brief and their public esteem is frequently low. Their critics include people who are quite convinced they could do the job better themselves but who typically have not spent a millisecond in the shoes of the school leader or policy maker they so vehemently criticize. When a board member or leader accepts the challenge of implementing standards, she has done far more than simply give her approval to the latest educational reform initiative. She has, instead, committed herself and her district to a comprehensive and rigorous course of action that influences teaching and learning for decades to come. This chapter outlines six key responsibilities of the leader and board member seeking to make standards work.

Create Ownership

Standards cannot be the exclusive product of the outside. Instead, standards must have broad ownership from every major constituency within the community. Even if your state has already adopted standards, each local district typically has the responsibility and the opportunity to develop its own standards, to be at least as challenging as the state standards.

The constituencies that should be represented in the standards development process include, at the very least, teachers, parents, community members, business owners and managers, colleges and universities, groups representing significant minority populations in the community, unions, and school administrators. The local history of your district may dictate inclusion of other key interest groups. In many communities, for example, the American Association of Retired Persons is a key voting group for school bond issues, and it would ill behoove any school district to exclude this group from any major educational policy initiative. Indeed, research on school bond elections indicates that support from the population frequently hinges on understanding that voting yes results in clearly understood educational results. Community ownership of standards is an excellent means to achieve this broadly based understanding.

Require Congruence

The superintendent and board of education must ensure that the policies they implement involving standards are congruent with other policy initiatives undertaken by the school system. In fact, the litmus test for every other educational initiative in the district should be, "Does this conform with our commitment to standards?" This means that in selecting textbooks and assessment instruments, conformity to district standards is essential. I know of one district in which a national assessment instrument vendor reviewed every single item in the assessment to determine the correspondence of those elements to the district's standards.

This is in marked contrast to the bland assertions of textbook and assessment vendors that their products are "standards-based." In fact, most textbooks and other curriculum materials are designed to meet the requirements of a great many states and thus pose an overwhelming amount of material for any individual teacher. The district leadership should specifically authorize curriculum directors, principals, and classroom teachers to use a textbook as a guide, not as a script. In the end, instructional leaders and educators are not responsible for the words they say but the results they achieve; thus the senior leadership makes it clear that there is a difference between delivery of prescribed material and the mandate to help all students achieve academic standards.

Congruence must also be ensured in personnel decisions. As leaders and other senior administrators contemplate the hiring, promotion, and tenure of teachers, administrators, and other key decision makers, the issue of standards must be part of the conversation. There are a number of fine teachers and administrators who do not believe in standards or who believe that they are a passing fad of minor significance. There are many places in the country for these people to work, but your district should not be one of them. Because this statement can be regarded by many as inflammatory, let me elaborate.

Standards are not just a good idea. They are essential if we are to achieve our national promise of equity and excellence for all children. If a school has a math teacher who is completely competent but who sincerely believes that Hispanic children can't do algebra, few leaders or school boards will hesitate to terminate the teacher. When it comes to matters of blatant discrimination, few people would argue, "Every teacher has the right to an opinion, and all opinions on the mushy field of education are equally valid." In this hypothetical case, we would conclude that competence in math isn't enough, and that the teacher must also be able to teach all students without prejudice.

What about a teacher who refuses to take a standards-based approach to education? Is this just a matter of personal opinion and professional independence? If we accept these tired claims and their twisted notion of professional independence, then any teacher can say, "I can teach the math, and it is the students' responsibility to learn the way that I teach." If such a statement is equated with

academic freedom and professional independence, then there is little recourse against the teacher who explicitly confesses prejudice
that is based on ethnicity or gender. In sum, teachers have a responsibility to teach all students, and leaders have a responsibility to
make decisions in the best interests of students. If we fail to lead
decisively, then teachers who take the risks and endure the work
of implementing standards soon get the message that the words of
their leaders are not congruent with their actions.

Congruence is also essential in using external evaluation. The
discipline of educational evaluation has too frequently depended
on the notion of expertise. This leads to a model in which the des-
ignated expert evaluates a program on the basis of her individual
understanding of what is good and proper rather than the criteria
of the district. In a standards-based district, however, the standards
have already set the criteria for evaluation; hence every external
evaluator should be expected to develop familiarity with district
standards. More important, it should be clear in every request
for proposal (RFP) for external evaluation that the standards
of the district—not the personal beliefs and prejudices of the
consultant—are the definitive guide for the evaluation.

Encourage Experimentation

One of the most frustrating things for a leader or board member is
the feeling of utter impotence in implementing a policy initiative
and then watching as nothing happens. Harry Truman remarked
that when General Dwight Eisenhower assumed the presidency,
Ike would be immensely frustrated by the contrast to his military
days, in which every order was followed by a salute and an action. As
president, Truman observed, the most powerful man on earth is frequently powerless in the face of the immovable federal bureaucracy.

Systemic change rarely occurs as the result of an order, a resolution, or a policy. Rather, change in a complex system occurs
when the various key decision makers (in this case, teachers, principals, students, and parents) decide that the new initiative is in

their best interest. This conclusion is reached most frequently by these many decision makers not from a persuasive speech by the superintendent but rather from their direct observation of use of standards in a classroom and school they know to be effective. As a result, using a pilot program is an important first step for standards implementation at the district level. During the pilot program, you can document your success, gathering testimonials from teachers, students, parents, and administrators. You will have a ready-made answer for every challenge, question, and inevitable complaint that "these ideas just won't work here."

Leaders are typically action-oriented; that is how they became leaders. Some of them, along with many board members who must stand for reelection in a short period of time, might ask, "If standards are so great, why not simply implement them throughout the district immediately? A pilot project just seems like a waste of time!" This question deserves a serious response.

• Pilot projects create enthusiasm among the key faculty leaders and principals. The best educational innovators in your district have probably been implementing some version of standards already, and it is essential that they be on your team.
• Pilot projects allow the initial bugs to be worked out of a system, which lowers the cost of errors. Many initial drafts of standards, including those approved at the state level, contain important omissions. Other drafts are not as clear as they should be. The pilot project allows a district to have the second draft of standards implemented districtwide, with the omissions and ambiguities corrected prior to large-scale implementation. Experienced computer users know that you never buy version 1.0 of anything. The same applies to districtwide implementation of standards: first, work out the bugs with a pilot project.
• The justification for a pilot project is leverage. There is an enormous professional development process involved in standards implementation. This challenge can best be achieved through teachers teaching teachers. The participants in your pilot project

have local credibility and direct experience in making standards work in your district. In addition, using an outside consultant can focus on a small number of schools, in workshops of a manageable size.

• Pilot schools are an ideal long-term source of mentors for student teachers. Few teacher-training institutions are offering any in-depth preparation for standards-based performance assessment. If this is a skill you expect teachers in your district to have, then it is essential that you build that expectation into the student teacher training program. It is also important that student teachers not be assigned to mentor teachers who are not actively conducting their classes in accordance with the district's academic content standards.

• Using pilot programs gives the district leadership an opening for public recognition and rewards for those who are leaders in the standards movement.

• To create systemic change, you must change the system of rewards. This includes not only appropriate remuneration for the extra meetings and time a pilot project entails but also public recognition, professional development resources, and special consideration for promotion and advancement. One certain way to effectively kill standards implementation in your district is for the leadership to talk about the wonders of innovation and academic standards, and then give the Teacher of the Year award to the person whose class had the best test scores on an assessment not related to your district standards.

Nurture Success

Requests for support probably constitute 90 percent of a superintendent's inbox. Standards implementation requires support in three specific ways: time, money, and protection. Management theorist Tom Peters has remarked that if he wants to see what a leader's priorities were, he looks no further than the person's calendar. If the days are consumed with meetings and presentations, then the headquarters staff (invariably large) is devoting its time and resources to preparation and elaborate presentation for those meetings. If, by contrast, the days are largely consumed with community associations, boards, and public posturing, then the leader is probably using the organization to promote his own image rather than using his leadership skills to promote the organization. Finally, if the leader is spending time doing what the organization actually does (make cars, sell toys, teach students) then (and only then) is the leader devoting the precious resource of time where it belongs.

Time

Surely no superintendent can get through many days without a meeting of some kind. But my observation is that too many school leaders are captives, rather than controllers, of their calendar. If the school leader is to make available the time essential for standards implementation, she or he must devote a significant amount of time for teacher collaboration. This is not simply a longer "planning period" but rather a specifically structured time in which the specific elements of student performance standards are reviewed. Some school districts that are successfully implementing standards devote two to four hours every week to this effort.

Just as Peters advocates a minimum of four hours each week for "management by wandering around," the superintendent focused on standards should similarly allocate a minimum of four hours each week to the subject of standards. Some of this time can be spent watching teachers in a pilot project struggle with their evaluation of student work. Other hours can be spent with members of the business community, improving their understanding and support for the standards movement in the district. Still other hours can be spent in extended classroom observation, sitting on the floor with some second graders.

The superintendent must be able to articulate what makes a standards-based classroom different. In one standards-focused district, the superintendent required every senior district-level administrator (including himself) to create and teach a block of standards-based instruction. This leader is putting his time where his rhetoric is.

Money

Support for standards by the district also means money. Specifically, standards implementation requires blocks of time (typically half a day per week) for teachers to review student work, devise scoring guides, and create new standards-based assignments. Allocating this time costs money. Given the workload of most teachers, their pursuit of a graduate degree in their nonworking hours, their family responsibilities, and the stress associated with a normal school day, it is unreasonable to expect that this half-day block should occur after the school day or on a weekend. (I have seen some effective standards implementation teams do this, but the participants ended the school year physically and mentally exhausted.) The best course of action is for the district to provide either long-term substitutes or other organized activities for the classrooms of these teachers so that the teachers can spend the half-day block at a consistent time and day. They can then devote their full intellectual energy to the hard work of standards implementation.

Protection

Finally, the support required of the superintendent and board is that of protecting the champions of standards. The resistance to standards implementation can be formidable and emotionally draining. This is particularly true at the secondary school level, where some students spend more hours and take more classes than has traditionally been the case to meet their requirement to demonstrate proficiency in all of the district standards. With more hours devoted to academic content standards, there are fewer hours devoted to nonacademic pursuits. Inevitably, some nonacademic classes and popular extracurricular activities suffer.

Rather than allowing a destructive division to occur between academic and nonacademic faculty members, the effective district leader must make clear that there is no such thing as a nonacademic faculty member. Every teacher, activity, class, and requirement makes a substantive contribution to students achieving standards. Teachers who effectively integrate academic content standards into their classroom activities need support and protection from the cynics, who always allege that some activities are outside the realm of standards. In the standards-based district, there are no such activities.

Leading Reluctant Followers

When a district changes its orientation from seat time to achievement of standards, it often takes time for many students to achieve these standards. This leaves some teachers, parents, and students asking, in a quavering voice, "Do you mean to tell me what I've been doing all these years isn't valuable because it doesn't meet the district's new standards?" The only response to this query is: "Your work is indeed valuable, because every class and activity, including yours (for example drama, music, art, woodworking), will now be linked to an academic standard. How can you enrich this class so that it will help our students achieve standards?" Some teachers and parents will respond, "But this just isn't an academic class, and it never has been!"

Faced with absolute intransigence, the superintendent and board must unhesitatingly make the decision to eliminate those activities or to do them in a strikingly different way. Such a position may make some educators apprehensive, particularly those who have viewed their field as nonacademic. Upon further reflection, however, educators in music, art, physical education, technology, and other areas that have been inappropriately stereotyped as nonacademic frills should be delighted that their classes are at last being recognized as possessing academic content and value.

They know from experience that many students (particularly those who are kinesthetic learners) can learn fractions, decimals, ratios, and many mathematical standards in home economics, industrial arts, and music classes. There are many students who learn these standards far better in such a hands-on class than they do in a traditional abstract math class. But some programs, supported only by tradition and popularity rather than commitment to achieving standards, have constituencies ready to conduct a wholesale attack on the standards movement.

The effective superintendent and board have no choice but to take swift and sure action to protect the champions of standards from these attacks and, ultimately, to eliminate inappropriate, unproductive, and wasteful activities from the district.

Focus

This heading is not a mistake. It is a repetition of early injunctions in these pages for leadership focus. My experience suggests that the message is important in every context and in virtually every chapter. Focus is one of the primary obligations of the leader because failure to focus places the mission at risk. Initially, the school board should consider seriously a one-year moratorium on any new initiatives in the twelve months following implementation of standards. Implementation of standards is a mammoth project; no complex system should attempt to undertake multiple major changes, particularly if there is a risk that some of the changes are contradictory. In addition, the board and superintendent should build into every agenda a progress report on standards implementation. This should specifically include an action report at the building-and-classroom level, where particularly effective examples of standards implementation can receive high recognition and appreciation. Just as many a board agenda begins with the Pledge of Allegiance and public recognition, so the standards-driven district gives consistent attention and priority to reports of successful standards implementation.

The leadership must ensure broad community ownership of standards. The content of meetings includes more than the words of the participants. Public wall charts in the board and superintendent meeting rooms, featuring standards achievement reports for the district and individual schools, also send a powerful message as these documents receive wide public attention. To implement standards effectively, the educational leader must do more than pass resolutions and articulate policy. He must insist that all policies of the district be congruent, and that the district standards be the filter through which all other policies must pass to ensure a high level of consistency. The leader must experiment with the early phases of standards implementation and use pilot programs to demonstrate the effectiveness of standards in the district. Support by leaders—meaning time, money, and protection—is essential in the standards-driven district. Finally, the leader must focus on standards, not only by eliminating distractions but also by devoting consistent attention, in meeting agenda and environment alike, to the district's focus on standards.

Leadership Reflections

1. Who owns your standards now? If your answer is "The state" or "The curriculum office," how can you create ownership among teachers, students, parents, and community members? Identify some specific actions such as communication and actual participation by multiple stakeholders in creating user-friendly standards and standards-based activities that begin transferring ownership from educational officials to your entire community.

2. Examine three recent decisions by the board and superintendent that were related to standards, curriculum, and assessment. To what extent do those decisions reflect congruence with your commitment to standards?

3. Identify two promising projects that are unproven but worthy of an experiment or pilot project. What is the risk (time, money, energy, embarrassment) of a failed pilot project? What is the risk if the district does not have the knowledge that a pilot project would produce? From this analysis of relative risks, make a recommendation for or against each pilot project.

4. Identify ten successes in your district regarding academic standards. They might be a success in the classroom by a spectacular teacher, one on the part of a principal, or in a curriculum office, or a successful experience with parent involvement in standards. Establish specific ways to recognize each success. At the very least, write a letter of appreciation to the ten people individually, and in the case of a school system employee ensure that the letter is entered into the personnel file. If you can find other ways to recognize and reward them—by newsletter notice, professional development opportunity, scholarship, or financial reward—then do that as well.

Chapter Nine

Redefining Educational Accountability

Leadership Keys

Identify what the leader must know

Measure leadership behavior

Develop essential leadership indicators

Link policy to leadership

Link leadership to student results

The information made available to educational leaders, particularly that related to student achievement, is overwhelming, voluminous, complex—and still insufficient. It is not that the quantity of information is insufficient; in fact, most student achievement information is presented in such prodigious quantity that the board and senior leader throw up their collective hands and leave the details to their research and assessment departments. The reason that this information is insufficient is that it is focused almost exclusively on test scores—the results of the educational system—without identifying the causes.

How we receive education information is analogous to the driver of a car who suddenly observes a light on the dashboard. "Warning!" the light flashes, accompanied by a synthesized voice saying, "The car is in trouble." Bewildered, the driver asks, "What kind of trouble? Am I low on gas?" The electronic voice repeats, "The car is in trouble." The driver persists, "Is the car overheating? Am I low on oil? Is one of my tires low on air?" "The car is in trouble," the droning voice continues.

If Franz Kafka were alive in the twenty-first century, he would surely give us short stories involving a man trapped in a nonresponsive machine; perhaps he would write one about school accountability. In the latter story, the secretary of education, state governors, superintendents, and board members would only know that their systems were in trouble. Each time they would inquire, "What kind of trouble?" the mysterious voice would only repeat that the system is in trouble. This is not, of course, a Kafkaesque fictional drama but the daily reality of accountability systems that are no more than a litany of test scores.

What the leader needs to know is not merely an announcement of results but the causes of those results. Those causes, as they are presently measured, are typically limited to demographic variables, and statisticians conveniently link variables such as income and ethnicity to student performance (Herrnstein and Murray, 1994). This educational equivalent of blame-the-victim analysis allows us to focus on students and their families as the cause of educational problems and deflects attention from the other factors at work: leadership, curriculum, and teaching practices.

Every leader has two figurative inboxes on the desk. One, quite large, is labeled "Things I Cannot Control." In that inbox is the family income of students, the language spoken in the student's home, the extent to which parents read to children and limit access to television, and a host of other variables far beyond the power of the educational leader's influence. The second inbox is much smaller and is labeled "Things I Can Control." Wise leaders focus their energy on the second box. In society at large, they can support policies and candidates who attempt to reduce poverty, and they can support educational programs that encourage parents to better nurture their children and support their education. But in daily professional life, the leader must focus on the areas over which some influence can be exerted; in education, this means the leader's own actions, the curriculum, and the teaching practices in schools.

Can Leadership Be Measured?

Just as some have argued that teaching is an art and not subject to measurement, others have concluded that leadership is an imponderable quality that one either has or does not have. One might be able to teach and learn a few management skills, but true leadership remains mysterious and elusive. Certainly, the argument goes, it is beyond measurement. It is not too much of a stretch to envision students making the same argument about an English essay of theirs, or a lab report, musical performance, or historical analysis. Our abrupt reply would be that student academic performance can be measured—indeed, measurement is essential in order to improve performance.

We would also note the advances in assessment in the past decade that allow us to measure student performance not just with a standardized test but with multiple measurements (demonstration, performance, written analysis). We would also point out that there are standards in English, science, and other subjects that establish objective criteria for students to meet. Therefore, we conclude with smug satisfaction, it is obvious that student performance can and must be measured. In fact, if any educator or school leader failed to measure student performance, that would be educational malpractice. Let us apply this logic to the subject of leadership, for here, too, we can establish standards, create multiple measurements, and use those measurements to improve leadership performance.

In the Leadership and Learning (L^2) Matrix (Figure 9.1), the vertical axis represents the results the organization wishes to achieve. For the educational leader, this typically focuses on student achievement data. The horizontal axis represents the degree to which the leader understands the antecedents of excellence, which are the causes that are related to results. Note that the name on the horizontal axis does not mean that the leader does everything right or perfectly executes every strategy. Rather, it

Figure 9.1. The Leadership and Learning (L²) Matrix

Organizational results	Lucky Good results, with no understanding of the reasons; replication of success not probable	Leading Good results, with clear understanding of the reasons; replication quite probable
	Losing Poor results, with no understanding of the reasons	Learning Poor results, with clear understanding of the reasons; replication of mistakes not probable

Antecedents of excellence

means that even if results are low, a high value on the horizontal axis indicates that the leader understands why the results are low.

Chapter Three of *The Daily Disciplines of Leadership* (Jossey-Bass, 2002) has step-by-step guidelines for creating such a matrix to analyze your own leadership performance. Briefly, the leader must first analyze the results to be measured, then identify the cause variables that are hypothetically related to the results, and then measure the relationship (correlation coefficient) between the two. The points on the matrix are plotted by the intersection of the results and the strength of the relationship. For example, if the leader achieves a high result and also demonstrates strong understanding of the antecedents of excellence by virtue of a high correlation between a cause variable and the result, then a mark is placed in the upper-right quadrant of the matrix. If the leader achieves a low result but still has a high correlation between the cause variable and the result, then a mark is placed in the lower-right quadrant of the matrix.

The lower-right quadrant, the "learning" portion of the matrix, is particularly important. In most cases, an organization does not discriminate between bad results that leave the leader clueless (the lower-left quadrant) and bad results that are understood by the leader and that can be avoided in the future. Moreover, most organizations do not discriminate between good results that are unrelated to the leader's actions (the upper left quadrant) and the good results directly related to leadership action (the upper-right quadrant). The Leadership and Learning Matrix, in brief, allows us to measure leadership variables and then test those indicators to determine the extent to which they are related to student achievement or other important organizational results.

Essential Leadership Indicators

If we are to have a usable description of what a leader should be, then we must articulate the results of effective leadership. For example, if we expect a leader to encourage community engagement and parent involvement, then we might measure:

- The percentage of students with a parent or significant adult who volunteers in school at least ten hours during the school year
- The percentage of students who have a parent or significant adult attending one or more parent-teacher conferences
- The percentage of school district committees and task forces that include parent and community representatives
- The percentage of students engaged in direct interaction with community and business partners on an academic project

If we expect a leader to be committed to the academic achievement of all children and not merely maintenance of an average sustained by students who come to school performing well, then we might measure:

- The percentage of students identified as one or more grade levels below their present grade in reading who receive individual academic intervention every day

- The percentage of students who are identified as nonproficient in mathematics on a diagnostic assessment who receive additional academic intervention every day

If we expect a leader to be committed to encouraging and recognizing great teaching, we might measure:

- The percentage of classes taught by certified teachers
- The percentage of secondary classes taught by teachers with a college major in the subject that they teach
- The percentage of teachers recognized as "distinguished" on the basis of a four-point analytical scoring rubric
- The percentage of teachers completing national board certification
- The number of teacher recognition programs sponsored by community and business organizations that specifically recognize teaching practice associated with improved equity and achievement

If we expect a leader to model leadership focus, we might measure:

- The percentage of cabinet agenda items that directly relate to academic achievement
- The percentage of information requests sent by the central office to schools and classrooms that directly relate to academic achievement
- The percentage of agenda items submitted to the board that directly relate to academic achievement

The list could go on, but the idea is clear. Defining leadership is an empty platitude without measuring specific indicators of leadership performance. Demands for educational accountability are hypocritical if the only measurement falls on the student. Do these measurements guarantee success? Certainly not, but using cause variables in your accountability system allows you to remain in the most productive quadrants of the Leadership and Learning Matrix.

As Figure 9.2 indicates, few if any leaders permanently reside in a single quadrant. Rather, they travel a continuum between quadrants. Some leaders float between good and bad results without ever measuring leadership, curriculum, and teaching, thus remaining on the left side of the matrix, traveling the "victim continuum." Other leaders remain permanently in the results cellar, occasionally understanding why they are there but not having the nerve, decisiveness, or ability to act on it; thus they travel the "random-acts-of-failure" continuum. The "illusion continuum" is theoretically traveled by the leader who has perpetually good results—a leader who exists only in the imagination of the school board hiring committee or superintendent recruiting organization. The most productive journey is represented by the "resilience continuum," in which results are not always good, but when the results are down,

Figure 9.2. The Leadership and Learning Matrix Continua

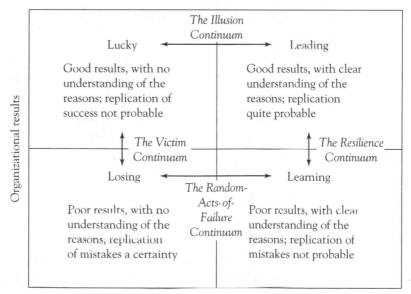

the leader understands why. Thus can mistakes be corrected and successes replicated.

As time goes on, you discard indicators and add a few new ones. You cannot drive down the highway with fifty gauges to monitor; neither can you drive with only a single undifferentiated warning light. Leadership indicators help you understand the antecedents of excellence; they also help you set a clear example for every administrator, teacher, and student. No one in the district is more accountable in measurable terms than the senior leadership.

Link Policy to Leadership

With each policy, resolution, and procedures, the leader or board member must ask three threshold questions:

1. Is this consistent with our mission?
2. Will the results be a measurable part of our accountability system?
3. To what extent will this requirement divert time, attention, and resources away from the things we told teachers, administrators, and students was the most important thing on the plate last month?

My experience is that leaders and policy makers are much better at addressing the first two questions than they are the third. When policies are accumulated over time, educational policies begin to resemble the Internal Revenue Code (with the exception of the fact that the IRS rarely goes after nine-year-olds). Just as the tax code can create a perverse incentive or send a contradictory message, so also accumulation of educational policies can do the same thing:

> Give early diagnosis and attention to special education students, move them into regular classes and, if they are successful, remove their special education designation. But remember that the district

receives supplemental funding according to the number of students diagnosed as special education, so if you are successful in removing the special education designation, your budget will be cut.

Increase test scores, as measured by the average. It doesn't make any difference whether the student has been in your school for one week or one year; we'll just look at the average test score. If a child comes to your school late in the year—say, a week or two before test day, of course (wink, wink)—you should welcome them into your school (wink, wink) and should not even consider suggesting (wink, wink) that they delay enrollment until after testing has been completed.

Promote and recognize great teaching, but the only way you can achieve an income sufficient to own a home and send your kids to college is to stop teaching and become an administrator, or leave the profession altogether.

The list goes on. Leadership and policy are linked, with the totality of policies, accumulated over decades, rarely reflecting the present priorities of the leader and the system. Before conducting any new initiatives or plans, the leader should consider a policy audit, in which every order, procedure, and policy is identified and reviewed. For every new policy, the board should consider a sunset provision that automatically retires a policy after a fixed amount of time. In this way, future board members must consciously renew requirements rather than unconsciously accumulate them.

The sunset provision can be applied retroactively so that the policy audit can be spread out over the next three years, with each past policy coming up for review at a certain time. Without specific action by the board, a policy is not renewed. This creates an incentive for administrators to collapse multiple policies into one and is an opportunity for the leadership and policy makers of a district or state to send a consistent message with every policy that is approved, extended, or allowed to expire.

Link Leadership to Student Results

Richard Elmore (2000) of Harvard is one of those rare professors who not only spend time in public schools but who express their conclusions in clear and unmistakable terms. The purpose of leadership, he argues, is improvement of teaching and student performance. We should therefore be wary of the attempt to romanticize leadership and duplicate the mistakes of the business press, which lionizes the leaders of mythic proportions one day, only to have them fall from grace the next. Effective leadership involves difficult and complex work, but its characteristics can be defined, measured, and learned. Schmoker (2001) notes the difference between the agenda of most leadership meetings and a focus on student achievement. He suggests that a typical presentation at a leadership meeting should be subordinated to four essential questions:

1. Do all teachers at all times during the school year know their limited number of annual improvement goals—to the number? . . . What evidence do you have of this?

2. Can every teacher, at any point during the school year, tell you precisely which areas of weakness their team is currently concentrating on during their regular team meetings?

3. When are your (at least monthly) improvement meetings scheduled?

4. What evidence do you have that the team's meetings are productive? What successful strategies are being generated, refined, and learned to promote improvement in the identified areas of weakness? (pp. 126–127)

Schmoker's documentation of the success of districts that persistently ask these questions speaks for itself. His evidence joins the research accumulated over decades (Haycock, 1998) that makes the point that leadership is not an ethereal blend of charisma and jargon, but a practical set of behaviors and decisions that can directly influence student achievement.

For a detailed examination of how to create an effective accountability system, see *Holistic Accountability: Serving Students, Schools, and Community* (Reeves, 2002b) and *Accountability in Action: A Blueprint for Learning Organizations* (Reeves, 2000a).

Leadership Reflections

1. Consider your own leadership role. What specifically do you need to know to determine if you are achieving your mission?

2. Identify indicators you can measure that will assist you in answering the first question. Your indicators should include both organizational results as well as measurement of specific actions you can control.

3. Review five policies that are related to your present leadership role. These might be departmental procedures, official board policies, state statutes, federal regulations, or policies that are related to your present role. For each policy, answer these questions:

- Is this policy consistent with your mission?

- Will the results of this policy be a measurable part of your accountability system?

- To what extent does this requirement divert time, attention, and resources away from whatever you told teachers, administrators, and students was the most important thing on your plate last month?

Chapter Ten

Assessing Leadership Performance

Leadership Keys

Establish the criteria for leadership assessment

Link leadership assessment to strategies

Use leadership assessment to improve organizational performance

Make senior leadership assessment part of policy governance

We have previously considered how rarely assessment has a forward perspective, such that a future leader can be identified and developed. It isn't really as bad as all that—it's worse. In fact, leaders (particularly senior leaders) are rarely assessed. And when they are it is frequently with an awkward and unprofessional approach. In general, the higher one goes in the organization, the less frequent and purposeful is the leadership assessment. The people who report to the superintendent are as busy as the superintendent, and none has time to write an evaluation report. After all, senior people don't need that sort of thing anyway, right?

This logic culminates with the current reality of superintendent evaluation being a national joke. Assessing the superintendent is typically done by the board in conjunction with a decision to renew or not renew a contract. It is a rare board that has formal periodic evaluation of the superintendent's performance, with specific goals and measurements.

Board assessment is even more haphazard, with an election that reduces complex issues to slogans. Wait a minute, the challenger says. However messy democracy may be, elections for school boards are superior to a process controlled by experts. Of course in a free society elections are important. Moreover (the challenger might continue) one cannot expect volunteer board members to engage in sophisticated leadership assessment.

The error in this dialogue is to associate assessment with hiring and firing, election and retention. In fact, the fundamental purpose of assessment is to improve performance. Thus the superintendent should be assessed frequently, long before a decision is made on contract renewal. Board members should evaluate themselves long before an election so that they learn to improve their performance and are worthy of reelection. Senior leaders should receive feedback that is explicit and oriented toward promoting their professional development. If we just take the time that senior leaders and board members spend talking about the importance of people and reallocate some of it from speechmaking to assessment, the job would be done frequently and well.

Leadership and Strategy: A Standards-Based Approach

For assessment to be fair and effective in the classroom, it must be based on clear academic content standards. It is not fair to assess a student unless everyone involved—student, parent, teacher—understands what the student is expected to know and be able to do. Therefore, to assess a leader with fairness and effectiveness, we must first establish standards for leadership performance. Academic standards are an excellent model, where creation of standards moves from the general ("students must communicate in writing to a variety of audiences") to the specific ("by the end of fourth grade, students must complete a three-paragraph persuasive essay that is well organized and mechanically correct and that clearly supports an argument with facts and examples"). Finally, we can design assessment that is linked to this standard so that the policy makers, leaders, and citizens know the extent to which students meet that standard.

For leadership standards, we might begin with a general state-ment such as "The leader will support teaching excellence." Then we consider how teaching excellence is supported by a leader. Here are some examples:

- The leader will create professional development opportunities linked to the individual learning needs of teachers.
- The leader will provide feedback to teachers, identifying individual strengths as well as areas for further development.
- The leader will identify teachers who are ineffective and produce an individual plan for their improvement, transfer to a nonteaching position, or dismissal.
- The leader will ensure equitable distribution of teaching quality so that each student in the district has approximately the same chance of drawing the highest quality teachers the district can offer.
- The leader will develop relationships with colleges and universities so that the teacher preparation curriculum of the institution reflects the needs of the district.
- The leader will create a mechanism to identify and reward superior teaching that is directly related to improved student achievement.

Beware the "Halo Effect"

None of these standards addresses the leader's rhetoric; all of them address actions that are observable and measurable. If we fail to measure leadership performance with this degree of precision, then leadership assessment becomes disrupted by what Sorcher and Brant (2002) have called the "halo effect," in which the evaluator prizes some characteristics and diminishes the importance of others. Sorcher, an organizational psychologist, found that traditional attributes such as personal dynamism (which can be defined as being an articulate public speaker) and being a team player (typically defined as someone who manages by consensus) are often negatively related to effective leadership performance. In fact, the most effective leaders were driven by a compelling vision that led them to disrupt the generally accepted consensus. If they were used to waiting until there was consensus, they were equipped to lead an organization that was permanently paralyzed by endless discussion and analysis. Those who lacked public speaking skills but had strong interpersonal skills and emotional intelligence were superior to those who displayed the reverse. The articulate public speaker is, however, more noticed than the empathic leader.

Standards, Not Platitudes

The key to beginning effective assessment of a leader is a focus on standards, not merely characteristics. This becomes particularly challenging when words such as *integrity* are used. Of course, every organization wants to have a leader with integrity, but what does that mean? Does it mean the leader never makes a mistake? Does it mean the leader makes mistakes but so far has been successful in having others in the organization take the blame? Does it mean the leader made some mistakes, including a major blunder or two, but learned from them and has not repeated those mistakes in the past five years?

The search for leadership perfection unguided by standards leads too many evaluators to equate integrity with an affirmative response to the first two questions, while the third criterion—the flawed person who admits, understands, and learns from mistakes—is likely to be a far more authentic leader and human being. Moreover, some of the standards associated with integrity might be at odds with the expectation that the leader builds consensus and follows the political winds carefully. It is hard to be a popular team player and meet a standard for integrity that reads "The leader favors effectiveness and principles over popularity and stands firm on a decision that supports the organization's mission and values, even if the decision is unpopular."

Translate Standards into Objective Observation

For each leadership standard, the evaluator must have a method of evaluating it. The typical method of evaluation is rather distant observation of leadership performance. A better way is explicit analysis of a specific situation. In this way, the leader as well as colleagues can focus on facts and evidence, identifying specific examples in which a leadership standard was met or missed. For example, if one of the leadership standards involves effective project management, then the leader and several colleagues might respond to these specific questions about a project led by the leader who is being evaluated. In each case, the evaluator is alert for the similarities and differences in how these questions are answered by the leader and the other team members:

- What was the purpose of the project?
- How did the project relate to the organization's vision and mission?
- What was the result of the project?
- Do you regard the project as a success?
- Was the project completed on time?
- Was the project completed on budget?
- What was the biggest error in the leadership of the project?
- What were the greatest lessons learned from the project?
- Who on the team gained sufficient skills during the course of this project to lead a project team today?
- What was the greatest contribution of the leader to the project?
- What did the leader do that could have been delegated to others?

Garvin (2000) suggests that the most effective organizations conduct such after-action analysis following every project, whether successful or unsuccessful. At the very least, a leadership evaluator must conduct this evaluation in a few areas for which the leader was directly responsible. Failure to do so allows generic description, platitudes, and excuses to predominate over factual analysis. The complexity of this analysis invariably yields a mixed bag: a leader who makes mistakes of varying seriousness and learns from them with varying success. Moreover, the introspection may not be comfortable for all parties concerned, particularly if a senior leader is being evaluated. Moreover, in an environment dominated by politics and fear, accurate responses from team members about a leader's performance are unlikely to be forthcoming (Pfeffer and Sutton, 2000).

To build your own leadership evaluation, start with Exhibit 10.1 (which as a purchaser of this book you are free to reproduce for your own use). Exhibit 10.2 is an example of a completed form.

The forms illustrate how a system might approach the leadership criteria of instructional leadership. First, we must identify the standards associated with effective instructional leadership. If the evaluation is to be fair, it must be specific and clear. What are the standards of effective instructional leadership, and what evidence helps us understand the extent to which the standard has been met?

Exhibit 10.1 is a start on such questions. For example, the first standard for instructional leadership is that "the leader ensures that the system provides a K–12 curriculum linked to state academic standards." This sounds like something right out of the state manual for school administrators. But what does it really mean in practice? In another instance, the leadership evaluator posed five questions. Each one must be answered with both words and numbers. There is an objectively measurable response to each question, but the inquiry itself no doubt reveals much more information that can best be described in qualitative terms. Together, the numbers and words give a complete picture of the extent to which this leader has really implemented K–12 academic standards, and ultimately the extent to which the person is an effective instructional

Exhibit 10.1. Developing Leadership Standards

Instructions: Use this form to create standards and identify performance evidence for each leadership criteria. Your organization will probably have several leadership criteria, such as integrity, supervision, planning, and communication, to name a few. For each criterion, use a separate form. In the left-hand column, identify the standards that describe in specific detail your expectations for the leader. In the right-hand column, write the evidence that you will collect for each standard.

Leadership criterion: _____

Standards	Evidence

Exhibit 10.2. Sample Leadership Standards

Instructions: Use this form to create standards and identify performance evidence for each leadership criteria. Your organization will probably have several leadership criteria, such as integrity, supervision, planning, and communication, to name a few. For each criterion, use a separate form. In the left-hand column, identify the standards that describe in specific detail your expectations for the leader. In the right-hand column, write the evidence that you will collect for each standard.

Leadership criterion: Instructional Leadership

Standards	Evidence
1. The leader ensures that the system provides a K–12 curriculum linked to state academic standards.	1.1 Does a survey of twenty pieces of randomly selected classroom work indicate that instruction is related to the district curriculum and state standards?
	1.2 Does a review of six classroom observations reveal that actual instruction is linked to the district curriculum?
	1.3 Does a review of twenty-six randomly selected teacher-created assessments (two from each grade level) demonstrate that teacher expectations as expressed in student assessment are based on state standards?
	1.4 Does a spot check of every building reveal that the district curriculum is present and available for use?
2. The leader provides assessment support from the central office so that assessments are used as a learning tool.	2.1 Does a review of the professional development calendar reveal that each teacher in the district has the opportunity to become proficient in developing standards-based performance assessments?
	2.2 Does the district provide sample assessments that are open; not secret; and easily available for use by teachers, students, and parents?

Exhibit 10.2. *(continued)*

Standards	Evidence
	2.3 Does the district provide common end-of-course assessments for every grade in the core subjects?
	2.4 Where common end-of-course assessments are provided, does the district create an opportunity for collaborative scoring to ensure consistency, quality, and fairness?
3. The leader personally and regularly demonstrates effective instructional techniques.	3.1 What classes did the leader teach during this evaluation period?
	3.2 What evidence did the teacher offer of effective instructional techniques, including standards, preassessment, differentiated instruction, assessment for learning, and the like that could serve as a model for every teacher in the system?
	3.3 How do meetings conducted by the leader model effective teaching and learning techniques?
4. The leader uses the personnel evaluation system to identify and reward superior teaching and to identify and correct unacceptable teaching.	4.1 What are examples of specific recognition of superior teaching linked to improve student achievement for which the leader was responsible?
	4.2 What are examples of ineffective teaching practices that were identified and corrected?
	4.3 What are examples of ineffective teaching practices that were identified but not corrected and that led to reassignment or a dismissal proceeding?
5. The leader demonstrates the qualities of emotional intelligence in personal interactions with students, staff, and community members.	5.1 What are examples in which the leader demonstrated self-awareness, including an understanding of personal strengths and weaknesses? Are there examples where the leader failed to do this?

(continued)

Exhibit 10.2. Sample Leadership Standards (*continued*)

Standards	Evidence
	5.2 What are examples in which the leader exercised self-control, avoiding outbursts and tantrums? Are there examples where the leader failed to do this?
	5.3 What are examples in which the leader persevered in the face of failure and discouragement? Are there examples where the leader failed to do this?
	5.4 What are examples in which the leader demonstrated empathy and respect for others? Are there examples where the leader failed to do this?
	5.5 What are examples in which the leader settled a dispute and encouraged cooperation and teamwork? Are there examples where the leader failed to do this?

leader. To assess just the extent of curriculum leadership, the evaluator asked:

- Does a survey of twenty pieces of randomly selected classroom work indicate that instruction is related to the district curriculum and state standards?

- Does a review of six classroom observations reveal that actual instruction is linked to the district curriculum?

- Does a review of twenty-six randomly selected teacher-created assessments (two from each grade level) demonstrate that teacher expectations as expressed in student assessment are based on state standards?

- Does a spot check of every building reveal that the district curriculum is present and available for use?

As is already evident, this is going to be a long evaluation. It takes time to complete and deserves substantial time for reflection. It is, however, the difference between the typical personnel evaluation full of perfunctory boxes and checkmarks, and an assessment designed to improve the performance of both the leader and the entire organization.

Strategic Leadership Assessment

If effective strategic leadership is to become a reality, then the criteria for effectiveness must be part of the leadership assessment system. We have defined strategy as a description of decisions linked to the mission, information, and results. We then said that effective strategic leadership occurs in the course of the simultaneous acts of executing, evaluating, and reformulating strategies, and focusing organizational energy and resources on the most effective strategies. Thus assessment of leadership performance remains incomplete if it does not require the leader to address three central questions:

1. What decisions have you made for the period of this evaluation that you reevaluated and changed? Describe the information and analysis on which you originally made the decision and what new information and analysis you used to change the decision.

2. How have you improved organizational focus by moving organizational energy and resources from one strategy to another?

3. What tasks and projects have you decided not to do?

In brief, strategy without focus is impotent, an exercise in filling binders and entertaining consultants. Strategy without focus is dangerous, as it inevitably involves making changes and moving resources. Focus requires speaking the unpleasant truth that some strategies are more effective than others, that not all initiatives are of equal value, and that healthy organizations and organisms must constantly undergo a process of shedding and renewal.

Leadership Reflections

1. Identify the criteria for leadership in your organization. Working with a team of leadership colleagues, complete the standards and evidence (Exhibit 10.1) for each of these criteria.

2. Examine the current forms and policies that are used for leadership evaluation, from assistant principals through the superintendent and board. For each position, describe the leadership evaluation system and the extent to which it does or does not reflect the criteria for effective leadership that you created in response to the first question.

3. Meet with the senior leadership of your organization, including the chief policy maker (probably the chair of the board of trustees) and the chief executive officer (probably the superintendent). Ask if they agree that the criteria you have identified conform to their expectations for leadership. Then ask if they believe that your current leadership evaluation system supports those criteria. If not, how do they react to your alternative of an improved leadership evaluation system? If they do not accept the proposed system for leadership evaluation, would they consider accepting the evaluation system for coaching, improving performance, and evaluating new and prospective leaders?

Part Three

Leadership Roles for Educational Standards

Chapter Eleven

The Role of the Superintendent

Leadership Keys

Communicate: from rhetoric to reality

Conquer: removing obstacles

Concentrate: the power of focus

Coach: challenger in chief

Coordinate: central office staff organization

Jeremiads concerning the impossibility of the superintendent's job are not new. Raise student achievement, but don't work my kid too hard. Make the busses run on time, but don't leave my kid stranded if he's a few minutes late. Have only healthy food in the cafeteria, but make sure it's the high-fat snacks that my kid likes. Give the teachers time to collaborate, but don't dismiss school early unless it's a holiday. John Holloway (2001) and his colleagues found broad agreement among both theorists and active superintendents that these expectations were widely accepted, in descending order of priority:

- Fostering school board relations
- Developing and maintaining an effective school and district staff
- Facilitating student learning
- Collaborating with and involving the community
- Providing organizational resources and operations

- Developing, implementing, and evaluating curriculum and instruction
- Conducting professional development for school and district staff
- Maintaining group processes
- Understanding and responding to the larger political issues

I've never seen a mission statement that reads "The primary mission of this school system is to have the board and superintendent get along," or "The mission of this school system is the care, comfort, and convenience of the adults," or "KIDS! They're number three, right after the board and the staff!" The anonymous respondents to Holloway's surveys knew that political realities trump mission statements more often than not. It is therefore easy for superintendents to succumb to cynicism and despair. I number among my close friends several superintendents who have followed the mission, raised student achievement, improved the educational and financial health of the systems they served, and then succumbed to the political heat that respects no accomplishment. The same, after all, could be said of many in public service. Why bother? Why suffer the indignities, the second guessing, the uninformed insinuation, the presumption of malfeasance? Why indeed. The answer is furnished by the legion of educational leaders who have confronted the fork in the road described by Paul Houston (personal interview, Mar. 28, 2002). Educational leaders, he argues, are dramatically different from functionaries, who view a successful day's work as executing the orders of the board—a worldview that rules out confrontation, disregards mission, and barely considers the intellectual challenge and development of students and adults in the system.

This chapter is for the leaders, not the functionaries. By attending to six critical functions, the superintendent can engage in strategic leadership, moving the system closer to the vision of excellence and equity that drives every successful superintendent.

Here are the five things the superintendent must do to become an effective strategic leader:

1. *Communicate.* Transform the vision of the system from rhetorical flourish to daily reality.

2. *Conquer.* Identify and remove the obstacles—including traditions, policies, prejudices, and personalities—that stand in the way of the mission. Conquering need not involve alienation and unpleasantness, but it definitely requires a continuous mental audit of all the demands from inside and outside the organization to determine whether those demands are consistent with the mission.

3. *Concentrate.* Focus energy, time, and resources on the most important initiatives, people, and ideas. Failure to focus is the Achilles heel of every leader.

4. *Coach.* Encourage the discouraged, challenge the complacent, and energize each individual in the organization toward a common mission.

5. *Coordinate.* Marshal the resources of the central office staff so that each department, division, office, and individual contributes directly to the mission.

Communicate: From Rhetoric to Reality

President Reagan was regarded (not always with approval) as "the Great Communicator." To his detractors, the implication was that communication was elevated over substance. A generation earlier, similar accolades and criticisms were given to President Franklin Roosevelt, who used radio as effectively as Reagan used television. But to associate their successes with voice and technology would be to miss the other qualities that made their communication so effective. These leaders mobilized a nation to action with messages that were clear, simple, and memorable. Eighty years later, school children still remember the words spoken in the midst of the Great

Depression: "We have nothing to fear but fear itself." Today's generation of students has not known of Communism as an international force, nor Eastern Europe as satellite states of the Soviet Union; but they should learn of the day Reagan stood near the Berlin wall and uttered the improbable (but astonishingly prescient) command, "Tear down this wall!"

Communication is the mission, vision, and purpose of the organization; it is at the heart of the goal for any leader. Goleman (2002) makes clear that the emotions conveyed by a leader are contagious. Just as a sour mood can infect an entire office, the leader's enthusiasm, resilience, and confidence influence leader and follower alike. An organization that has survived self-styled reform, reinvention, reengineering, and revolution is the breeding ground of cynicism.

Educational leaders who wish to improve achievement, set and achieve high standards, enhance accountability, and establish educational equity run into the same negativism that has greeted every change movement since the Renaissance—and probably, if we knew the history better, since the wheel. The rhetoric of negativism is appealing, as it resonates with the fear that individuals feel whenever change is in the wind. Plans for change carry with them the implication that the present state of affairs is less than optimal; the cynics will seize upon this to cry out, "Does this mean that everything I've been doing for twenty-eight years is suddenly wrong?" Placed on the defensive, the would-be change agent instinctively offers reassurance; slows the pace; says that, after all, these things take time; and like the *Titanic* slipping into the North Sea, another opportunity for change sinks into oblivion. Rather than succumbing to the cynics, the leader must anticipate the rhetoric of negativism and be prepared to confront it.

Confronting Negativism

The most frequent question I receive when addressing educational groups throughout the nation is, "How can we get buy in? How do we motivate people to change?" These groups are almost always surprised when I respond, "You don't."

Let me explain. The great myth of change is that if the leader is sufficiently inspirational, then every cynic will hit his forehead with the palm of his hand and exclaim, "Of course, you're right! Now that you've given me such an illuminating explanation, I'll acknowledge the error of my ways and immediately become an acolyte in the change movement." As the kids say: Yeah, right. Leaders must engage the hearts and minds of followers with a compelling vision, not with the policies, procedures, and daily tasks that accompany change.

In fact, those daily tasks are hard work and not terribly enticing. They are the organizational equivalent of diet and exercise—things that we do not do because shredded carrots are our favorite food or the treadmill is our favorite pastime, but because the results of those choices are preferable to the alternative. Weeks and even months can elapse before the results of a healthy choice become apparent, and during that awkward interim healthy people persist in making healthy choices not because they are motivated or enlightened. As Bill Habermehl (personal interview, Mar. 21, 2002) says, they "just do it" because they trust the vision. Ultimately, success breeds on itself; few people ask for help in motivating a staff that has already tasted success. It is the motivation of the group on the way from mediocrity to success that is the greatest leadership challenge. The best way to meet that challenge is to stop placing buy-in on the pedestal that it now occupies in most organizations. Collins (2001) explains that when leaders have first identified the right people and a compelling mission, motivation is not necessary. If people need to be motivated to do what is right, then you have the wrong people in the wrong positions.

Confronting Error

Let us return to the first cause of negativism, the fear and defensiveness embodied in the expression, "Does this change effort mean that everything I've been doing for twenty-eight years is wrong?" Let's think through that statement for a moment. It is more worthy of the inquisitors challenging Galileo than it is of an educator or any other professional. It is difficult to imagine the captain of an ocean liner rejecting use of a global positioning system because she prefers stellar navigation ("I've been finding my position success-fully with a star map for all of these years, and now you're going to tell me that I'm wrong?"). What would we say of a physician who rejects modern anesthetics because "I'm really more comfortable using whiskey, and besides, the practice of medicine is an art, and I have to do it my way"? Leaders of ship lines and hospitals would not patronize such reasoning with bland reassurance. They would confront the Luddite captain and the dangerous doctor. They would not be easily assuaged by self-congratulatory articles in the *Inquisition Monthly* and the professional journals of the Luddite Association that proclaimed that all was well. Educational leaders must do the same. Here are descriptions of some of the most fre-quent errors that impede strategic leadership.

"One Mistake Implies Universal Blunders." This is the error made by those who, having found an academic standard that is poorly worded, declare that the entire standards movement is fatally flawed. When they find an error on a test, they decry all testing. When they find an incompetent teacher, they condemn the entire profession. This logical fallacy is common in education, where the kernel of truth in a single anecdote soon becomes a widely cited research study that represents the whole of the educa-tional establishment. Thus does a reference to chemical elements in the California academic standards become the putative require-ment for every fifth grader in the state to study the periodic table of the elements. Inconsistencies in evaluating performance assess-ment on the part of a teacher learning the practice becomes an irre-deemable flaw inherent in all performance assessment. Misuse of accountability and test scores by an administrator becomes an indictment of all testing and accountability systems. The strategic leader knows better. Because she uses multiple sources of information, she does not generalize from a single piece of data and does not tolerate the faulty logic of those who do.

"People Who Disagree with Me Are Evil Conspirators." In this error, the otherwise innocent endorsement of a curriculum by business executives becomes, to the opponent of that curriculum, a cabal of the Fortune 500 and the educational establishment to train a workforce for the brave new world of automatons. The suggestion that students solve real-world math problems is, to the opponents of anything beyond basic mathematics, an embrace of fuzzy math, foisted on us by ivory-tower intellectuals and lazy teachers. The requirement that states determine once a year the reading proficiency of schoolchildren becomes, to the opponents of standards and testing, an invasion by the federal government into the prerogative of local control of schools. A variation on this theme is the conclusion that "People who disagree with me are incompetent and stupid." This is the stuff of cheap laughs and hearty applause at an education convention, where labels, sarcasm, and invective frequently substitute for evidence.

"If You Are Successful, It Is Because You Tortured the Kids into Submission." When forced to confront the evidence of successful student performance, particularly when the method used is unpopular or the student population is not typically associated with success, the opponents of reform use this all-purpose error. It is a convenient complement to the first two errors. If a leader in educational reform makes a mistake (as leaders always will), then he suffers the arrows of overgeneralization in the first error and character assassination in the second. If the leader in educational reform is successful, he runs into the third error, which asserts that any success must have come at a price far too dear to be reasonable.

In this thesis, the only way a school can have high achievement is for the institution to become a dreary boot camp. In fact, even schools led by critics of standardized testing who reject test prep and focus on thinking, analysis, reasoning, and engagement demonstrate every year that such an approach is consistent with, not antithetical to, high test scores. Moreover, the work of Csikszentmihalyi (1990) and his colleagues make clear that the highest level of personal satisfaction and self-esteem comes not from false affirmation and avoidance of challenge but from success after a series of trials and errors. To those who embrace the fallacy that student success comes only at the price of unpleasantness, the prospect of students and teachers who work hard, achieve well, and enjoy themselves must be truly frightening. The critics depend upon unhappiness and failure to feed their screed, and the facts and faces of student success are an unpleasant intrusion on their rhetoric.

Strategic leaders are worthy of the name because of their consistent linking of evidence to decision making. Thus they respond to these challenges not by scoring rhetorical points but by consistently elevating evidence over assertion. When the critics of standards and assessment call effective educational leaders an ally of Joe Camel and a member of some vast and inevitably pernicious conspiracy, it is tempting to call the accusers ill-informed bigots. But such an exchange is ultimately unproductive. The strategic leader must instead challenge the fundamental premises of the argument. In the present case, the fundamental premise is that no one has time anymore for good teaching techniques that require reasoning, analysis, thinking, and communication. The only path to success on mandatory state tests, the rhetoric goes, is mindless academic boot camp, endless test prep, and drills that substitute for intellectual development.

If these premises are true, then the schools that pursue intellectual development, including reasoning, analysis, thinking, and communication should have terrible test scores, and those that engage in mindless test drilling should have superior results. These are hypotheses that beg to be tested, and the evidence presented in Chapter One demonstrates that the hypotheses are not supported. In fact, a higher level of student achievement is associated with a greater level of student writing, thinking, analysis, and reasoning.

Strategic leaders need not be classical rhetoricians. Their communication skills lie not in mastering polysyllabic blather but in words that are simple, precise, and clear. They impress not with complexity but with transparency. Their message resonates at every level of the organization.

Stan Scheer, the same superintendent who puts himself on the substitute teacher list several days a year to walk in the shoes of classroom teachers in an extended and authentic manner, also regularly shows up at his school system bus garage at five in the morning, coffee and donuts in hand. The professional drivers entrusted with safe and timely transportation of students play an essential role in accomplishing the mission of the school district, and the superintendent reminds them—and everyone else—of the importance of drivers in that mission. Fourteen hours later, Scheer may present a complex financial plan, assessment data, and personnel policy to a board meeting.

Superior communication is among the many characteristics shared by great teachers and effective strategic leaders. Although leaders rarely think of themselves in this light, Noel Tichy (1997) asserts that teaching is the primary leadership function. David Garvin (2000) contrasts the typical planning meetings that "seldom encourage active engagement or new thinking" (p. 194) with learning forums. The learning forum is an opportunity for many people to address complex issues and conduct the debate, constructive confrontation, and detailed examination that rarely occur in a meeting where, most participants concede, the decisions are preordained. Successful learning forums include new information, using previously untapped sources of data. They encourage different points of view, sometimes assigning this role to a participant so that no idea, premise, or conclusion goes unchallenged. This bestows analytical rigor on the process, and it also creates an atmosphere in which contention becomes a normal, welcome, and necessary part of the decision-making process.

Alternative hypotheses are routinely considered and different inferences from the same data are placed on the table for review. This is an uncomfortable setting for traditional inhabitants of an organization in which mindless affirmation of the status quo is the rule. Discomfort also results, at least temporarily, in an organization that has held to the ethic that every disagreement is personal and, as a result, unpleasant and offensive. Constructive contention in the learning forum is never personal but always focused on the ideas, evidence, premises, and conclusions. Individuals and organizations build skills through challenge, never through false assurance that all is well when the evidence is decidedly to the contrary.

In sum, the communication imperative is not about speech making or persuasive skills, though the strategic leader frequently needs to develop such skills. The essence of communication beyond rhetoric is the essence of strategic leadership: a decision based on evidence that supports a compelling vision that everyone in the organization can understand. This common understanding occurs because the leader is constantly evoking the mission, to bus drivers and board members. The strategic leader is sharing the evidence supporting a decision and change with teachers, parents, and food service workers. A decision in this context is the result of a transparent process that blends mission and evidence, not the result of a popularity contest or tradition. The result of this unending communication effort is an organization that does not ask "Will they like it?" but rather "Will it be an effective way to help us achieve the mission?"

Conquer: Removing Obstacles

The leader cannot establish any new initiatives without first identifying and removing the obstacles that stand in the way. Time is certainly a zero-sum game in an organization, with every moment that is devoted to one activity is unavailable to another. The strategic leader must conduct an inventory and audit of the demands placed on every part of the organization. This should include a physical list of every single report demanded by and generated by the central office and school board. In most cases, the sheer length of the list is surprising, as is the widely varying utility and necessity of the items on the list. When the leader asks, "Why are we doing that?" the answer, in at least a few cases, is "I don't know; we've just always done it that way."

The leader must also inventory and audit meetings. At the start of any new initiative, one of the most powerful acts of a leader can be the instruction during a meeting for people to get out their calendars. "Here she goes again—another meeting!" the crowd will mumble. At this point, the leader finds a meeting that is already on the calendar, ceremoniously rips the page out of her date book, and says:

> I can accomplish everything I need to with a memo, and holding that meeting does not contribute directly to our mission. Besides, you need the time reserved for that meeting more than I do. It is therefore cancelled. Now, leave your calendars open and everyone find at least one meeting or other activity that is on the calendar but is not making a contribution to our mission. We are adjourned when every one of you has identified such a meeting in your book and shared it with the group. We will leave this meeting with more time available to focus on our mission.

By removing the time-honored obstacles of meetings, activities, reports, and requirements, the strategic leader conducts an organizational spring cleaning. Just like the annual event that clears the winter's accumulation of dust and trash from a home, the organizational spring cleaning must be conducted periodically—at least once every two or three years—so that the accumulated obstacles that have no more value are discarded, giving those that remain the time and attention they deserve.

The Knowing-Doing Gap (Pfeffer and Sutton, 2000) is one of those rare books in which the title precisely matches the subject. The authors assemble an impressive amount of evidence to support a simple but stunning conclusion: knowing what to do isn't enough. Most organizations know what works, but the failure of leadership to confront and remove obstacles to change prevents advances that would bring obvious benefits to the organization. This trend certainly is confirmed in education, when personal taste, tradition, and strong opinion remain frequent obstacles to a decision that is based on research and evidence. Among the obstacles that separate knowing from doing are talk as a substitute for action, fear of speaking the truth, and internal competition, all of which can occur in an individual school and certainly in the central office of a school system.

There may be other obstacles to progress as well, some of which are within the leader's control and others that are beyond it. Changes in personnel take time but can be accomplished. Changes in negotiated contracts and state legislation, for example, may require years. Changes in local politics and attitude may require longer than that. Thus the strategic leader focuses on decisions that she can make and processes that she can influence rather than a wish list of things that are beyond her control. The leader can exert the greatest influence over how she spends her own time, and from that starting point she can identify those areas of each organization where she can exert the greatest and most immediate influence.

Concentrate: The Power of Focus

One of the popular myths surrounding leadership effectiveness is that of the chronically multitasking executive who simultaneously handles multiple priorities. Given the diffuse nature of educational leadership, with demands for attention coming from many entities and the label of "highest priority" accorded to so many activities, such a model of frenetic leadership may seem appealing. It is, instead, doomed to failure. The strategic leader does not do more; he accomplishes more important things by deliberately focusing his efforts on fewer tasks, fewer projects, and fewer priorities. This is why, for example, a strategic plan with twenty strategies and two hundred action plans is not strategic.

The Rule of Six

I am skeptical of generalization. Nevertheless, when I observe the same phenomenon on repeated occasions in a variety of contexts, I begin to suspect a pattern. One such pattern is the "rule of six," which states that neither an organization nor an individual can focus effectively on more than six priorities at any one time. In practice, this means that a school should not have more than six goals at the same time, because this is the maximum number of goals that can be measured each month, monitored with care, and be the focus of the leader and the entire team. Since the days of steel magnate Andrew Carnegie, time management theorists have advised that a key to effective time management is identifying the six most important things one proposes to do during the day, writing them down in priority order, and completing them. In my own observation of activities ranging from a strategic plan to professional development to policy objectives for a board of education, I find that when attempting to answer the question "What are your priorities?" the list begins with clarity, specificity, and compelling urgency. After the speaker has articulated half a dozen priorities, however, clarity turns to mud and specificity is replaced by ambiguity. As a result, the compelling urgency that characterized the early priorities becomes just another wish list that is unlikely to be realized.

If the rule of six is ignored, cynicism and negativism find fertile soil. A leader without focus has neither the time nor the ability to engage in the necessary confrontation to fight negativism. The rule of six is hardly an empirically supported law of nature, but it is a good guideline. Some of the most remarkably effective leaders I have observed get by with fewer than six priorities; none of them have more than six. If your list is longer, or if the leaders in your organization are unable to narrow their focus to six priorities, then some reflection is in order.

There are other areas in which the number six continues to appear. Leaders, particularly superintendents, who are in a new position enjoy a period of no longer than six months in which they can institute major changes that are based principally on their authority and trust. After that time, institutional inertia takes hold and change becomes more difficult. If there is a major change in central office staff, board procedure, or a strongly held tradition that the new leader wishes to make, then sooner is better than later. New leaders carry with them high expectations along with a high level of tolerance. Familiarity breeds contempt, and after six months the new leader has descended from savior of the system to just another administrator.

Focus in Action

Leaders can demonstrate their focus by rendering their own decision making transparent. The three areas where focus can be most apparent are time, meetings, and evaluations. The most obvious decision a leader makes is in use of time. When he periodically tracks his time and displays the result of his self-examination, it speaks volumes about the true priorities. The leader who gives an oration about lifelong learning but whose time log reveals little or no time for reading and learning does not value lifelong learning. Meetings are an executive function that dominates the life of many a leader. Ask yourself: When was the last time you cancelled a meeting because it did not conform with your priorities and mission? When was the last time you terminated a meeting within minutes because it was obvious that the participants were not going to contribute to an informed decision that supported your mission? When was the last time you doubled the length of a scheduled meeting because the issues at hand required more thought, reflection, and time?

The third area where the focus of a leader is readily apparent is written evaluation of colleagues and review of evaluation conducted by colleagues. If, for example, your organization has primary objectives of student achievement and educational equity, are there measurable indicators of those two objectives noted on every written evaluation for every leader? Despite significant advances in teacher evaluation (Danielson, 2002), evaluation of educational leaders is typically unspecific, untimely, and unproductive. This is particularly true at the most senior level, where "It's time to evaluate the superintendent" is frequently equated with "It's time to find a justification for the decision we have already made to fire the superintendent." The strategic leader approaches personnel evaluation the same way he does other decisions, with an explicit link between the decision, data related to the decision, and the mission and values of the organization. It would be inconceivable to the strategic leader to sign an evaluation form that does not make explicit reference to student achievement and specific decisions undertaken by the person being evaluated that relate to student achievement.

However obvious this may seem, I have personally witnessed the abrupt transition of a superintendent who talked the talk of student achievement one moment and then conducted thirty consecutive principal evaluations without a single mention of student achievement in even one of them. This example is neither isolated nor extreme. Try this experiment: conduct a simple frequency count of the issues, behaviors, and performance measures addressed in a dozen leadership evaluations in your own district. Create a pie chart displaying the relative emphasis of each area discussed. If your chart is similar to ones I have created from similar observation, it reflects a mission and vision that are not focused on student achievement and equity, but instead on employee relationships, parent relationships, physical appearance, compliance with central office rules and regulations, and meeting attendance.

A school administrator who excels in those categories can be regarded by central office decision makers as a superior educational leader even if she continues to deliver mediocre student achievement results. Conversely, the innovative principal who delivers strong improvement in excellence and equity but does so at the expense of some union grievances, parent complaints, and dollars diverted from painting the hallways to conducting academic interventions for students might be regarded as insensitive and "not a team player."

Joyce Ford Bales, one of the nation's leading superintendents, was the recipient of a standing ovation from the Colorado legislature when she was recognized for her exceptional achievement in transforming a district with chronically low achievement into one of the highest-performing school systems in the state. Her focus on standards, assessments, and accountability gave new hope and confidence to a system that had long used poverty, language, and ethnic identity as a convenient excuse for low achievement. Eight years after her arrival, poverty and language are still significant issues, and the ethnic identity of students is celebrated with pride. But student achievement is a nonnegotiable issue. During her first year in the district, I heard people complain, "All she ever talks about is standards, standards, standards." On the back of her door she maintained charts of the most important goals of the districts. It was impossible to have a meeting with her for even a few minutes without gaining a sense of her priorities. It remains true today. She is a walking example of the power of focus.

Coach: Challenger in Chief

Most successful people can identify a coach, mentor, or other influential person who challenged them to accomplish more than they had thought possible. The standing joke in administrator meetings is how common the first name Coach is, but the fact is that an effective coach who inspires extraordinary performance from ordinary people is a model of strategic leadership. A successful coach does not offer universal praise or condemnation but instead specific feedback. He is unequivocally clear about the mission and objectives and is, above all, a great teacher who identifies each step that takes the team from vision through execution to success. Lest the athletic aspect of coaching be overdone, let me illustrate the point with an unlikely coaching model, the concert pianist and Harvard faculty member Ludmilla Lifson, whose exceptional artistry is matched only by her patience. I know this because I am her student.

I am an experienced pianist, used to Chopin, Debussy, and applause. "Not so fast," Professor Lifson reminds me. I can play the notes proficiently and become complacent, but to the ears of an experienced musician I am merely pressing the buttons. "There is just playing the notes," she says, "and then there is music." She helps me to find the inner voice in a Bach fugue and the mystery in a Chopin nocturne. In other words, she guides me on the difficult journey from performance that is proficient to the elusive one that is exemplary. In this way, she holds my interest, makes me reconsider my assumptions, challenges my complacency, and helps me do my best work.

There are many superintendents whose colleagues are proficient. They are experienced in their field and have a wall full of plaques attesting to their prior success. They have met the expectations of their supervisors and exceed the performance of many of their peers. Yet the superintendent has the uncomfortable feeling that she should not settle for the academic equivalent of merely playing the notes. To guide her staff to a higher level of performance and to challenge their acceptance of proficient performance, she must provide feedback with specificity and accuracy. There is a gap between where we are and where we wish to be, and every member of the organization bears a responsibility for bridging that gap.

Professor Lifson does not command me to "Be Rubinstein!" but gently and clearly shows me the difference between where I am and where I wish to be. She guides me to recordings of the masters, just as a superintendent who wants her colleagues to improve their performance guides them to the best literature in leadership, organizational development, and education. Although great musicianship, like great leadership, may appear to be mysterious, my piano teacher knows that Edison's formulation for genius applies in this realm as well: "One percent inspiration, 99 percent perspiration." Thus Edison's numerous failures are less well recalled but were nonetheless an essential antecedent to his successes. Hemingway went through multiple drafts to produce *For Whom the Bell Tolls*. Great teachers and coaches in the rank of Ludmilla Lifson practice every day, placing themselves in the role of student. Their empathy as well as their skill informs their ability to serve as a model for students, teachers, and educational leaders.

Great coaches also develop other leaders. They create a strong cadre of potential leaders long before a leadership crisis because they systematically identify prospective leaders throughout the organization. What would happen if, outside of the parameters of formal evaluation, we asked every person in the organization every six months, "What can you and the organization do together to advance your career? Would you like to be considered for a leadership position in the future?" There is nothing wrong with a person answering the second question in the negative, but merely posing it would allow a school system to identify a much larger leadership pool throughout the organization, from the classroom to the finance office, than is presently the case.

Coordinate: Central Office Staff Organization

The traditional organization of the school system is undergoing radical reconsideration. In the past, the industrial model was the norm, in which the school was a factory. Few people admit to such a model because the terminology is so offensive, but when the functions, duties, and roles of each participant in the system are examined, the factory analogy is hard to avoid. The only question is whether it is a modern and humane factory of the twenty-first century or one of Dickensian proportions. In this model, students are a product to be shaped and molded. Teachers are the assembly line workers who follow the rules and make the products. The principal is the foreman who enforces the rules. The central office is the factory owner to whom all obeisance is paid and whose principal role is creating the rules and supervising the foreman. There is a better way.

Strategic Analysis: Functions Versus Objectives

Most central offices are organized around functional analysis. There are departments for food service, transportation, technology, special education, curriculum, assessment, research, community relations, finance, personnel, and so forth. The presumption of this organization is that function defines organizational placement, and this presumption carries with it a certain logic. After all, doesn't it make sense that the technology people be together in a homogeneous group, as with the finance people, personnel people, and curriculum people? If the criterion for decision making is the care, comfort, and convenience of the adults in the system, then this homogeneous organization makes sense.

If, however, the criteria for decision making are the principles of strategic leadership, some new options become available. Because the strategic leader makes decisions by linking information to the mission and necessary decisions, the question is not "How do the functions fit together?" but rather "How can we best organize to accomplish the mission?" The traditional homogeneous organization appears to be purposefully opposed to the mission because it is so self-absorbed. There is a better way. Here are three examples to illustrate typical challenges and strategic responses to them.

Challenge Number One: Computer Integration. The challenge is that computer integration seems impossible because the business and personnel offices use PC-compatible machines while the curriculum and assessment personnel use Apple Macintosh machines. Each school makes its own choice, with some principals preferring Macs and others preferring IBM. Some use Microsoft network software while others use Unix, and still others prefer

Linux. Using a blend of information and prejudice founded in the difference among these machines in the 1970s, neither side budges and the prospects for an integrated computer system appear to be hopeless.

The resource and personnel requirements of the technology office grow each year, as do complaints about poor service, as they attempt to meet the needs of a bewildering array of users with varying software and inconsistent hardware. Meanwhile, anyone who suggests that the district adopt a consistent technology standard is accused of threatening the authority of department heads and principals. The director of technology reports to the assistant superintendent in charge of services—the same person who supervises transportation, personnel, and food services—and thus has no direct link to the curriculum people anyway.

Strategic Response Number One: Technology as a Tool. Technology is a tool, not a department. Can you imagine having a Department of Pencils in the nineteenth century, as pencils replaced slate? Computers are no more than the pencils of the twenty-first century; they are tools for learning. If you have a chief technology officer, then this person should report to the chief learning officer, who should be the superintendent or chief deputy superintendent. A better approach is to deploy each person in the technology department to the functional department(s) they should serve. Thus the technology people who are best equipped to work with assessment data report to the director of assessment, those who are best equipped to work with finance report to the director of finance, and those who are best equipped to work with human resources data report to the director of personnel. The skeletal crew that remains in the technology department sets standards so that every department, school, and classroom uses interchangeable parts. The urban myths of the 1970s ("Only Macs can do graphics"; "Only IBMs can do business") can be safely challenged and abandoned. In fact, both platforms are perfectly serviceable machines; each school system should pick one and be done with it.

Challenge Number Two: Shortage of Substitute Teachers. The district is chronically short of substitute teachers, yet the personnel office only accepts applications once a year. From the time an application is submitted, it takes at least three months for the fingerprint card to be processed and the background check to be conducted.

Strategic Response Number Two: Change Personnel to a Learning Function. The research is unambiguous that the quality of teaching is the variable most related to student achievement. Once personnel is a learning function rather than an administrative function, the district can accept substitute teacher applications every day of the year, accept them on the Internet, conduct interviews by videoconference, and complete fingerprint checks in twenty-four hours.

Challenge Number Three: Paperwork. The curriculum and assessment department generates reams of documents and hours of professional development programs that are ignored in the classroom and the school. A quick review of the evaluation of principals reveals the reason: there is no organizational connection between the administrator incentives and curriculum. An administrator is praised for a clean building and good "organizational climate" (a code word for no grievances to the union). Implementation of curriculum innovation, use of assessment data, and improvement in student achievement receive scant attention in evaluating principals, assistant principals, and teachers.

Strategic Response Number Three: Reorganize for Learning. Radically change the organization of the central office to refocus the reporting, evaluation, and supervision in a way that emphasizes student learning. In some districts, this involves identifying a chief academic officer, who is in charge of curriculum, assessment, and instruction. In other districts, evaluation of school principals has been transformed from the judgment of a central office administrator to achievement of goals related to learning, teaching, and student achievement—all areas that the curriculum and assessment office can directly influence. The role of the curriculum and assessment office is not to police school compliance with central office demands, but rather to support each building and classroom in achieving its goals. This creates a symbiotic relationship in which the principals and teachers need the academic program support offered by the central office, and the central office treats each school and classroom educator as a valued customer whose needs must be met.

Putting the Mission First

The people in these examples of challenge are not malicious. They are doing their job to the best of their ability, but they have misidentified their constituents and their role. In each example, the central office leaders believe that their constituents are their employees and their role is their function. Not a single one of these leaders is focused on the mission of improved student achievement. They'd like to be more helpful, they explain, but their hands are tied. The superintendent may implore, persuade, and plead, but in the end bureaucratic inertia trumps the exigency of the mission every time. What is needed is a fundamental restructuring of the central office in a manner that places the mission first and function last. In each of these examples, there is a solution that involves strategic leadership, in which the traditional organization is subordinated to the needs of the learning organization.

The strategic leader has neither the time nor the patience for a bureaucratic fiefdom or personal empire. When the organization is focused on improving student achievement, each central office leader is expected to ask the same question regularly: "How can we better organize to meet the needs of students, teachers, and schools?" Through such a question, the organization is self-renewing, constantly adapting and changing, and with each evolutionary development it more closely aligns to the mission, is more closely attuned to available information, and becomes more responsive to the imperatives of the mission. In this organization, the care, comfort, and convenience of the adults is not the priority. In fact, the inconvenience, challenge, and disruption associated with change and reorganization are an exciting prospect and an expected part of a day in the life of the central office. The focus is not on self-aggrandizement, but on the mission. The heroes are not those with the largest number of direct reports and the biggest budgets, but those who have recreated their function in a way that is more supportive of the mission.

The Superintendent's Primary Challenge: From Knowing to Doing

University of Washington researchers Paul Hill and James Harvey (2002) have observed school superintendents for more than twenty years. Their extensive interviews reveal a range of programs, initiatives, and ideas. The leaders knew what they wanted, understood the research, and saw how to achieve the mission. They espoused values of equity and excellence and articulated specific strategies to achieve their mission. With the candor permitted by a confidential research design, these wise and capable school leaders were nearly unanimous that "badly needed reforms are mostly a pipe dream" (Hill and Harvey, 2002, p. 32). They reported their inability to control the budget, the calendar, an agenda, a union, and even the central office personnel (who, in theory, report to the superintendent). In brief, understanding of effective practice is a necessary but insufficient condition for effective strategic leadership. Success requires creating an organization that relentlessly examines each element of each process and systematically roots out the barriers that separate knowing from doing (Hammer, 2001).

To be sure, there are some external forces that constrain the actions of the superintendent. They include state legislative decisions, school board policies, and votes by the community. But the superintendent is not an innocent bystander, merely an actor in a play doomed to recite the lines written by others. The effective strategic leader plays a significant role in designing the strategies, not merely executing them. When confronted with obstacles, the leader changes them, sidesteps them, or obliterates them. At every turn, the leader asks whether the value of the obstacle is greater than the value of the mission. If the answer is in the affirmative, then it is clearly time for a change in the mission statement. If the answer is in the negative, then the mission wins hands down.

Just once I'd like to see a superintendent print a mission statement for consideration by all the interest groups—board, business leaders, union, building administrators, and central office staff—that reads, "The mission of our school system is slavish devotion to processes and procedures that systematically elevate the care, comfort, and convenience of the adults in the system over the values of student achievement and educational equity." If people decline to support such a mission statement, then they must also decline to engage in conduct that conforms to it. Finally, the superintendent must regularly ask the board and community, "Do you want improved student achievement in our schools?" Upon hearing the inevitable affirmative answer, the leader must state clearly, emphatically, and repeatedly, "Then support me as we make some changes, because we cannot improve results without also improving—and that means changing—the system that delivers those results."

Leadership Reflections

1. Consider your most challenging communication gap. Write a brief statement of what you intend and another brief statement of what your stakeholders are hearing. Using the principles of communication discussed in this chapter, outline the steps to move from rhetoric to reality.

2. What are the primary errors that are so-called common knowledge in your organization? How will you confront each of these errors?

3. Complete Table 11.1. In the first column, list five things that you already know need to be done. You don't need any more research, studies, or opinions; you know the kids who can't read need help and you know that teachers who don't know mathematics cannot teach math. Find those clear and obvious needs for your present leadership situation, and list them. In the middle column, list the obstacles—money, time, tradition, institutional inertia, and so on—that prevent you from moving from knowing to doing. In the right-hand column, devise a way to change the obstacle, sidestep it, or remove it.

4. Look at your calendar for the last two weeks. List the six most important things to which you gave time and how much time you devoted. If you worked ten-hour days and five-day weeks (chances are you put in many more hours than that), that's a total of one hundred hours. What percentage of those one hundred hours were devoted to the six most important areas of your professional life?

Table 11.1. The Obstacles Between Knowing and Doing

We Know We Must Do:	Obstacles Between Knowing and Doing	How I Will Deal With the Obstacle (Change It, Go Around It, or Remove It)

5. Examine the board agenda for the past two months. List the six most important things that the board considered. What percentage of the board agenda is represented by the most important issues that your policy makers must confront?

6. Identify a person who directly reports to you, and consider a specific area in which that person can improve performance with your coaching and encouragement. Write in specific detail the contribution that this person would, with ideal performance, make to the mission and vision of your organization. With that ideal performance in mind, identify the specific steps that this person must take to move from his or her present state of performance to the ideal state.

7. Without looking at one, sketch the organizational chart for your school system. Ask three colleagues—a central office administrator, a teacher, and a principal—to do the same. You now have four charts, so compare each of them to the official organization chart. How are they similar and different? What specific changes should you make in central office organization or in your communication about the central office organization?

Chapter Twelve

The Role of the Board of Education

Leadership Keys

Define the stakeholders

Represent the underrepresented

Find the devil in the details

Focus on strategic action

Model effective internal communication

Deal decisively with diversion

The striking demographic shifts in the American population are evidence of the fact that the population is aging. The impact that this has on the election, policy, and role of the board is striking. Whereas the stakeholders of a school system in decades past may have been limited to students, parents, teachers, and administrators, it is now clear that every element of the community, including those who have no direct participation in the school system, are in fact stakeholders.

To the extent that school leaders and board members ignore a stakeholder group, they have virtually guaranteed hostility toward economic and political support for educational needs. In *The Key*

I am particularly indebted to Anne Bryant, executive director of the National School Boards Association, for her thoughtful advice on the role of the school board in strategic leadership. In addition, I have been significantly influenced by the work of Katheryn Gemberling, Carl Smith, and Joseph Villani, authors of *The Key Work of School Boards Guidebook*, and extend my appreciation to these scholars for their work.

Work of School Boards Guidebook, Gemberling, Smith, and Villani (2000) make clear that the involvement of stakeholders extends far beyond board members and school administrators. They argue that the vision of the school system is disconnected from the vision of the community unless aggressive efforts are made to involve parents, community leaders, representatives of higher education, the business community, governmental agencies, and other key stakeholders. Of course, an established vision is impotent unless it is communicated effectively throughout the community and becomes the cornerstone of school board policy and school system operation.

Diverse communities require diverse channels of communication, and successful community outreach requires multiple methods and iterations of communication (Anne Bryant, personal interview, Apr. 3, 2002). There is an enormous difference between, on the one hand, a community gathering in which the educational leader announces plans and seeks to communicate to the audience, and on the other hand, a process that, over the course of time, involves active listening to the community. In far too many cases, "community involvement" is a code phrase for expecting a passive audience to support decisions that have been predetermined by the superintendent and board. This is a prescription for cynicism and disengagement, and ultimately for community opposition to educational progress.

The power of communication was made clear by the observations of the Iowa School Boards Association. In districts of similar demographic characteristics, the highest student achievement occurred in those where there was a strong sense of shared vision. "Every teacher and board member knew the vision and goals of the district," Bryant said, "and understood the relationship between curriculum and professional development." This is consistent with the observations of Terry Thompson (personal interview, Apr. 8, 2002), who explicitly links information on student achievement, professional development, and districtwide goals with leadership evaluation. In the most effective systems, the stakeholders and leadership perceived a direct connection between their actions and the results of the system. In the least effective systems, the stakeholders perceived the most important variables to be outside of their control, blaming families, students, communities, and environmental factors for poor results. I have described this else-where as the "victim continuum" (Reeves, 2002a), in which lead-ers notice that results change from bad to good to bad again but lack understanding of the root causes of those changes and thus are unable to replicate success or avoid repeating failures.

Represent the Underrepresented

School board members, whether elected or appointed, serve every member of the community: those citizens who voted for them, those who voted for their opponents, and those who did not vote at all. In fact, each board member has an affirmative obligation to represent those stakeholders who are not represented by a political action committee, who paid no heed to any newspaper endorse-ment, and who do not follow each development in educational policy. After all, eight-year-olds do not vote—but they are among the most important people every board member represents. When-ever I hear a board member say "I represent the taxpayers" or "I rep-resent the teachers" or "I represent the business community," it is clear that her focus is narrow and her thinking is rarely on the entire system.

Representing the underrepresented is not easy. The usual sus-pects are always willing to volunteer for a task force on strategic planning, accountability, or building design. Thus the local cham-ber of commerce, teacher's union, administrator's association, or major employer always finds a place at the table. Less likely to find a seat on a task force or committee are parents of students who are eligible for free or reduced lunch, parents whose primary language is not English, senior citizens who have not had a direct connection to the school system for many years, and small business owners whose schedule rarely permits a meeting in the middle of the day.

Each of these groups, along with members of the media, clergy, political leaders, and (lest we forget) students, is a vital part of the community and yet is chronically underrepresented in most decision-making bodies. Each time the school board commissions a task force, committee, or other body that has the obligation to make policy recommendations to the board, it must ensure that the views represented are not insular and self-perpetuating. The value of outsiders, including those who may be regarded as uninformed on history and local politics, is that they view data, decisions, and questions with a fresh approach unencumbered by the prevailing wisdom. The advantage of broadening the scope of community representation is that someone is more likely to challenge conventional wisdom and open the door to new insights not only for the committee but for the board and community at large.

Details Matter: Between Abdication and Micromanagement

A common axiom is that school board members establish policy but do not become involved in the details of administration. Horror stories abound in which board members become embroiled in cafeteria colors, the salary of the football coach, and (in a notable example from Kansas) the method of grading term papers in an English class. On the other hand, a board that has taken the view that it is above the fray and need not become involved in the mundane details of policy has presided over the Enron debacle. There are, to be sure, a number of "educational Enrons," in which the officials entrusted with oversight were overly deferential to administrative initiatives. Where is the balance between the ideal of policy making and the responsibility to see that policy is implemented appropriately?

Bryant argues that the school board bears the burden of linking data to decisions. "A consideration of data without specific goals," she argues, "is irrelevant fluff, and a discussion of goals without data is an exercise in forever spinning wheels" (personal interview,

Apr. 3, 2002). Thus board members must, at the very least, create accountability systems that give them a steady flow of information about their goals and the processes that lead to their goals. If they have a goal of student achievement, then an annual report on the matter is hardly sufficient. Not a single meeting should pass without some inquiry into a specific process that links a specific action by students, teachers, and school leaders to the goal of improved academic achievement.

By asking specific questions about the most important goals and examining each report about the links between cause and effect, board members can enforce the "grocery store" test. If a school leader cannot explain his initiative such that it can be posted at the local grocery store and parents and other citizens can understand it, then his communication is inadequate. Many school reports, from student report cards to systemwide accountability reports, are incomprehensible to a reader unaccustomed to educational jargon. Board meetings must be declared a "jargon-free zone" in which clarity of speech is the rule and the obligation to communicate to stakeholders outside the world of education is taken seriously.

Surely this does not mean that every board member must become an expert in curriculum, assessment, school finance, and personnel. It does mean, however, that the administrators in charge of those areas have an obligation to translate their processes, duties, measurements, and results into language that the board can understand. The befuddlement that accompanies many administrative reports, particularly on such crucial areas as student assessment and school finance, opens the door to potential disaster. Board members must be forthright enough to issue the challenge, "I don't have any idea what you are talking about, and unless you can make it clear to me what you are talking about, I'm not going to vote to approve your report." University graduate schools sometimes place a premium on language that is arcane and distinctly unfriendly to the lay audience, yet every senior administrator has devoted many years to succeeding in the university environment, composing a thesis or dissertation in which obscurity was the rule, elliptical reasoning was praised, and the imponderable was endlessly pondered.

This is not a distant indictment, as I fully confess to being part of the problem for part of my professional career. As a former professor advising these graduate students, I assume personal responsibility for my part in this state of affairs. Eventually, however, I started asking questions:

- Why do we insist that students write a study of collaborative learning entirely alone and without collaborating with their colleagues?
- Why do we require students to master varying learning styles but model only a single method of teaching and learning in a graduate school class?
- Why do we require students to learn the value of feedback, followed by improved performance, and then give a one-shot final exam and dissertation defense that are the antithesis of constructive feedback?

Board members can be similarly iconoclastic. They can ask the commonsense questions that are rarely posed. Some people would regard such questions as inappropriate, since they threaten the turf of administrators and teachers. Common sense, however, is not heresy, even if it is uncommon. Here are a few examples of questions that a board member should ask:

- If a high percentage of our students are not proficient in reading comprehension with our current schedule and curriculum, why are we planning the same schedule and curriculum next year?
- If a high percentage of our students are not successful in ninth grade algebra now, how will next year's algebra classes be different? What changes are we making in our middle school curriculum to improve success in high school?

- If a substantial percentage of our middle school students are not coming to middle school with the skills that they need, how will next year's curriculum for fourth and fifth grades be different in order to better prepare students for middle school?

- If the information we receive from the state is too late to be used for good diagnostic information, what will we do as a school district to supplement that information?

- If we have district and state standards, why are the expectations, assessments, and curricula so highly variable from one school and classroom to the next?

This is a good start. Too many board members fear that posing such questions is beyond their level of expertise and an inappropriate imposition of the board into administrative decision making. The acid test is this: Do these questions relate to the fundamental mission and vision of the system? If so, then the inquiry is totally appropriate.

We are not talking about colors on the cafeteria walls, but about the fundamental issues of equity and excellence, the heart and soul of board policy, mission, and vision. As the previous chapter indicated, superintendents and school administrators have a difficult time challenging the status quo. Board members can support administrators who are willing to ask uncomfortable questions and explore the outer limits of conventional wisdom. They can, in sum, challenge what everyone believes to be true but in fact is false.

Strategy Versus Tactics: Focusing the Board on Strategic Action

An important theme of this book has been to differentiate effective strategy from typical decision making. Effective strategies, we have come to learn, are those linking decisions to information and the organization's mission in a process of simultaneous evaluation, focusing the resources of the organization on those areas with the greatest impact on the mission. Kaplan and Norton (2001) offer numerous examples in business and nonprofit organizations where a focus on a handful of processes and strategies is linked to appropriate balance between a board that is so hands-off that it is clueless and one that is so hands-on that it is micromanaging.

To achieve this balance, the board must decide in advance which measure to watch and then focus on those measurements and the monthly changes in them. As a vital principle of measurement, it is more important and effective to measure a few things consistently and well than to measure a great many things once a year. Most boards, however, take the latter course. They examine the entire budget, often in excruciating detail, annually. Then they rarely follow financial matters unless there is a crisis or another annual review that is due. The board examines test scores, often in a soporific report from the assessment office, and recognizes excellent or poor performance annually, but it fails to consider the impact of month-to-month strategies in teaching and learning. The reason many boards are reluctant to examine data monthly is that the details can be overwhelming; and besides, they reason, those monthly decisions are mere tactics and best left to the administrators. The failure of a board to consider critical information frequently results from confusion about what strategies and tactics really are.

The essential link between the role of the board and tactical decisions is this: the mission, values, and strategies of the board drive the tactics of administrators and teachers. Tactics are the daily, even hourly, decisions that are made in the classroom, building, and department. These decisions are, to be sure, almost always inappropriate for board discussion. Though some boards do want to get involved in student grading, which players are on the varsity football squad, and which teachers are assigned to which rooms, these tactical decisions are clearly the responsibility of the administration. However—and this is the critical link—the strategy that establishes those responsibilities and decision-making criteria is the result of teamwork between the board and superintendent. In each case—assessment of student work, extracurricular activity, and teacher work assignment—the mission and values of the district are either reflected or flaunted. Thus the board must be so relentlessly clear, in its focus on the mission and vision as well as on the decision-making strategies that stem from the mission and vision, that even tiny decisions made every hour throughout the organization reflect the board's focus.

Internal Board Communication

Board communication has become increasingly problematic in the era of the Internet and restrictive open meeting laws. Some critics have suggested that when board members communicate with one another (particularly if one sends a message to all other board members), they may be engaging in a form of communication that would violate the statutes of some states. Another form of technology, television, has distorted the atmosphere of the public open meeting, transforming discussion into speech making and posturing. Thus it is absolutely essential for a board to create a forum in which inquiry, discussion, challenge, and honest admission of error are possible and even encouraged. The most effective board members are able to say regularly, "I blew it" (Anne Bryant, personal interview, Apr. 3, 2002) and effective organizations regularly have a forum devoted to "honest bad news" (Reeves, 2002c). The researcher's maxim is that error is far better than uncertainty; yet the forums in which most board meetings take place are rarely conducive to constructive discussion of error. When error is discovered in a board meeting, the question is rarely "What can we learn from this?" but rather "Who is to blame, and what will be the consequences for this malfeasance?"

Human nature is unlikely to be suspended once one is appointed or elected to a board, and discussion of error—particularly one's own—is not easy. Thus the organization itself must create the opportunity to promote and encourage productive and constructive discussion. The ideal setting is a board retreat, a meeting of two or three days, preferably away from the district. Some boards combine the retreat with another professional development opportunity, such as the meeting of a national or state association. More often, however, the board fears that an out-of-town meeting just looks bad, as if the members were having fancy meals at a resort and enjoying recreation at the taxpayer's expense. Other boards resolutely refuse to engage in any professional development opportunity or meeting of their state or national association, convinced that travel cannot be justified in a time of limited resources.

In fact, every school system in every year always has limited resources. The issue therefore is not to wait for the theoretical period of abundance in which the board can improve its professional knowledge, but rather to recognize that the body charged with administering a multimillion dollar budget must invest a tiny fraction of it in improving the members' own knowledge, interacting with other board members around the nation, and gaining context and perspective for its own decisions. If travel or a retreat is impossible, then the next best thing is for the board to plan a "study session" in which members take no votes, do not hold a public hearing or receive comment, or otherwise follow the formality of a typical meeting. The purpose of the study session is precisely as the name implies: to study and learn a particular issue. Ideally, a study session is confined to a single issue. From this study session, the board can maintain a continuous link between the details that its members learn and the broader focus of the mission, values, and strategies of the organization.

In a monthly study session, a board might profitably consider a yearly cycle that includes a number of areas of learning:

- School finance, including the relationship between state policies and board action
- Special education, including the relationship between federal and state requirements and board action
- Student assessment, including the particular strengths and challenges of the district

- Classroom strategies for teaching and learning, including a focus on the best practices already taking place in the district and strategies the board could undertake to encourage replication of those best practices

- Union bargaining issues, including federal and state fair labor practice requirements that affect board decision making

- Parent and community involvement in schools, including a focus on schools and programs where this has been particularly effective, and strategies the board could apply to broaden the impact of those practices

Diversion from Standards, Equity, and Excellence

Examine the minutes of your school board for the past three months. Count the total number of items, and then calculate the percentage of those items that relate directly to the priorities of academic standards, equity, and excellence. Chances are that there are many agenda items, among them many that are legal mandates, or an area of deep public interest, or a topic that is particularly important for your community. Responsiveness to community needs is one thing, but never-ending engagement in the paralysis of analysis (Peters and Waterman, 1982) is something else.

A striking example of this occurred in my town, where the school committee has been debating the disposition of one property since 1936, with people of goodwill and intelligence suggesting in the early days of the twenty-first century that the matter needs more process, more time, and more deliberation. A board cannot avoid diversion from its priorities, but it can manage those diversions. First, the board can dictate the sequence of agenda items, placing those items that directly reflect its priorities early in the meeting. The traditional sequence of "reports, old business, new business, etc." rarely reflects board priorities; this sequence is supported not by legislative mandate but by hoary tradition. Second, the board can establish a filter for matters to come before the board. It is reasonable, for example, that every decision have a one-page cover sheet that includes a summary displaying the decision posed in a single question, followed by a set of alternatives. The relationship of this decision to the organization's mission and values should be clearly spelled out. This is followed by a summary of the data related to the decision. This simple format requires that every decision by the board be linked to mission, values, and data.

Astonishingly, these three factors are commonly supplanted by reams of information or terse recommendations from the administration. Such recommendations are appropriate and necessary, but the decision-making process that the board must control should be one that improves the probability of implementing an effective strategy. This occurs only if a decision is habitually linked to the mission and values of the organization and supported by relevant data. If matters cannot be brought to the board that fail to meet this threshold, then the board meeting is shorter, the board packet is lighter, and board deliberations are more focused.

Leadership Reflections

1. Analyze the relationship between the stakeholders in your system and communication with the board. The Stakeholder Participation Matrix in Exhibit 12.1 can assist you. What inferences do you draw from it? For those stakeholder groups associated with blank boxes—that is, stakeholders who have been identified but who are rarely represented in official communications with the board—how would you characterize those communications, compared to the stakeholders who are actively represented and frequently communicating with the board?

Exhibit 12.1. Stakeholder Participation Matrix

Directions: In the left-hand column, list all the stakeholder groups that you can think of for your community. They might include students, parents, the taxpayers association, teachers union, administrators association, and other stakeholders relevant to your community. Across the column headings, list the major influence groups that regularly bring matters to the board. These might include the accountability task force, the strategic planning committee, the community relations committee, and other groups that interface between the board and community. Write the number of participant stakeholders represented in each group for each column. If there is no representation, leave that box blank. Use this tool to identify which groups are most and least represented in communication with the board.

Stakeholders:							

2. On the basis of your analysis in Exhibit 12.1, identify the underrepresented stakeholders. What can the board do to proactively include those groups? What are the consequences of underrepresentation of those groups? What is the risk of taking steps to include them now? What is the risk of failing to include them?

3. Determine the level of detail you need for a board decision. In some cases, such as personnel matters or a student expulsion, the law clearly establishes the nature and extent of information and evidence the board must have to make a decision. What about other board decisions, where there are no such clear legal guidelines? Consider recent agenda items in student assessment, curriculum, finance, promotions, technology, and other important areas for your school system. For each of these, list the minimum information necessary for you to make an informed decision. From your review of the minutes of the past three months of board meetings, did you have the information you needed? What would be the risk of postponing a decision until you have adequate information? What is the risk of making a decision promptly but without adequate information?

4. What are the open meeting requirements for your board in state law and board policy? Are e-mail communications to multiple board members permissible? Is a study session that is not an official meeting and in which no decision or vote is taken permissible? Is an offsite retreat permissible? Within the guidelines, policies, and laws of your area, how can the board have time for reflection, learning, study, and communication outside of a formal board meeting?

5. Return to the minutes of the past three months of board meetings. Which items were not related to your core mission? Which items could have been removed from the agenda or handled as a block without taking excessive time during a board meeting? What policy does this suggest for filtering items that come before the board in the future?

Chapter Thirteen

The Role of State Leadership

Leadership Keys

Balance local control with state mandates

Admit it: Do you really have standards?

Pursue compliance by design, not by default

Get constructive feedback from state test data

The governor's new role in educational leadership

The new federalism of the last two decades of the twentieth century witnessed a remarkable transfer of power from the federal government to the states in areas such as welfare, Medicaid administration, and even parts of environmental protection. In 2002, educational policy became the capstone of this trend. Critics maintain that the reauthorization of the Elementary and Secondary Education Act was a power grab by the federal government because it required annual reading and math tests for some students; but the plain language of the law makes clear that its most significant impact is the transfer of authority from the federal government to the states. Although the federal government retains an interest in equitable treatment of students who are poor, members of ethnic minorities, or disabled, much of the daily decision making that had for thirty years been the domain of federal government agencies is largely shifted to states.

Thus state educational leaders now stand at the threshold of an exciting opportunity. Some will use their new flexibility to engage in bold new initiatives (Christensen, 2001) and others will merely replace the bureaucracy of Washington, D.C., with one located in their state capital. In the latter case, the flexibility and local control that were hoped for as a result of a shift from federal to state control will be largely illusory.

There is an unfortunate trend toward attempting to characterize the federal role in education according to one's support for or opposition to the person signing the legislation. The facts must, in this case at least, interfere with our political predisposition. The "No Child Left Behind Act" was, indeed, signed by President George W. Bush, but it would not have appeared on his desk without the affirmative votes of ninety out of one hundred senators and more than 90 percent of the members of the House of Representatives. Senator Edward Kennedy accompanied Bush on the celebratory bill-signing tour, and Senator Hillary Clinton offered several amendments to the legislation that were unanimously approved. To call this the Bush Bill is as accurate as calling it the Kennedy Bill or the Clinton Bill, as it is the product of broad bipartisan support.

In the early days of implementation, critics have identified the provision that they least like and then associated those provisions with the politician that they least like. This may be personally satisfying, but it does not represent accurate analysis.

Balance Local Control with State Mandates

Freedom Within a Framework

For many years, the easy applause line that a politician could issue in any education debate was a sentence extolling the virtues of "local control" of education. Now that the federal government has transferred enormous authority to the state level of government, the question of what local control means and where it resides is more problematic. The notion that the states are closer to the action than the remote federal government is may sound appealing, but the distance between the state capital and local district can seem equally immense in matters of educational policy. The concept is thus plagued with ambiguity much in the same way that the phrase *academic freedom* receives nods of approval until it is used to justify low expectations, incompetence, or insubordination. In fact, neither local control nor academic freedom is an absolute concept, but both occur within a framework. Academic freedom, for example, prevails only within the boundary of state academic content standards. The teacher is not an independent agent who can choose to ignore state standards on the basis of presumed freedom, nor is the teacher free to invoke the concept of freedom to expect less of a child who is poor or a member of an ethnic minority. Similarly, a school district exerts local control only within the framework of state and federal guidelines. Local control does not, for example, allow a board of education to engage in gender discrimination or to ignore the rights of disabled students.

The Need for Specificity

This tension between prescriptive standards and individual discretion, whether by an individual or an organization, is directly analogous to the dilemma teachers face daily. If they are too prescriptive, then they risk crushing the creativity, independence, initiative, and motivation of students. If they are insufficiently prescriptive, then students may fail to meet the academic requirements necessary for future success. Wise teachers strike a balance by making the boundaries clear. Each time they give an assignment, the expectations for success are absolutely clear; such a practice is the very essence of standards. No student need guess what is required, nor must any student worry about whether her work is superior to that of other students. Rather, the student focuses on a singular objective: attainment of the standard.

Similarly, state and federal officials should give consideration to using standards and scoring guides for implementing state policies. They can begin by envisioning what an ideal district might do in implementing state or federal policy and labeling such ideal conduct as exemplary. Then state officials can contemplate what adequate implementation of policy would look like and label it proficient. As of this writing, a minority of states have complied proficiently with federal requirements promulgated in 1994 (General Accounting Office, 2002); without improved communication patterns between the federal government, state departments of education, and local school districts, the prospects for improving on this record are bleak. Mere establishment of regulations is not enough, any more than the teacher's creation of a syllabus is magically translated into student learning. Rather, teacher and policy maker alike must articulate a vision of success, describing in rich detail various levels of compliance and implementation success.

The Binary Fallacy

To achieve this objective, state and federal leaders must move beyond the binary approach that now dominates policy implementation. In this worldview, states and school systems are relegated into two categories, those in compliance and those out of compliance. The real world is more complicated, of course. Implementation of federal and state requirements can be arranged on a continuum from exemplary compliance that acknowledges both the letter and spirit of the law to proficient compliance that passes inspection, and then on to compliance that is close to acceptable, and finally to brazen defiance and willful disobedience. If such a continuum analysis is considered, leaders and policy makers can engage in a more thoughtful approach to policy implementation. They can, for example, document and leverage the strengths of an exemplary school system. Most state departments of education and a great deal of energy at the federal level as well is focused on catching people doing things wrong.

There is, in fact, far more power in identifying, documenting, and replicating best practices. By assembling a large body of examples of successful classrooms, schools, and districts, policy makers can disprove the frequently asserted hypothesis that compliance is impossible and that success is a pipe dream. Of equal importance, policy makers and leaders can focus their energy appropriately. Strategies must vary for those schools and districts that are close to compliance—they know what is required, know how to do it, and are close to success—and those that either do not know what to do or, more commonly, know what to do and insist that it is impossible and unpopular and therefore will not do it. If we change the context of this discussion to talk about board of health inspection of restaurants, then the difference at hand is between a restaurant that receives a warning because the temperature of meat was off by five degrees and a restaurant that has a cockroach-infested kitchen and a chef belligerently indifferent to city health requirements. The former is given a warning, and the latter is shut down.

State and federal resources cannot be focused on every school. They must be placed where the reward is greatest. By using a continuum analysis for compliance, leaders and policy makers can focus on the bookends of the system. They can identify, nurture, recognize, reward, and replicate exemplary schools and districts. They must also assist those districts that are almost, but not quite, proficient. They have to take decisive and immediate action for those districts, schools, and individuals that are so far out of compliance that they will not make progress without aggressive intervention. Once again, the analogy to the classroom is apt. Consider the eighth grade teacher who has a student reading at the fourth grade level. The child does not have a learning disability but has simply slipped through the system, barely decoding words and never reading on grade level. Here are four ways of responding to the problem:

1. "Sure, he can't read—never has, never will—so what do you expect from a kid in that neighborhood?"

2. "I know that he's below grade level and I collected assessment information on it, and we'll send him to summer school if he doesn't straighten up."

3. "We know that progress is not sufficient. Therefore we have made drastic changes in his eighth grade curriculum, providing intensive intervention, three hours a day of literacy, multidisciplinary literacy, personal academic coaching, and regular reassessments to evaluate our progress."

4. "We've been monitoring this student since the fourth grade. It took years for the child to get into this problem, and we've established a multiyear plan to resolve it. In addition to providing intensive intervention, three hours a day of literacy, multidisciplinary literacy, and personal academic coaching, we also conduct parent assistance and weekly assessment to measure progress. We have identified this student's younger siblings for assessment to identify any additional literacy challenges as early as possible. Finally, we have offered special training in literacy for all teachers so that, even in eighth grade, every teacher focuses on reading and literacy. Our data, gathered weekly, indicate that this program is successful because we have dramatically reduced the percentage of students who are not proficient in reading on grade level."

Clearly, these four teacher responses require vastly different leadership responses. Analysis that simply says the first two are "not meeting standards" and the second two "meet standards" is superficial and unhelpful. A more careful reading reveals that the first teacher deserves to be terminated; contrary to popular myth, termination of incompetent and bigoted teachers is entirely legal and possible even within the most unionized environment (Lawrence, 2001). In the last case, we need to document the success in some detail, publicize it, reward it, and replicate it. In evaluating successful policy implementation, states face a similarly complex range of options and thus must develop not only a set of rules but a continuum of evaluation for implementing those rules, ranging from exemplary implementation through a level of defiant nonimplementation that begs for an authoritative and unequivocal response.

Admit It: Do You Really Have Standards?

The grand fantasy of standards—or for that matter any policy at the state and federal level—is that establishing a law or policy is equivalent to implementing it. Speeches, wall posters, campaigns, and incessant pleas for buy-in follow the change initiative, but the chasm between the policy maker's wish and implementation at the classroom level remains deep and wide. Every one of the fifty states has academic standards. The often-cited exception, Iowa, has standards at the district level rather than the state. Although states vary in specificity, quantity, and style of standards, there has been unanimity among state policy makers for almost a decade that clear expectations of what students should know and be expected to do are a fair and effective manner in which to educate children.

Yet for all the talk of standards and the many years in which any sentient being in the educational world has had the opportunity to learn about the standards-based approach to education, my phone rings daily with the plea from a superintendent or other educational leader who complains that "We just don't have support for standards here" and "Our teachers don't see the benefit of them" and "Our community just doesn't buy into this notion yet." In such an environment, the standards fantasy prevails only in Rotary Club speeches and formal reports to the state department of education.

How do you know if you really have standards? Exhibits 13.1, 13.2, and 13.3 present checklists for evaluating implementation at the classroom, school, and system level, respectively. It is unlikely that you will find a classroom, school, or district that qualifies for exemplary implementation on every criteria. Rather, you will find a rich mix of strengths and challenges and thus can focus leadership energy where it yields the greatest return on investment of your time and resources.

Pursue Compliance by Design, Not by Default

As states assume more authority and responsibility, they must also review the accumulation of requirements and reports of the past few decades. With the dramatic increase in the sheer quantity of data accumulated at the local level and processed at the state level, and with stagnant or declining staffing numbers at the state department and school system central office, it is imperative that state officials

Exhibit 13.1. Classroom Checklist
for Standards Implementation

☐ Standards are highly visible in the classroom.

This need not imply every standard related to that grade level or subject, but it certainly must include the standards that are being addressed in the class during the current week. Students have a right to understand the expectations they are to meet, and teachers have a right to understand the parameters within which their instruction takes place. This serves not only to focus students and teachers but also as an antidote to administrators and policy makers who are sometimes tempted to suggest extras for the classroom.

To put a fine point on it, school leaders must think twice before taking a good idea such as character education and transforming it into an additional curriculum in the school day. Teachers can reasonably ask, "Which standard on this wall shall I take down in order to make room for the new requirements?"

The same is true for myriad curriculum requirements that, by themselves, seemed innocent but taken together form a mountain of time requirements for classroom instruction and inevitably compete with academic content standards. Examples I have heard are the obvious ones of character education; drug, alcohol, and tobacco education; and also newly established mandatory curricula, including sensitivity training, bully-proofing, diversity training, free enterprise education, sexual orientation tolerance training, and a host of other items requiring curriculum documents, assemblies, and even assessments.

When these ideas are implemented as part of a curriculum in critical thinking, social studies, or health education, that is one thing. When they have the practical impact of reducing the amount of reading and writing in a classroom and, overall, reduce the focus on achieving academic standards, then leaders must confront the divergence between, on the one hand, those of their principles that are based on the value of fairness and the practice of standards-based education and, on the other, the reality of a fragmented day in which some students succeed, some students fail, and teachers frantically bounce from one curriculum area to another like a pinball in a poorly leveled machine.

☐ The standards are expressed in student-accessible language.

A few states, such as Illinois, have taken the time to express a few of their standards in language that makes sense to students—and, for that matter, to parents not immersed in the jargon of standards. The work of most states, however, can be charitably described as the result of the efforts of a very earnest committee. Membership in this committee typically excludes

Exhibit 13.1. (continued)

fourth graders, and as a result the wording of the standard not only eludes our students but also strikes their parents as obscure.

The remedy for this problem is not to complain about standards but to add value to the standards by restating them in language that is clear and accessible to all students. There is ample precedent for this. Teachers do not put the state criminal statutes on a poster at the front of the room, nor do they display the local board of education disciplinary code. Instead, they display the class rules, using language that students, parents, and teachers alike can understand. This should be the model for expressing standards and expectations for student academic proficiency.

☐ Examples of proficient and exemplary student work are displayed throughout the classroom.

In some schools, this is called the "wall of fame," in which the work of present and former students is displayed. Some schools even use the trophy case for this purpose, making it clear to parents and visitors that student achievement is valued and that students in this school have already demonstrated that success is possible.

Some of these displays do not include student names. The purpose of the display is not to elevate one student over another, but rather to give a model to all students of what successful writing, mathematics, science, or social studies work looks like. Success in these schools is never a mystery. The display of student work clearly links the standards to real student work. These displays have the added advantage of allowing school leaders to check that each classroom has the same level of quality expectation, and that expectations for student proficiency are always linked to the standard rather than to idiosyncratic judgment about students.

☐ For every assignment, the teacher publishes in advance the explicit expectations for proficient student work.

Although a full scoring guide may not always be necessary, it is absolutely essential that students enter every academic activity knowing in advance what success means. They need not guess, nor must students merely attempt to beat other students. They know precisely what is expected, whether through a rubric, checklist, or other document that clearly establishes the rules of the assignment.

☐ Student evaluation is always done according to the standards and the scoring guide, and never on the curve.

When I ask students, "How did you get that grade?" I frequently hear an honest reply: "I don't know." In a standards-based classroom, this is never

(continued)

Exhibit 13.1. Classroom Checklist
for Standards Implementation (*continued*)

the case. The rationale for grading is not the mysterious judgment of the teacher, but a reflection of a scoring guide that is based upon a clear set of standards.

☐ The teacher can explain to any parents or other stakeholder the specific expectations of students for the year.

Parents must be able to ask, "What does my child need to know and be able to do in order to be successful this year?" They should receive an answer that is consistent and coherent. Although the initial impulse to reply "Work hard and follow directions" may be tempting, parents and students deserve more detail. In any activity outside of school, parents would expect a clear definition of success, and they deserve the same within the school. Leaders can profitably devote the first few faculty meetings of the year to role plays in which the leader assumes the role of a parent and asks that question. Teachers and leaders can collaborate in crafting the best response to the query regarding what students must know and be able to do to succeed. The time to answer the question is at the beginning of the year, not after there is a controversy about a grade or curriculum decision.

☐ The teacher has the flexibility to vary the length and quantity of curriculum content daily to ensure that students receive more time on the most essential subjects.

This criterion is counterintuitive to many teachers and leaders, particularly if they have assumed that implementing academic standards implies standardizing teaching practice. In fact, an integral part of successful standards implementation is greater flexibility for teachers. Because student needs vary from one classroom to the next, the greatest need is flexibility in timing and emphasis, provided that it does not lead to flexibility in expectations. Therefore, administrators should devote more attention to classroom assessment and teacher expectations, not to whether each teacher is delivering the same lesson at the same time on the same day.

☐ Students can spontaneously explain what "proficiency" means for any assignment.

Larry Lezotte asks the question well when he inquires, "What are you learning about today, and how do you know if you are learning it?" If students are unsure or hesitant, it may be time to allow them to play a greater role in restating standards and creating scoring guides. My experience suggests that when students have the opportunity to create

Exhibit 13.1. (*continued*)

expectations, the requirements are clearer and more rigorous than when the job of articulating requirements is left exclusively in the hands of adults.

☐ Commonly used standards, such as those for written expression, are reinforced in every subject.

In other words, spelling, capitalization, and grammar always count. When teaching mathematics, whether to elementary students or graduate students, I would begin the semester by explaining: "Mathematics is about describing the universe using numbers, symbols, and words. We will use all three this semester, and all three are important enough that we will express them correctly." Symbols, including inequalities, exponential notation, periods, and commas, are important. Words and letters, whether in an algebraic equation or an English sentence, are important. The same emphasis on clarity of expression applies to science, social studies, physical education, and music. There is, in other words, no class in any school in which English expression is unimportant or in which thinking, reasoning, and communication are extraneous.

☐ The teacher has created at least one standards-based performance assessment in the past month.

Training teachers in standards and standards-based assessment is not enough. The real question is whether the training is being used in the classroom. With respect to the issue of determining whether standards are really in use, the question is not whether the teacher likes standards or had a good attitude about the last training session. The only relevant question is whether the assessments the teacher creates and uses in the classroom are related to state academic standards.

☐ The teacher exchanges student work with a colleague for review and collaborative evaluation at least once every two weeks.

Collaboration is the hallmark of effective implementation of standards. In fact, standards have never been implemented by virtue of a colorful wall chart from the state department of education. Standards have only been implemented successfully when professional educators and school leaders agree, through intensive and consistent collaborative efforts, on what the word *proficient* really means.

☐ The teacher provides feedback to students and parents about the quality of student work compared to the standards, not compared to other students.

School leaders will be called to deal with this criterion when aggrieved parents notice that their child received the same score as another child,

(*continued*)

Exhibit 13.1. Classroom Checklist
for Standards Implementation (*continued*)

and the other child had to submit the assignment several times to be proficient. "That's not fair," the parents will assert. "Our child got the problem right the first time, and that child only got the problem right after working hard, respecting teacher feedback, meeting the standard, and resubmitting the work. That just can't be fair!"

Leaders must support teachers as they offer two clear rejoinders to this complaint. First, in a standards-based school, teachers never compare the work of one student to that of another student. "I'll devote an entire hour to comparing your child's work to a standard," the teacher might say, "but I will not spend a single moment comparing your child's work to that of another child. That sort of discussion is out of bounds, and I won't do it." Second, the teacher might say: "I'm quite familiar with the academic standards of this state, and not a single one of them requires that our students complete proficiency quickly. In fact, not a single standard refers to speed, but all of them refer to the quality of work. Therefore, I evaluate student work on the basis of the standards and the quality of work, never on a comparison of one student to another."

☐ The teacher helps to build community consensus in the classroom and with other stakeholders for standards and high expectations of all students.

National polling data make clear that teachers are trusted purveyors of information, particularly about educational policy. Voters trust teachers more than they trust board members, state policy makers, or school administrators. Teachers therefore bear a particular responsibility for carrying the message of the fairness and effectiveness of academic standards. Effective leaders give teachers the tools, time, and opportunity to practice effective communication with the community at large. Role-playing dialogue with skeptical community stakeholders is excellent practice for a faculty meeting or professional development seminar.

☐ The teacher uses a variety of assessment techniques, including extended written response, in all disciplines.

Although I believe in performance assessments, I am not a zealot on the subject. In fact, there is a time and a place for multiple-choice items, short answers, extended response, demonstrations, and projects. Effective teachers use all of these assessment techniques.

Exhibit 13.2. School Checklist for Standards Implementation

☐ Faculty meetings are routinely devoted to collaborative examination of real student work compared to academic standards.

☐ There are schoolwide assessments administered to every student in the same class (secondary) or grade (elementary) at periodic intervals.

☐ Professional development is based on analysis of teacher familiarity and application of essential skills in standards-based instruction.

☐ Student performance in key standards is posted monthly or quarterly, with the "percent proficient or higher" tracked during the year.

☐ Eighty percent or more of the faculty agree on the standards-based scoring of an anonymous piece of student work.

☐ The principal personally participates in evaluating student work at least once a week.

☐ Students who do not meet academic standards receive immediate and decisive intervention, including mandatory tutoring and schedule adjustments.

☐ A review of the agenda and minutes of faculty meetings, grade-level meetings, and department meetings reveals an overwhelming focus (90 percent or more of agenda items and time) on academic achievement and collaborative scoring of student work.

☐ Faculty meetings are held jointly with other schools at least once a quarter to ensure that there are comparable expectations for student achievement.

☐ Teachers evaluate student achievement on the basis of the performance compared to standards and not on the normal curve, any comparison to other students, or average performance during the grading period.

☐ The grading reporting system allows teachers to give a narrative explanation for student work, including an alternative explanation for a letter grade.

☐ Analysis of data, including test data; classroom assessments; and professional practices in teaching, curriculum, and leadership are regularly reviewed. The building leader can readily articulate specific changes made since the previous semester that are directly related to this data analysis.

☐ The building leadership regularly identifies best practices, documenting in detail successful practices in teaching, curriculum, and leadership, and sharing those practices with all faculty members.

(continued)

**Exhibit 13.2. School Checklist for Standards
Implementation (*continued*)**

☐ The building leadership conducts a "weed the garden" exercise at least
once a semester and can identify initiatives and activities that have been
dropped in the past six months.

☐ The school analyzes data at the classroom and building levels to
analyze the relationship among teaching, curriculum, and leadership
indicators and student results. These results are analyzed on the
Leadership and Learning Matrix, and the most effective practices are
shared with all faculty members.

☐ School goals are obvious, regularly measured, and understood by faculty
and students. List school goals here and note evidence of regular
measurement:

Exhibit 13.3. District Checklist for Standards Implementation

☐ The district curriculum clearly reflects state academic content standards and adds value to those standards through prioritization and focus.

☐ The district has gathered a consensus from every building on the standards for each grade that are essential for the next level of instruction. The consensus "power standards" have been shared throughout the district.

☐ The district regularly identifies and shares best practices in standards-based teaching, assessment, and curriculum.

☐ The district regularly conducts a weed-the-garden exercise and can specifically identify initiatives and activities that have been dropped in the past six months.

☐ The district monitors the information requests and other requirements from the central office to classrooms and buildings; it reports to the superintendent monthly the nature of those information requests and other requirements and their relationship to student achievement.

☐ The district accountability plan includes not only test scores but also building and classroom-based practices in teaching, curriculum, and leadership.

☐ The district regularly identifies the relationship between effective practice and student results using the Leadership and Learning Matrix.

☐ The board has established standards for its own conduct, including standards regarding communication with faculty members and information requests from buildings, classrooms, and central office departments.

---

engage in a thorough review of every report and requirement now on the books. The plain fact is that there will not be 100 percent compliance with all state regulations, just as there as been a low rate of compliance by the states with previous federal requirements.

Strategically, a state has two choices as it reviews the totality of the mandates for the school system: compliance by default or compliance by design. In the first case, compliance by default, a school district is overwhelmed by mandates and thus complies with as many as possible before running out of resources, staff, and time. In the second case, compliance by design, the school district focuses on a narrow set of the most essential state requirements. Because state officials are not stretched to the breaking point, there is time for technical assistance, intermediate feedback, and early warning indicators long before a district fails to meet state obligations.

Leadership Focus

The high failure rate of new initiatives generally and of compliance with governmentally mandated initiatives in particular is, in popular wisdom, due to a lack of resources. The term *unfunded mandate* has been a virtual mantra directed by the states toward the federal government, and by school systems toward the states. In fact, there are never sufficient resources. The root cause of the failure rate of most initiatives is not only the lack of resources but also the lack of leadership focus. The result of this unfocused leadership is that the resources available are scattered in so many directions that no initiatives get the time, attention, and resources that are necessary for success.

The obstacles that must be removed if state policy makers and leaders are to succeed in implementing standards and any other student achievement initiative include the overlapping examinations and audits now in place that pull districts in multiple directions. Within a period of a few months, a school system can be evaluated by a state inspector, a regional accreditation agency, a financial audit, a building safety inspection, and a variety of federally sponsored inspections on matters ranging from special education to gender and race discrimination. Each inspection invariably results in further reports, plans, and meetings.

Toward a Presumption of Compliance

The presumption of such a Byzantine inspection system is noncompliance. If this were effective, one would expect to see a greater level of compliance, but the quantity and complexity of federal and state requirements has outstripped the ability of most school systems to comply. Given the inevitability of limited resources at all levels of government, the fundamental presumption of the regulator must change from noncompliance (leading to a comprehensive inspection regime) to compliance. If governmental authorities presume that a district will comply, they can stop asking for response to inspections and begin requiring creation of a self-monitoring system. The dynamics of an inspection system are "catch me if you can," while the dynamics of a self-monitoring system are that each school system and ultimately each school takes responsibility for understanding and complying with state and federal requirements.

Knowledge of these systems is not restricted to technical experts far removed from the local level. Each school becomes the learning organization that it should be. Transferring compliance from a central bureaucracy to the local level, where services are provided, is becoming increasingly common in successful businesses (Garvin, 2000) and one can plausibly argue that if the complexities of compliance can be managed by a customer service department or shipping dock, in a highly unionized environment or an old organization steeped in tradition, then the central office of a school district and schools themselves have the intellectual ability to do the same.

Get Constructive Feedback from State Test Data

State education departments are a rich source of data. Despite a proliferation of seminars called Data-Driven Decision Making, use of state test data for constructive feedback to improve teaching and learning is the exception rather than the rule. In some cases, the information from the state is difficult to read and interpret; in most cases, it is delivered to the school and classroom many months after the students took the test. In still other cases, teachers complain that the test is insufficiently related to the standards, textbooks, and curriculum that are used in the classroom. Despite these shortcomings, there are four positive steps that state leaders can take to help teachers, principals, and school system leaders use state data strategically and constructively. First, states must make complete information available, including subscales and item analysis. Second, they must distribute the information in such a way that schools can easily import it into their own data systems. Third, states must use one format for all test information. Fourth, they must accumulate cause data along with effect data from schools.

Complete Information

"We really need to work on those test scores," the principal complained. I inquired which scores he was talking about. He replied, without amplification, that he was concerned about reading and math scores. All that the district had distributed to principals and teachers were average test scores for the building. The principal did not know which teachers had high scores and which had low scores; she did not know whether students had more difficulty in language mechanics or reading comprehension; and it was not clear whether the students needed more assistance in measurement, problem solving, or calculation.

Then the principal requested and received a somewhat larger package that, she was assured, contained more detailed test data. In fact, the package did contain information on subscales with labels such as "number sense" and "verbal reasoning." When I asked the principal what those labels meant and which specific test items were associated with them, she confessed that she did not know, but she speculated that it was something about computation and reading comprehension, respectively. Finally, when the principal asked for the information on specific test items—on which items the students entered the right answer and which wrong answers were selected—she was told that item information was not available from the testing company. This saga is played out every day in virtually every school in the country.

State officials have literally millions of pieces of information accumulated from tests, but principals and teachers do not have the information they need to transform that data into an instructional strategy. Exhibit 13.4 presents, in plain language, a guide for state educational leaders to use in helping teachers, principals, and system-level leaders use data wisely. The most sophisticated test in the world is of limited value if a teacher cannot use the information to improve classroom practice. Announcing that math scores are low is not nearly as helpful as a report that helps teachers understand that their students are strong in mathematical calculation but weak in measurement, particularly in the metric system. The exhortation to "work harder on reading" is not as illuminating as a clear report that allows the teacher to understand that students need particular help on drawing an inference and summarizing.

The gulf between the reading reports now offered by the state to the school system and the school's response to those reports is best illustrated by the fact that schools have invested hundreds of millions of dollars on reading programs that help students recognize letters and enunciate words and, according to local testing, show significant improvement in reading skills. The schools are then disappointed by flat test scores from the state department of education—which, it turns out, is not measuring whether students can read aloud quickly in a classroom or master their consonant blends, but rather is testing whether students can comprehend what they are reading. Certainly letter recognition is important, as is reading aloud. But those skills do not constitute "reading" as state academic content standards define it. Without a clear link from what the test data say to what the information means for teaching and learning, we have little more than a weather report: something that people listen to with bemused interest, but something that no one does anything to change.

State educational leaders are the customers in the huge and growing business of standardized testing. Their customer role should give them the clout to demand information that is clear, complete, and usable by the ultimate customers: students, parents, teachers, and school leaders. We should be able to ask, for individual students and for groups of students, "How many questions

**Exhibit 13.4. Guidelines for Providing Constructive
Test Data to Schools**

State policy makers and educational leaders can use this checklist to ensure
that test companies, universities, or other providers of test data give
information to schools in a form that is usable:

☐ Test data are coded with a unique student number so that if the student
moves from one school to another, the history of test performance can
easily follow the student.

☐ Test data are coded with the name of the classroom teacher for
elementary students and the name of the subject-matter teacher for
secondary students so that results can be analyzed and sorted by teacher.

☐ Test data are in a form that can be easily integrated with school
information systems. This means that, in addition to or instead of paper
reports, the test information exists in a spreadsheet or commonly used
database format so that teachers and schools can import the state test
information and conduct additional analysis of test results on the basis
of such local characteristics as curriculum, attendance, classroom grades,
and other important student variables. The ideal format for test data is
for each student name and unique number to appear in the rows, and
each test item and other information to appear in columns.

☐ Complete test data are provided to each school, not merely to the
district research department. Complete test data includes a name and
student number, along with the actual response the student made for
each item, whether the item was right or wrong, the raw score
(percentage correct), the scale score, and any subscale score that
represent groups of items. Where subscale scores are available, the
items that are part of the subscale must be clearly identified.

☐ The state academic content standard is identified to which each item is
related.

---

were correct, and what percentage is that of the total?" without
being given a lecture by a psychometrician about why we really
don't need that number. I am well acquainted with the reasoning
behind scale scores and the other information typically packaged
by testing companies. Nevertheless, at the classroom-and-building
level, as a teacher and as a parent I still want to know which items
my students answered correctly and which items were incorrect.

I want to use this information not to mindlessly teach to a particular test question but to look for trends that help me discover which practices in teaching, curriculum, and leadership are most and least effective. The persistent failure of testing companies to make this information available at the level of the classroom and school is, at best, lousy customer service; at worst, it is corporate arrogance.

Importable Information

State test data are frequently furnished in a manner that is inaccessible to local school systems. There are some notable exceptions: Wisconsin and Virginia, both of which put at least some of their test data on the Internet in a form that can be downloaded into a teacher's computer for the most commonly used spreadsheet program, Microsoft Excel. More frequently, however, principals and teachers receive reams of paper, which a few of them reenter by hand into their own computer so that they can analyze it.

The reason additional analysis is necessary is that average test scores reveal little or nothing about instructional and leadership practice. The strategic leader, charged with linking information to decisions, must know more than the score. For example, the principal and teacher need to sort the scores by rate of student attendance, data that typically reside at the school rather than the state department of education. The most meaningful information that relates test scores to school curriculum, after all, is for those students who actually attended class at least 90 percent of the time. In addition, the principal must be able to identify which instructional practices were associated with the greatest level of student success; thus the principal must be able to sort student results by teacher and curriculum. If, for example, a school has four fourth-grade classes, all with similar demographic characteristics, but two of those classes use the core knowledge curriculum and the other two use a teacher-selected curriculum, all parties should be able to

quickly and easily identify the extent to which curriculum variation is associated with variation in student achievement score.

The failure of the test vendor to provide information that is easily importable and usable by teacher and principal alike is the cause
for enormous waste, on two counts. It is wasteful of the time and
energy of those extraordinary teachers and principals who, despite
the obstacles placed before them, analyze the data by hand or reenter the data into their own computer. It is even more wasteful, however, for the much larger number of teachers and principals who
find the task overwhelming and who, as a result, simply do not use
available test data to influence learning, teaching, and leadership.
Because the test data are not used, the time, money, and resources
devoted to testing are largely wasted. The leader then wonders why
the same mistakes are repeated year after year in school.

Consistent Format

Closely related to the previous criteria is the need for consistent
assessment format throughout the state. Teaching a generation of
teachers and principals to analyze test data—something that was
never part of their university undergraduate or graduate school
curricula—is difficult enough under perfect circumstances. The problem is compounded when the state uses three tests—perhaps one for
reading, another for writing, and yet another for mathematics—and
all three use different terminology and measurements to describe student proficiency. There should be a single range of scores and a single
set of terminology to describe student proficiency. Because the tests
should be linked to state standards, the norm-referenced clutter associated with most test reports—stanines, quartiles, and percentiles—
is largely irrelevant. The most important information at the level of
the classroom is the extent to which students are proficient. Some
states have a clear definition of this level, describing students in
both cumulative terms (advanced, proficient, progressing, and not
meeting standards) and numerical terms (percentage of test items
correct).

Cause-and-Effect Data

Although a few states conduct site visits and make other observations about the environment in which test scores occur, the fore-
most feature of most accountability reports is the test score. The
predominance of test scores as the sole feature of an educational
accountability report is analogous to a report on the health of a
patient with notations on weight and blood pressure, but not a word
about the patient's habits in diet and exercise. Moreover, if in the
next report the patient has lost twenty-five pounds, but again there
is no information about the cause, the reader of the report does not
know if the patient began a regimen of diet and exercise or has
fallen victim to an eating disorder or drug use.

The argument is sometimes made that teaching is an art rather
than a science and thus is not amenable to precise measurement.
The same argument was no doubt made, before the Enlightenment,
about medicine. There is certainly an art to great teaching, but a
great many teaching practices, curriculum choices, and leadership
decisions are subject to objective measurement; the relationship between these decisions and student achievement can be
explored and used to promote improved student achievement. At
the very least, the state can gather information on the curriculum
in use and whether the student was taught by a fully certified
teacher. Around the nation, education officials note with disap-
proval the continued low test scores of some schools and then
purchase consulting services, special programs, and expensive technology for these schools. They even pursue curricula that, the vendors announce, are specially formulated for the needs of poor and
minority students. What they do not do is increase the percentage
of certified teachers who are in those classrooms; nor do they
explore specific professional practices that are associated with high
and low student achievement.

Thus it comes as no surprise that student achievement, despite
the apparent efforts of state and local officials, frequently does not
improve. Researchers have consistently demonstrated that the

quality of classroom teaching is the most profound influence on student achievement (Ingersoll, e-mail). Because that variable is the most difficult and expensive of all to address, the unending pursuit of cheap alternatives remains in vogue. Famed Green Bay Packers coach Vince Lombardi was fond of saying, "If you've got a cheap head, buy a cheap helmet." Replace *head* and *helmet* with *children* and *teachers*, and the point is made.

The Governor's New Role in Educational Leadership

Education ranks with the economy as the issue most likely mentioned by sitting and aspiring governors. The power of the governor to influence educational policy has, in the past, been fragmented. Now the nation's governors have the opportunity to become the most powerful influences on education in history. Whether they take advantage of this extraordinary opportunity or cede the initiative to a combination of local interests, tradition-bound state departments of education, and unchecked federal demands remains to be seen.

This section of the chapter describes the potential for the governor to play a personal and decisive role in improving student achievement and thereby improving our nation's economic and cultural viability. As this book goes to press, major structural reforms are under way that significantly affect the power of the governor in educational governance (Education Commission of the States, 2002). Nine states—Colorado, Georgia, Hawaii, Indiana, Maine, Maryland, Minnesota, North Carolina, and Ohio—are now being joined by many others contemplating less significant changes. The need for structural change is overdue, as students and teachers are whipsawed by competing and often conflicting demands. The situation is particularly acute when the governor favors one type of assessment but the state department of education prefers another, or the state board of education favors one set of standards and accompanying curriculum but legislators oppose it and are thus unwilling to adequately fund the state board and department.

The Governor's Remedy for Chaotic Governance

The chaotic state of educational governance has, at least, helped policy makers understand that there is a profound difference between listening to a variety of points of view in formulating policy and having dissenting voices institutionalized as part of the process of implementing policy. A successful military organization knows the value of contention until the moment a decision is made; then it requires unity of command and unanimous support for the decision once it has been made. This principle of constructive contention before a decision, followed by total teamwork after the decision, is the hallmark of any effective organization.

In education, however, the battles continue long after the war has been won. Academic standards are now part of the law of all fifty states, but I continue to hear disgruntled parties at the state and local levels refer to it as a passing fad. Although annual testing in reading and math is now a federal requirement supported by more than 90 percent of our elected representatives and a similarly strong percentage of the general public, progress toward improved student achievement remains stymied by opponents who are unable to acknowledge that this is one policy dispute they have lost. It is as if the line at the post office could not proceed because the clerk remains unhappy about the Elvis stamp. State departments of education, no matter how carefully organized and well led, do not carry the weight of authority that a unified executive branch of government can offer. This means that the governor, the state board of education, the chief education officer, and the senior leadership and employees of the state department must all support the same policies.

The source of the governor's power is the rarely noticed Tenth Amendment to the U.S. Constitution, which reserves for the states all powers not explicitly given to the national government. Because the Constitution does not address education, it is one of the many unnamed "reserved powers" of the states. Even the significant recent federal legislation, the No Child Left Behind Act,

includes explicit prohibition of the use of a national test and consistently places the burden on the states to establish standards and
create assessments to measure the extent to which students meet
those standards. The flexibility in the law extends not only to standards and assessment but to school governance as well (Reeves,
2001a), as the law encourages expansion of charter schools and
programs of school choice within the public school system.

The influence of the governor and other state educational officials has a dramatic impact on the effectiveness of educational programs. The General Accounting Office (2002) found that the
involvement of state leadership was one of the most significant con-
tributing factors in those states that were able to successfully meet
federal goals. In addition to the governor, the GAO study singled
out business and community leaders, legislators, and state department of education leaders as crucial players in program success—
and their lack of active involvement as an almost certain sign of
trouble.

One important power enjoyed by most governors is that of
appointment. In some cases, this is the appointment of state board
of education members, while in other cases it is the power to
appoint the commissioner, superintendent, director, or otherwise
named leader of the department of education. Governors who wish
to successfully implement their policies must establish a strategic
alignment in which policy making is done by legislators and state
board members and policy implementation is attended to by the
leadership and staff of the department of education.

The Governor's Impact on Educational Standards and Testing

Governors are busy people and thus must focus their time and
influence on those few areas where it has the greatest impact. In the
field of education, the greatest leverage is in final approval of academic standards and testing policies. These may appear to be mere
details that should be delegated to others while the governor

focuses on the big picture, but the fact is that standards and testing are the biggest picture of all. These documents and policies influence what happens in the classroom every day in a way that no other action by the governor or legislature can.

State Communication of Standards

States have produced widely varying versions of standards, with some weighed down in educational jargon and full of complexity well beyond the interest of most lay readers. Other states, by contrast, have gone to an extraordinary length to make their standards documents and accompanying notes for parents clear and useful. The clarity and usefulness of standards is not a function of political affiliation.

Some of the best examples of user-friendly standards and accompanying parent documents come from Florida, Massachusetts, Arkansas, and California, four states whose political partisans might resist finding much in common with the other three. Florida produces clear standards, practice tests accessible by students and parents, and user-friendly parent guides published in Creole and other languages. Arkansas has the aptly named "refrigerator curriculum," in which lengthy documents are replaced by a single piece of paper suitable for mounting on that traditional educational display, the refrigerator door. California offers superior information for teachers and parents not only on the standards and testing program but also for a variety of special needs that students may have. Massachusetts takes the mystery and fear out of standards and testing by giving every parent in the state a clear guide, free of jargon, that helps them discuss important academic issues and concepts with children.

There are surely other examples of exceptionally fine work by state departments of education, but I select these four to make the point that the ability to create clear and coherent communication is not a function of geography, politics, or the demographic characteristics of the state. These four states represent the prosperous and depressed, urban and rural, east and west. What they have in common is commitment to educate children and communicate with parents.

Revision of Standards: An Opportunity for the Governor

Creating and revising standards is a dynamic process. As a state continues to revise and improve its standards, the governor has a wonderful opportunity to focus on two areas that dramatically improve the quality and usefulness of state academic content standards: readability and prioritization. The governor is, as noted, busy, but should—just once a year—read a form in every department of government that is intended for the general public and ask, "Do I really understand this?"

So, Governor: read a tax form, read an unemployment form, read a public assistance form, read a business license application, and yes, read your state academic content standards. If you don't have time to read all of them, just pick one grade, as if you were the parent of a child of that age, and read all of the standards for that grade. Do you know what your child is expected to know and be able to do to be successful in school? If you have any questions at all, how must the parents who do not have your level of education, background, interest, and expertise feel? In the next revision of standards, you have the opportunity to insist that they pass "the governor test." In other words, if you can't read them, understand them, and apply them to your own children or grandchildren, then it's back to the drawing board. Too many first drafts of standards were designed to impress others in the academic arena (as if the drafters were paid by the syllable). In the next draft, the writers need not impress you, but they absolutely must communicate with you.

In addition to improving the clarity and readability of standards, the governor can dramatically improve the quality and usability of academic standards by insisting on prioritization of those standards. Establishing standards is a political process. The word *political* in this sense is not intended with the typical sneer, but in the best sense of the word: the political process involves listening to a variety of points of view and accumulating great ideas from a broad cross-section of constituents. Even as good ideas accumulate, however, the time allotted to the school day remains fixed. Ironically, each good new idea receives fewer minutes of attention, as the numerator of school time is divided by an ever-increasing denominator of standards. Ideally, some standards should be eliminated, but because this may not be possible in the political process in which standards are created, the next best solution is for a prioritization process to take place.

This prioritization is absolutely essential because of an essential truth: no teacher—not a single one in any state—covers every standard to perfection. Some standards receive more attention than others, and some are omitted entirely. Teachers complain of a persistent lack of time, of students who come unprepared so that the teacher must first cover the previous year's standards, and of students who take longer than expected to master the standards. Thus some standards will be omitted; the challenge for state leaders is whether those omissions occur as a result of careful prioritization or as a result of random selection, personal taste, and the exigencies of the calendar.

One means of prioritizing standards is to use the concept I have labeled "power standards" (Reeves, 2000a). There are three filters useful in reducing a large set of unprioritized standards into a smaller subset of power standards.

First, we ask if the standard has endurance. That is, does the standard represent knowledge or skills that will endure long after the assessment for the year? For example, the skills that students acquire in reading comprehension and the knowledge that they gain about measurement are likely to endure throughout a lifetime, while memorizing the difference between the Articles of Confederation and the Constitution is likely to have a shorter duration. This does not mean that we necessarily forget about the Articles of Confederation, but it emphatically means that before teachers spend a great deal of time talking about *The Federalist Papers*, they devote sufficient energy to ensuring that their students can read them.

The second threshold for prioritization is leverage. Standards with leverage give students the ability to improve in many standards. The most striking example of a standard with leverage is nonfiction writing, which is associated with improved student achievement in mathematics, science, social studies, and reading (Reeves, 2000b). Another example is the development of skill in creating and drawing inferences from tables, charts, and graphs. In addition to helping students meet mathematics standards, proficiency in this area also assists students who must achieve standards in science, social studies, and verbal reasoning, all areas that use tables, charts, and graphs.

The Standards Paradox: Too Many and Too Few

The third filter for prioritization of standards is readiness for the next grade level. I frequently ask teachers this question: What are the knowledge and skills that your teaching colleagues in the next lower grade must impart to their students so that they can enter your class next year with success and confidence? Not once has a teacher responded that colleagues in the earlier grade must cover every standard. Instead, teachers uniformly create a list that is brief and balanced. They rarely list more than a dozen standards per subject per grade. Moreover, their list is balanced with consideration of content area information, literacy, and behavior.

In this way, teachers resolve the standards paradox in which there are simultaneously too many and too few standards. There are too many standards because they typically represent more content than can be covered adequately in a single school year. There are too few standards because they typically omit essential skills in time management, organization, and teamwork. To return to our previous example, I have never heard a high school history teacher say that a student failed because she was unable to recall the details of the Hamilton-Jefferson debates, but I have heard many teachers speak of failure associated with time management, organization, and behavior. If these criteria are added to the official standards, the result is an air of reality and practicality in the documents that is noticeably absent in many cases.

Transforming the Public Dialogue on Education

Beyond the authority granted in the state constitution, a governor has a power that offers exceptional influence—that is, the power to guide public conversation. This does not mean excluding disagreement, but it can certainly involve explicit limitations on unproductive and vitriolic attacks on motives, which so frequently predominate in a debate over educational policy. It is not sufficient, to these combatants, to present alternative policy points of view. They must give them unflattering labels and speculate that they are part of a conspiracy of evildoers associated with the forces of perdition, ranging from Joe Camel to Disneyland (Ohanian, 1999). The governor can open the public dialogue widely while, with the dignity of the office and flawless personal example, demonstrating that disagreement without rancor is possible and even necessary. The governor can, in a word, establish standards for the dialogue. As a fundamental moral principle, the participants in a debate over standards for children should not enter the fray unless they are first willing to establish and achieve standards themselves.

Civility and respect are not the only way in which a governor can influence the public debate on educational policy for the better. Strategic leadership depends on wise decision making, to be sure, but also on explicit links among information, mission, vision, and decisions. Thus the governor can maintain focus on those decisions that are exclusively related to the mission and vision and that have information to support them. There are a variety of opportunities for discussing opinions unsupported by evidence and for interesting ideas that are irrelevant to the primary educational mission of the state. But a forum convened by the governor on educational policy is not such a place. The governor's framework should include several filters, such as those listed below, that can address both the ideas and the people who advocate them. Perhaps we could label the list "Standards for Grownups When Discussing Policies About Kids":

• Is this related to our primary mission of improving student achievement for all children in the state? It is not sufficient that the idea have merit or that one feel strongly about it. It must be related to the primary educational mission.
• Is this supported evidence that can be independently verified? The phrases "research proves" and "studies show" must be associated with detailed evidence and citations. The standard should be the "preponderance of the evidence," rather than a set of dueling rhetoricians, each of whom has an article, anecdote, study, or glib assertion to support a point of view.
• Can the advocate answer thoughtful questions from the other side, or merely parrot a prepared speech?
• Can the advocate respond to challenges with thoughtful answers in an environment of civility and respect?

By guiding the dialogue on educational policy, the governor can move from the typical work of government to what Heifetz and Linsky (2002) have described as adaptive change. The work of technical change traditionally undertaken by a governmental entity involves assembling experts (and consequently excluding the general public) and, when the work is completed, announcing the solution. With the repetition of such a pattern, people come to believe the function of government is to solve their problems. As the governor moves to address challenges through adaptive change, it is the people with the problems—parents, students, employers, educators—who take responsibility for the work. Although this process surely includes experts, it does not exclude those without a degree or specialized training. The governor's role is not to satisfy a series of unhappy customers, but instead to challenge people to question their assumptions, contribute to the solution, and commit to one another.

Building Social Capital

In his landmark book *Bowling Alone: The Collapse and Revival of American Community*, Harvard professor and president of the American Political Science Association Robert Putnam (2000) assembles a powerful case for developing and nurturing social capital. Political participation, civic engagement, club membership, volunteer activities, social connections at work and in the neighborhood are all indicators of the extent to which a society's social capital is strong or depleted. Putnam's research brings bad news and good news. The bad news is that social capital has been eroding alarmingly for the past five decades. The worse news is that this decline is directly related to a variety of social ills, ranging from crime to ill health and dependence on public assistance and low level of education:

> States that score high on the Social Capital Index—that is, states whose residents trust other people, join organizations, volunteer, vote, and socialize with friends—are the same states where children flourish: where babies are born healthy and where teenagers tend not to become parents, drop out of school, get involved in violent crime, or die prematurely due to suicide or homicide. Statistically, the correlation between high social capital and positive child development is as close to perfect as social scientists ever find in data analyses of this sort. States such as North Dakota, Vermont, Minnesota, Nebraska, and Iowa have healthy civic adults and healthy well-adjusted kids; other states, primarily those in the South, face immense challenges in both the adult and youth population [Putnam, 2000, pp. 296–297].

Although the governor cannot influence much of the social fabric of his state, he can wield immense influence over some of these seminal causal variables. He can encourage membership in parent associations and, wherever necessary, invent and sponsor such groups. The governor can recognize volunteerism not only among the peripatetic parents in the suburbs but among parents who have never even considered volunteering in a school, and in schools where parents rarely volunteer. The governor can promote and nurture social networks not through a governmental bureaucracy but through microgrants in which the difference between a successful series of meetings and the absence of participation might be the cost of child care and coffee for the parents who take time to attend. Governors can recognize extracurricular activities—some of the early sources of social capital and human connectedness among students—with particular emphasis on the most inclusive activities. If only the state championship basketball team has lunch with the governor, it sends one message. If the school that has every single student involved in one or more extracurricular activity receives a visit from the governor, it sends quite another.

Putnam's research is exhaustive and stunning. Even after taking into account the variables that are typically regarded as intractable—poverty, unemployment, adult educational level, state budget support for education, family structure, and many others—the influence of social capital on childhood welfare and educational success remains. He finds the same impact in low-poverty neighborhoods as in high-poverty neighborhoods. Social capital—our connections to other human beings that are placed at risk each time we displace a human connection with a television, or allow cynicism to gain the upper hand over personal commitment and participation in society—is a profound influence on our own children and on every child in the nation. Social capital can be operationalized into specific actions that each governor can take, and many of those actions can be undertaken independently of legislative authority or extraordinary expenditure; developing, nurturing, recognizing, and promoting social capital is one of the most important things that any governor can do to foster education and improve the vitality of a state.

Leadership Reflections

1. Identify one state policy that is of particular importance to you. It might be curriculum and standards, special education, school facility maintenance—whatever you have personal interest in. Describe in rich detail compliance with that policy that is *exemplary*. This implementation meets the letter and spirit of the policy and then goes beyond it. You would use this example as a model for everyone in the state to see ideal implementation of your policy. Write your description in such a way that a teacher or school principal who desires to comply with this policy can read your words and know precisely what to do without asking for additional assistance.

2. Refer to the same policy you have examined in the first question, and now complete a scoring rubric for policy implementation. Describe implementation that is *proficient*. It is not the ideal that you described earlier, but it meets all state requirements. Describe implementation that is *progressing*. It does not quite meet state requirements, but it is close enough so that with a few modifications the school or district will be in compliance. Write a description for *not meeting standards*, the level at which the school or district appears to not even understand the requirements of the policy and needs intensive and immediate assistance.

3. Choose the checklist in Exhibits 13.1, 13.2, and 13.3 that represents standards implementation in the classroom, school, and district, respectively, and apply it to an actual classroom, school, or district. Discuss your findings with the teacher, principal, or superintendent.

4. On the basis of your discussion of the checklist in question three, add additional criteria for effective standards implementation that are appropriate for your area.

5. Ask a teacher in your area for the state test information that is readily available in the classroom. Ask a principal for the same thing—the state test information that is readily available. This does not mean whatever they get after several phone calls to the district office, but what they have immediately at hand. Compare the test data to the criteria listed in Exhibit 13.4. What would be required from the state or district office to give the classroom teacher and school principal the information they need to use state test data constructively?

6. What are the greatest impediments to the strategic alignment of policy development and implementation in your state? For each of these impediments, identify if it is structural (that is, a legislative or constitutional change is required) or administrative (an administrative order of the governor is sufficient to change it).

7. Read the standards of your state for just a single grade. Do they pass "the governor's test" for readability? Are they prioritized?

8. If your standards are not prioritized, ask a teacher (someone who has a history of success in teaching the next higher grade than the one for which you reviewed state standards in question two), "What are the knowledge and skills that students must acquire in the prior grade in order to enter your class with success and confidence?" Compare the response to that question with the list of standards that you read in question two. What is the same? What is left out? What is added to the essential list from the teacher that does not appear in the state standards?

9. If you were to host a governor's forum on educational policy, what standards would you establish for the participants?

10. Does your state have a clear educational mission? If so, write it down. Does it meet the criteria of brevity and passion that we have previously established for mission statements? If not, how would you revise it? If you do not have a clear educational mission, write one that conveys your essential mission with clarity, brevity, and passion.

11. Identify how the governor of your state can build social capital. Focus on ideas that do not require legislative action but can be undertaken immediately and unilaterally by the governor. (Social capital, as Putnam defined it, involves an improved level of trust, joining organizations, volunteerism, voting and other civic participation, and socialization with friends.)

Chapter Fourteen

The National Leadership Imperative

Leadership Keys

Follow the money: new strategies in federal influence

The limits of federal involvement in education

Set the record straight about federal policy

Use standards to close the gap between expectations and
  reality

Apply economic incentives to improve local schools

Understand the limits of federal policy

It is difficult for some people to reconcile the prerogatives of
the state government and local school board with the power of the
national government in educational policy. They are suspicious of
any federal intervention in educational matters and—perhaps on
the basis of other experience they have had with agencies ranging
from the Internal Revenue Service to the Bureau of Alcohol,
Tobacco, and Firearms—deeply distrust anything labeled *federal.*
This chapter is not an exhaustive analysis of federal education policy; it summarizes some of the myths and realities associated with
the role of the national government in education.

It is also necessary to respond to a surprising number of critics
of the political left and right who have joined forces to criticize new
federal education legislation. Both of these forces, who agree on
hardly anything else, invoke the mantra of local control to support
their viewpoint, with only the metaphors changing. For the right,

the requirement for annual testing of students in reading and math conjures up images of Black Hawk helicopters, fresh from a gun confiscation mission, now dropping tests onto schools—yet another encroachment of liberal government into private affairs. For the left, the same requirement for annual testing represents the distrust of teachers and public education that is typical of the right-wing conservative establishment. From the intensity of their rhetoric and the stridency of their claims, one would never know that 73 percent of teachers and 92 percent of principals support standards-based reform in schools (Ravitch, 2001). In addition, 76 percent of parents and 81 percent of the general public support a high school graduation test, provided that students have several opportunities for success. Perhaps this explains why more than 90 percent of the members of Congress supported legislation on standards and testing.

Nevertheless, in my frequent travels and conversation with literally thousands of teachers in hundreds of schools, I continue to hear skepticism and resistance to standards. The plain fact is that a presidential signature on a law overwhelmingly approved by Congress and widely supported by the American public is not enough. Standards will not reach their potential of bringing equity and excellence to schools if leaders do not confront the opposition and continue to make the case that this is the best way to educate children.

A disturbing myth about the federal role in standards is that the standards themselves are imposed by the government. Here is the fact: there are no federal academic content standards, period. There is no federal test, period. The only thing that comes close is the National Assessment of Educational Progress (NAEP), which will be periodically administered as a method to report on the relative rigor of state tests but which cannot be used to create any consequence for students, schools, or school districts. In fact, the NAEP results are not even reported for individual students, schools, or districts, but only for the state as a whole. It is true that the federal government requires each student in grades three through eight to take a reading test and a math test once a year, but they must be of the state or district's own making and must be based on state, not federal, standards.

Those who argue that this is an extraordinary imposition by the federal government must be prepared to answer this question: Does your opposition imply that, in the absence of a federal law, you are unwilling to tell parents just once a year if their child can read on grade level? Without a federal law, would your school not administer a math test at least once a year? Of course, the critics retort, we test reading and math, but we do it our way. That is precisely the point. The new federal legislation allows each state to test "our way," but it also requires that those tests be based on the academic content standards of the states and not the idiosyncratic expectations of individual teachers and schools.

Research by Sylvia Ybarra (2000) makes the point about how widely expectations can differ among teachers and schools. She studied more than six thousand pieces of student work using a simple methodology. She compared the grade level of the work, as identified by the classroom teacher, to the grade level of the work as described in the state standards. Figures 14.1 and 14.2 tell the tale. With each passing grade, less schoolwork given to the child represents work on that grade level. If we do not ask students to do grade-level work, how will we ever know if they are capable of doing it? I talked with Ybarra recently, and she informed me that her database has grown to 250,000 pieces of student work. But the conclusions presented in Figures 14.1 and 14.2 remain depressingly the same.

When teachers view this slide, they immediately counter with the argument, "These kids come to us far below grade level, so we have to meet them where they are." The charts make clear the consequence of this logic. With each passing year, students receive less instruction on grade level and thus fall farther and farther behind. Thus it is not surprising that when a student is unable to read on grade level in the eighth grade, there is an 85 percent probability of

Figure 14.1. Language Arts Grade-Level Gap

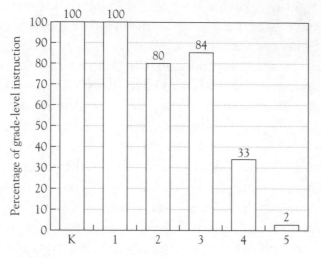

Source: Ybarra (2000).

Figure 14.2. Mathematics Grade-Level Gap

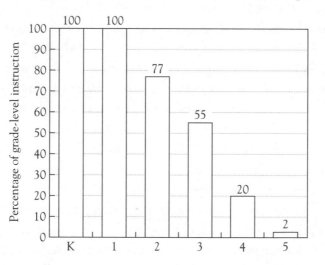

Source: Ybarra (2000).

the student remaining in that situation throughout high school, with a high likelihood of a lifetime of adverse consequences (Capella and Weinstein, 2001).

This problem is perpetuated by the substantial disconnection between student performance on the standards that represent the state's expectations of knowledge and skills on the one hand, and on the other the presumed student performance (on the basis of teacher evaluations in the report card). I recently reviewed data on more than twenty-two thousand students in thirty-five schools in a Midwestern district. Figure 14.3 shows the difference in two groups of students on state proficiency tests in four content areas: reading, mathematics, social studies, and science. For each test, students responded to multiple choice questions, as well as questions requiring short answers and extended response. Thus there were twelve measurements—three types in each of four content

Figure 14.3. Performance on Standards: Do We Tell the Truth with Letter Grades?

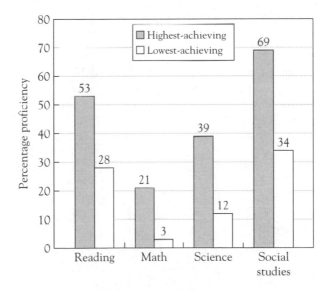

Source: Reeves (2001b).

areas—for each student. I first separated the students into two groups according to their performance on the state standards. As is starkly clear in Figure 14.3, the highest-achieving group outperformed the lowest-achieving group by a substantial margin.

Such differences are not particularly remarkable. Indeed, in a system dedicated to offering direct assistance and meaningful academic intervention to students in need, differences must be highlighted and understood. In this district—which, I am convinced, is not exceptional in this regard—any attempt at meaningful intervention could be stifled by the conflicting messages sent from teachers on report cards. Figure 14.4 shows the relative difference in grade point average, which is only about one-tenth of a point.

Throughout the nation, I regularly hear of students who are in danger of failing a high school exit examination but who have been on the honor roll for years. I hear of other schools where, the principal announces with pride, "Everybody is on the honor roll," but fewer than half the students are reading on grade level. Somebody, sometime, must tell children the truth. Perhaps it will be an employer; perhaps a high school teacher; perhaps a college dean

Figure 14.4. Grade Point Average of Highest- and Lowest-Performing Students

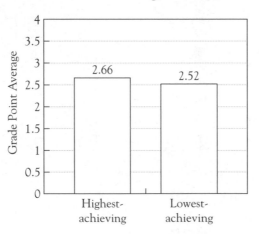

explaining why a student is not ready for college; or perhaps a trade union leader explaining that skills in reading, writing, and mathematics are necessary to become an electrician, plumber, or sheet metal worker.

One important element of the standards-based approach to education is that we retain enormous amounts of freedom, creativity, and discretion in planning and delivering curriculum, but no one has the freedom, creativity, and discretion to lie to children. We must tell them and their parents the truth about their proficiency at least once a year, at least in grades three through eight, at least in reading and mathematics. This is not the act of a heartless federal bureaucracy, but the act of a sound policy maker, wise teacher, and good parent.

Follow the Money: New Strategies in Federal Influence

Since the original Elementary and Secondary Education Act was passed in 1965, the traditional system of federal funding was that the government funded programs. After all, there did not seem to be much other choice. The programs were created at the federal and state levels, gained advocates in Congress and successive administrations, and took on a life of their own. By the end of the twentieth century, there were more than sixty federal education programs. The reauthorization of that legislation signed by President Bush in 2002 takes a strikingly different approach. If a school fails to achieve its goals of adequate yearly progress, then federal dollars do not fund the program; rather, they fund the student. In the legislation's final form, those dollars cannot follow the student to a private school in the form of a voucher, but the federal funds can follow the student to another public school, thus setting the stage for schools seeking successful implementation of standards to attract students and the funds that accompany them.

Such a market-oriented approach may strike many as the hallmark of a Republican administration. People are therefore surprised to see, at the bottom of Executive Order 13153, the signature of

President Bill Clinton, on May 3, 2000. The order requires the federal Department of Education to take action to improve low-performing schools and specifically requires sanctions if a school fails to improve for two consecutive years. A cornerstone of the Clinton order was the alternative of school choice programs, so that students can transfer out of a school identified for improvement without regard for district boundary or student assignment policy (Reeves, 2001a). It turns out, then, that neither standards in general nor promotion of student choice and sanctions for ineffective schools is the exclusive domain of one political party or philosophy.

The Limits of Federal Involvement in Education

Despite the enormous power of the federal government to wield money and influence, the walls of the school are strong in many ways and are a barrier sometimes impervious to outside influence. The institutional resistance to outside forces is the heart of the concept of academic freedom, in which scholars need not pander to popular taste. The genesis of academic freedom was in the centuries after the Reformation and Counter-Reformation, in which professors who espoused unpopular beliefs were lucky if they lost only their positions and witnessed the burning of only their books. The atrocities visited upon thinkers whose only crime was thought is an enduring shame of our civilization from its past five hundred years. Even in the putatively more enlightened twentieth and twenty-first centuries, the wrong thoughts, the wrong ethnic identity, the wrong residence, or the wrong workplace can all be a death sentence. Neither resolutions of the United States and the United Nations nor solemn speeches and grave threats by world leaders have stopped hate, a uniquely human trait that eludes legislation.

The same distance between governmental action and human results exists in the realm of economic and racial bigotry, the true source of the chronically low expectations that prevail where students are predominantly poor and members of an ethnic minority.

Almost half a century ago, the U.S. Supreme Court ordered the Board of Education of Topeka, Kansas, to desegregate its schools. The oral arguments began on December 9, 1952, and featured many articulate advocates, including the young attorney Thurgood Marshall, who later sat on the dais himself as the first African American justice of the Court. In reviewing the oral arguments before the Supreme Court (Friedman, 1969), I was startled to notice the similarities to contemporary debate over educational changes. The recurring argument by the defendant school districts was that treatment of the races was a local affair and not the appropriate concern of the federal government. Several district courts had sided with them, even awarding court costs to the states and school districts.

Before the Supreme Court, attorneys for the defendants alternated between statements that everything was fine and that, after all, the "Negro schools" (the prevailing phrase employed by both sides) were just as good as the white schools; they threatened grave consequences if the races were mixed. One attorney from South Carolina flatly said that he would not send his children to a Negro school even if ordered to by the Court. Another attorney said, "if the appellants' construction of the Fourteenth Amendment should prevail here, there is no doubt in my mind that it would catch the Indian within its grasp just as much as the Negro. If it should prevail, I am unable to see why a state would have any further right to segregate its pupils on the ground of sex or on the ground of age or on the ground of mental capacity" (quoted in Friedman, 1969, p. 51). Girls and boys with the same opportunities? Allowing students with diminished "mental capacity" into our schools? Allowing Indians in the schools? Surely, the attorney thought, the prospect of such horrific consequences would bring the Court to its senses.

When the Court's decision to overturn the prevailing separate-but-equal doctrine was published in 1954, the attorneys returned to argue about the remedies, with the defendants pleading for a gradual approach that would be locally supervised. In one remarkable exchange, the attorneys argued that one could not, after all, over-turn the attitudes of teachers and society just by legal fiat. Justice Felix Frankfurter interrupted to ask, "Would it not be fair to say that attitudes in this world are not changed abstractly, as it were, by reading something, [but] that attitudes are partly the result of working, attitudes are party the result of action? . . . You do not fold your hands and wait for attitude to change by itself" (Friedman, 1969, pp. 412– 413).

There is inevitably tension between government as a force that reflects the will of the people and government as a force that leads, influences, and directs that will. Philosophers have contended that people cannot create a government better than themselves. On the contrary, we have the obligation to create a government, including school boards, legislators, state and federal officials, and Supreme Court justices who collectively challenge us to be better than we are now. When Chief Justice Earl Warren delivered the opinion of the Court in *Brown* v. *Board of Education of Topeka*, he did not say, "We can't really make any major changes unless we get buy-in from the teachers." He did not say, "Unless we get financial support from the federal government, we should not expect this new deseg-regation plan to work." He did not say, "Come to think of it, this racial equality stuff is probably just a passing fad, so why don't we wait to see if it's going to stick around before we make a federal case out of it?" The Court ordered, in simple and clear language, the end to racial segregation with these words: "We come then to the question presented: Does segregation of children in public schools solely on the basis of race, even though the physical facilities and other 'tangible' factors may be equal, deprive the children of the minority group of equal educational opportunities? We believe that it does" (quoted in Friedman, 1969, p. 329).

Will today's leaders bend to the prevailing threats against implementation of standards to promote equity and excellence? Will they listen to the predictions of doom that echo those of the attorneys for the defendants in the *Brown* case? Will they listen to the constant stream of complaints, allegations, and assertions that combine into the single notion that demographics are determinative and that poor and minority children cannot be expected to achieve at a high level? The next time you hear such challenges, hear the words, "The next thing you know, they'll be letting girls, Indians, and special education kids in here." If you wince at such a quotation, then the screed of the antistandards movement should make you equally uncomfortable. This is not a disagreement over policy but a matter of values, and it is our values that must prevail.

Leadership Reflections

1. What are the arguments against federal support for standards-based education that threaten to impede progress in your area? Write each argument as a statement from the opposition. For each of these arguments, classify the statement as a fact or opinion. (This is, incidentally, part of the critical-thinking standard for elementary students in many states.) If the statement is a fact, identify the evidence that suggests that the fact is true. How does that evidence compare with the evidence you have observed in reading this book or elsewhere? If the statement is an opinion, estimate the number of decision makers—voters, parents, teachers, community leaders—who share that opinion. If the opinion is widely shared by decision makers in your community and, as a result, threatens successful implementation of standards, what can you do to either respect the opinion and move on or change the opinion?

2. How can you create choice within your system now? Whether you are considering a single school, a system of schools, or an entire state, how can you encourage public schools to give choices to parents and students so that each time they walk in the door they are saying, "I got what I wanted and I choose to be here"?

3. Identify ten students who were not proficient on your last state test. Choose them at random so that you get neither the best nor the worst of the nonproficient students, but simply a random selection of them. Now collect copies of the report cards or transcript grades for each of those students. Did the information in the report cards or transcript grades adequately warn the students and parents that these students were genuinely at risk of failure?

4. Identify ten students on your honor roll. Again, select them at random, so you identify neither the highest- nor the lowest-performing honor roll students. Now find the scores for each of these students on the last state tests. Are 100 percent of these honor roll students proficient or higher on your state standards? Are you sending the same message in the honor roll that you are in the form of state standards? If you wish to give positive recognition to students who have exemplary behavior and attitude but who need help academically, is there another way aside from inaccurate grades and false statements on the honor roll that this recognition can be extended?

5. In a collection of student work, find five examples that the teacher regards as proficient at the fourth, fifth, and sixth grade levels. The work should all be the same, perhaps a one-paragraph persuasive essay. Have a colleague code the grade levels for each paper, remove all references to the names and grade levels of these students, shuffle the papers so that they are not in grade-level order, and give the student work back to you. Now, try to identify which of these proficient papers are from the fourth, fifth, and sixth grade. How many of the actual sixth grade papers did you identify as being from the fourth and fifth grades? What inferences do you draw from this analysis?

Conclusion

The Enduring Values of Leadership

Leadership Keys

Ask *why* before *how*

Pay your intellectual and emotional debts

Rise to the inevitable challenge

In the darkest of times (which all leaders face), values endure while policies, procedures, and the quotidian details of daily life fade into obscurity. These values did not emerge from a void, but from our personal stories. People in your organization know that you are passionate about your mission, but few of them know why. They see you as a person of authority and certainly as a person who, by virtue of your position, is successful. They do not, however, know the story behind the passion, and I would like to make the case that effective leaders must be vulnerable enough to share those stories. Because of our misplaced honor for the individual, we risk isolating the leader, placing her on a pedestal, and making the mission dependent upon her rather than the enduring values of which she is merely the custodian. An essential task of the leader is to elevate the mission and values over the person of the leader.

Reflect on your own history. Surely you have had some disappointments. If you are a senior leader, you have probably lost a job or two, or at least feared termination as a result of a board change or political crossfire. At the very least, you have witnessed an initiative fail, a colleague change from being supportive and collaborative to being disruptive and cynical. You certainly have seen changes in student achievement in your career, not all of which were positive. What made you persist? Take a moment to complete this sentence: "Even after a rotten day, I still get up the next day and come back to work passionately engaged in the mission because . . ." If you keep a journal, then how you complete that sentence deserves a journal entry. Perhaps it merits a small card on your desktop, not for display to others but as a reminder to yourself of why you work so hard and care so deeply.

Before you undertake your next challenge, ask *why* before *how*. Before analyzing the project and listing the tasks, launching the initiative and waging yet another battle, ask why. Review your story, your journal, or the card on your desk. It will lighten the load. As you become more comfortable in asking the *why* question in solitude, begin to share your story with others and ask them the same question. "Why do you still do it? How have you endured disappointment? What is the key to your persistence?" These conversations are not idle; they are the source of the emotional energy that will sustain your mission and vision long after you are gone. The conscious discipline of *why-before-how* is a great legacy you can leave to the organization and the children that you serve.

Paying Your Debts

As you review your own story, certain names and faces of the past who were part of the energy that drives you today will pop up. Some are obvious, since they are represented by pictures on your desk. Others are a little more subtle, as they are only names on a chart or on the cover of a book you keep close at hand. Many are almost forgotten, perhaps filed away in a drawer with other miscellaneous correspondence or in the deep recesses of memory. Collectively, these memories represent your emotional and intellectual debts. As part of your reflection on the energy that sustains you, an inventory of these debts is in order.

I do not have to look far to be reminded of the debts I have accumulated. As I look out my window, the first thing I see is an

American flag, with Boston Harbor in the background, reminders of the determination required to launch our nation out of colonialism and the resolve required to protect it today. My file still contains letters from some of my favorite teachers, one of whom was, in a time of deep despair, my most faithful correspondent. On my wall is a painting by a mother who, into her eightieth year, creates beauty with every brush stroke and reminds succeeding generations that the obligation to learn, share, and create beauty never stops. On the adjacent wall is a picture of an open hut, covered by a thatch roof and furnished only with handmade log benches. It serves people in East Africa as a school and church and brings to mind my vivid recollections of children there clutching books as if they were the greatest treasures in the world.

Close by is the Buddha given to me by one of my students in rural China, an extraordinary sacrifice for her family in a culture that values teaching and learning in a way that should shame anyone who considers teaching a profession unworthy of the name. Next to my desk is my father's award of professor emeritus; I cannot approach my own desk without remembering how long he remained at his desk after retirement, with no more remuneration than the confidence that he influenced a generation of students. In the center of my desk is a statuette of a dog jumping through a hoop, given to me by my wife the day I completed my doctorate.

These are but a fraction of the emotional and intellectual debts of which I am reminded every day. You and every other reader have a similar story, and it is well that we keep track of such accounts. Our awareness of them prods us to action, convicts us of the occasional inadequacy of our efforts, and imparts the energy necessary for the task even when the well appears dry.

Rise to the Inevitable Challenge

Just as we are on the brink of significant educational progress, I am dismayed by the extent of temporizing that threatens the very foundation of educational standards. Otherwise-thoughtful writers express misgivings about the progress of poor and minority students, caving into the demographics-as-destiny belief that I thought had been buried under the weight of thirty years of evidence. Otherwise-resolute leaders, weary of too many fights with unions, parents, and politicians, seek to find a middle ground on standards and hesitate to change too quickly. Just as a strong majority in congress approves standards for every public school in the nation (an action that polls reveal is widely supported by the American public), the backlash against standards has never been stronger. The backlash is a staple of a growing number of meetings that masquerade as professional development but are in fact political rallies designed to undermine established public policy. Every strategy, every standard, every leadership action is threatened if the leader fails to rise to these challenges. Because change is inevitably uncomfortable, opposition to change is equally inevitable.

Imagine for a moment that your responsibility is not public education, but public health. You find in the course of your daily routine a restaurant that is dangerously unclean, a water main that leaches lead into the public drinking supply, and a break in a sewer line that threatens an entire neighborhood with disease. How do you react to the challengers who suggest you take a gradual approach? How do you respond to people who appeal to you to get more buy-in from the stakeholders before you proceed with your plan of action? What do you say to those who challenge your efforts ("Well, those may be your health standards, but they are not my health standards and you have no right to impose them on me")? How would you react to a colleague in the health department announcing that he will not close a restaurant, ensure clean drinking water, or save the neighborhood from dysentery because he prefers that you "just close the door and let me practice public health my way—after all, I've been doing this for twenty-eight years and have seen a lot of health ideas come and go"?

Of course, when public health is on the line, the answers are clear. We brook no opposition, tolerate no insubordination, and do not ask if our decisions are popular. We are, after all, charged with improving the public health, and what could be more important? That is precisely the question. Is your educating mission as compelling as that of your local health inspector? Are you convinced that the children who fail in your system face a lifetime of health risks as surely as if they drink unsafe water or eat in a foul restaurant?

The evidence is clear that your job is this important, and more so. People can recover from food poisoning, but recovering from the neglect of an educational system that fails to implement adequate standards may not be possible. In the few years that we have children, we shape a lifetime of opportunity or a lifetime of consequences. When I wrote the first edition of *Making Standards Work* several years ago, these words closed the volume; they are as appropriate today as the day I wrote them by the light of the setting sun in rural China:

> In some cases, the opposition to standards is based on misunderstanding and misinformation. That opposition can be dealt with by effective communication and patient dialogue. But there are also times when the differences between the advocates and opponents of standards cannot be dealt with by explanation, persuasion, or compromise. The differences are deep, personal, and sometimes bitter. Examples of these objections:
>
> • "What do you mean, 'All children can learn'? That's a bunch of malarkey. I've been around kids for thirty years, and some of 'em just can't do it. Why can't you just admit that?"
>
> • "Standards are just another way for the feds to get their hands in education. They are taking away local control and anything to do with standards is simply one more denial of my rights as a parent."
>
> • "Standards, schmandards. It's just one more piece of paper on the principal's desk, and I'm doing twelve hours a day of paperwork for the district already."

- "Standards are just a politically correct method of bringing every kid down to the lowest common denominator because educational bureaucrats won't admit that some kids are always going to do better than other kids. My kids have always been above average, and you just can't stand the idea that white kids have higher math scores, so you invented standards to prove that everybody's 'equal' even when common sense tells you that's hogwash."

- "Just leave me alone and let me teach. I didn't get into this profession to have some state legislator trying to tell me what to do in my classroom."

I could go on, but you get the idea. These are comments reflecting a fundamentally different value system than that held by the leaders of districts that are committed to standards. However sincerely held, deeply felt, and articulately presented, these comments are emphatically wrong. There are times when leaders need to confront the advocates of such positions and make the case for standards.

When faced with comments such as those above, the effective leader (who already has made many other attempts at communication and persuasion) does not say, "Gee, Mr. Jones, maybe you have a point there. Let's study the matter some more." The effective leader confronts the issue directly. This confrontation does not take place with the oratorical flair of a Daniel Webster or the plaintive plea of a James Stewart.

A better model for delivering a proper response is the late Barbara Jordan, the member of Congress who first came to national attention as a member of the House Judiciary Committee during the impeachment hearings of President Richard Nixon. Unlike many of her colleagues, Jordan did not engage in hyperbole or appeals to emotionalism. She spoke in even, measured tones that said, with every syllable, "This is serious business, and these words are not rhetoric but fact." Were Barbara Jordan a school superintendent faced with challenges such as those above, she would have first tried reason and discussion. When that failed, however, I think she would have said something like this:

> There are times when both sides of an issue have merit, but this is not one of them. This district has some fundamental beliefs that are bone deep. If this were thirty years ago, and the comment was made that black and white children just can't learn together in the same school, I would not temporize, but I would say that such a comment was wrong and was contrary to my beliefs and the beliefs of this district. That is the case now.
>
> You say, "Not all children can learn." You are wrong. Our jobs as educators have never been simply to help the students who are the best and brightest, but to reach out to every single child in the school and ensure they have the chance to prove to themselves they can do things that, a short while ago, they would have sworn they could not do.
>
> You say that standards are the result of intrusion from the federal government. You are wrong. These standards were developed by people in our community, including your neighbors, colleagues, and friends. The standards are the expectations of our community about what our children must know and be able to do to be productive citizens and participate fully in our democratic society.
>
> You say that you have too much to do to implement standards. You are wrong. You have too much to do because you have not defined what the primary focus of your school should be, and standards will help you to do that. If you cannot manage your priorities in order to start implementing standards, then I will find someone who will.
>
> You dismiss the belief that all children can achieve as a "politically correct" idea and suggest that only certain students, usually the white upper class, are the only ones who can really compete. You are wrong. Any district of which I am the leader is committed to the principle that every child can excel, and that those who have done well in the past can do even better. The test scores your children have achieved in the past, or the scores their parents and

grandparents achieved, don't cut much ice with me. In fact, we have had too many children with good test scores who cannot meet our standards, but their test scores have confirmed in their mind and yours that they are doing well. I am here to tell you that they are not doing well. If they cannot meet our standards, then they are not satisfactory. And if I were you, I would go home and tell your "above average" child to get busy.

You say, "Just leave me alone and let me teach." You are wrong. Ours is an inherently collaborative profession. We need each other. When you close the door on our requirements for academic standards, you close the door on fairness, opportunity, and achievement. I will not allow those doors to be closed in this district.

I do not know if a superintendent or board president will ever deliver this speech, but I have dreamed it at least a hundred times. At the dawn of every great educational reform, the discussion eventually moves from conception to reality, and that is when the trouble starts. The leader of a standards-driven district is willing to tolerate a certain amount of this discomfort. If, after every attempt at conciliation and dialogue has failed, you deliver your version of this speech, I will be cheering for you.

Appendix
Leadership Tools, Checklists, and Forms

A note about reproducible forms: purchasers of this book are granted the authority to copy and use the forms in this Appendix for educational use within their school or district. This authority for reproduction is limited by the following stipulations:

- All forms must be reproduced in full, including the copyright notice and the stipulation that reproduction is limited for educational and noncommercial use.

- Reproduction is explicitly not authorized for commercial use, including resale of these forms or packaging of these forms into professional development handouts that are sold or marketed by any other entity, whether commercial, nonprofit, or educational.

Forms in This Appendix

A.1. Student Achievement Form

Achievement indicator: _____

Data source: _____

Date of administration: _____

Class	Indicator	Result (Percentage Proficient or Higher)

A.2. Educational Practice Form

Practice: _____

Data source: _____

Date: _____

Classroom	Indicator	Measurement (Frequency, Percentage, Etc.)

A.3. Leadership Practice Form

Leadership practice: _____

Data source: _____

Date: _____

School	Indicator	Measurement (Frequency, Percentage, Etc.)

A.4. Curriculum Practice Form

Practice: _____

Data source: _____

Date: _____

School or Classroom	Indicator	Measurement (Frequency, Percentage, Etc.)

A.5. Data Analysis: Ordered Pairs Linking Professional Practice to Student Achievement

Professional Practice	Measurement (Horizontal Axis)	Achievement Variable	Measurement (Vertical Axis)

A.6. Worksheet: Leadership and Learning Matrix Data

Antecedent of Excellence	Relationship to Student Achievement (R^2, Correlation Coefficient, or Other Indicator of Relationship Between Cause and Effect Variables)	Student Results Indicators	Percentage of Students Proficient or Higher, Using Scale of 0 to 100%

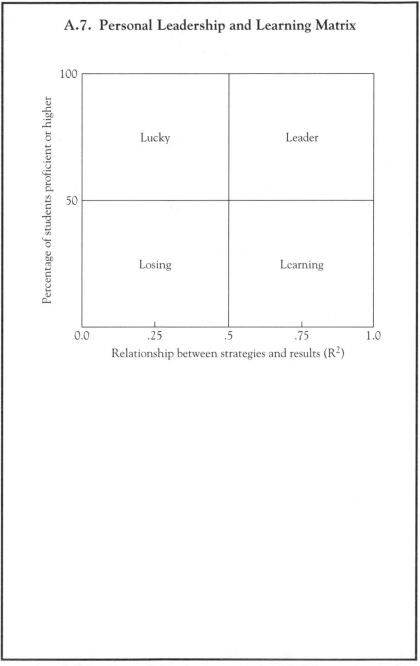

A.7. Personal Leadership and Learning Matrix

A.8. Professional Practice Inventory

☐ Frequency of writing assessment

☐ Frequency of collaborative scoring

☐ Percentage of agreement on scoring of anonymous student work

☐ Time required to reach 80 percent consensus in scoring

☐ Percentage of lessons integrating technology

☐ Percentage of non–language-arts lessons involving student writing with editing and rewriting

☐ Frequency of feedback to students that resulted in direct action by students based on that feedback

☐ Frequency of updates in student writing portfolio

☐ Frequency of updates in student reading assessment (Running Record or similar folder)

☐ Percentage of student portfolios in _____ (name of academic subject) receiving comparable evaluations by colleague or administrator

☐ _____

☐ _____

☐ _____

☐ _____

☐ _____

☐ _____

☐ _____

☐ _____

☐ _____

☐ _____

☐ _____

☐ _____

A.9. Leadership Practice Inventory

☐ Percentage of faculty meeting discussion and action items relating to student achievement

☐ Percentage of professional development activities directly related to classroom practice supporting student achievement

☐ Percentage of parents who agree or strongly agree with the statement, "I feel welcome to visit my child's classroom at any time."

☐ Frequency of recognition of teacher best practices

☐ Percentage of A-level tasks on daily prioritized task list directly related to improved student achievement

☐ Percentage of faculty members with student achievement practices in assessment, curriculum, and instruction at the "distinguished" level according to a collaboratively scored rubric of professional practices

☐ Percentage of available time by certified staff members devoted to student contact

☐ Percentage of students with identified academic deficiency who are rescheduled for additional assistance within thirty days of the identified need

☐ Percentage of leader-initiated parent contacts related to academic achievement

☐ _____

☐ _____

☐ _____

☐ _____

☐ _____

☐ _____

☐ _____

☐ _____

A.10. Curriculum Practice Inventory

☐ Percentage of students who are one or more grade levels below current grade in reading who receive targeted assistance

☐ Percentage of classrooms that allow multiple opportunities for student success

☐ Percentage of failing finals that were subject to resubmission and potential success

☐ Percentage of students participating in advanced classes

☐ Percentage of students participating in "preadvanced" classes

☐ Percentage of leader visits in which the actual activity corresponds to the planned activity

☐ Percentage of physical education classes incorporating academic content and assessment in writing, reading, mathematics, or science

☐ Percentage of music classes incorporating academic content and assessment in writing, reading, mathematics, or social studies

☐ Percentage of art classes incorporating academic content and assessment in writing, reading, mathematics, science, or social studies

☐ _____

☐ _____

☐ _____

☐ _____

☐ _____

☐ _____

☐ _____

☐ _____

☐ _____

☐ _____

A.11. Factors Influencing Student Achievement, Not Controllable by Leader

Factor	Student	Environment/ Family

Other

A.12. Factors Influencing Student Achievement, Subject to Influence by Leader

Factor	Teaching	Curriculum	Leadership

A.13. Parent Communication Checklist

Multiple channels of parent communication are available:

☐ Face-to-face meetings at school

☐ Personal meetings at nonschool locations, including

_____

☐ Incoming phone calls with personal response

☐ Incoming phone calls with voice mail

☐ School-initiated calls by teachers

☐ School-initiated calls by administrators

☐ School-initiated calls by other student advocates

☐ Internet-based communication

☐ E-mail initiated by parents

☐ E-mail initiated by school

☐ Other channels of communication:

☐ _____

☐ _____

☐ _____

☐ Student achievement results are communicated to parents with more information than letter grades.

☐ Student achievement results for students in danger of failure are communicated at least every week to parents.

☐ Student achievement results for students previously in danger of failure who are now demonstrating exceptional progress are communicated at least every week to parents.

☐ Teachers identify a watch list of students in danger of failure; a team approach, including parents, is used to monitor and improve student performance.

☐ Parents have multiple ways of becoming engaged in school support activities.

☐ More than 90 percent of students have a caring adult who is regularly involved in school support activities.

☐ Parents have the opportunity to participate in scoring student work using standards and scoring guides.

☐ Parent scoring of student work is comparable to teacher scoring of student work.

☐ Test information is sent to parents in a timely and understandable form.

☐ _____

☐ _____

☐ _____

☐ _____

☐ _____

☐ _____

A.14. Faculty Communication Checklist

☐ The primary method for faculty announcements is a written or e-mailed list, not a verbal announcement in a meeting or during classroom time.

☐ The focus of faculty communication in faculty meetings, grade-level meetings, and departmental meetings is achievement of a professional consensus on the meaning of *proficient* in student work.

☐ The degree of faculty consensus on student proficiency is regularly monitored and posted.

☐ If the level of faculty consensus is below 80 percent, special leadership attention is devoted to improving scoring guides, reducing ambiguity, and increasing clarity until the 80 percent consensus level is restored.

☐ Schedules are set in such a way that, even for final examinations, faculty members have time to collaboratively score student work, communicate with students, and allow students to respect faculty feedback as well as improve the quality of their own work.

☐ Faculty members are clearly and specifically authorized to change schedules and lesson plans to assist students in meeting the requirements of academic content standards.

☐ Faculty members are clearly and specifically authorized to reduce curriculum content to focus on the most important "power standards" and essential skills.

☐ Faculty members regularly share best practices, documenting specific successful practices. Aside from collaborative evaluation of real student work, this documentation and sharing of best practices is the dominant feature of faculty meetings and professional development sessions.

☐ Faculty members personally lead professional development sessions for this building and for other buildings.

☐ Faculty members routinely collaborate with staff from other buildings, including grade levels above and below their current grade level.

☐ The results of schoolwide and districtwide common end-of-course and end-of-grade level assessments are published, discussed, and used to inform future practice.

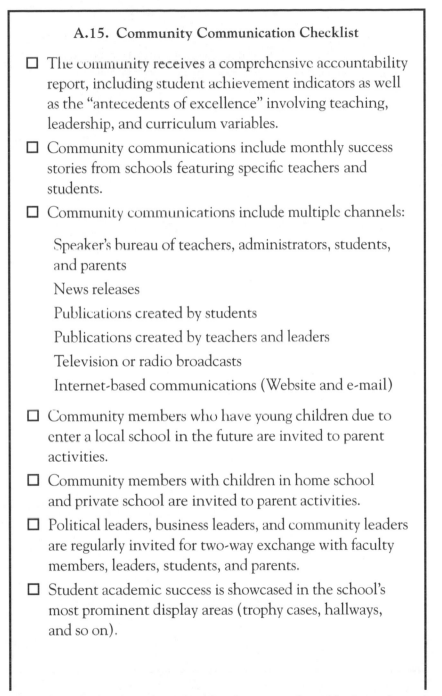

A.15. Community Communication Checklist

☐ The community receives a comprehensive accountability report, including student achievement indicators as well as the "antecedents of excellence" involving teaching, leadership, and curriculum variables.

☐ Community communications include monthly success stories from schools featuring specific teachers and students.

☐ Community communications include multiple channels:

Speaker's bureau of teachers, administrators, students, and parents

News releases

Publications created by students

Publications created by teachers and leaders

Television or radio broadcasts

Internet-based communications (Website and e-mail)

☐ Community members who have young children due to enter a local school in the future are invited to parent activities.

☐ Community members with children in home school and private school are invited to parent activities.

☐ Political leaders, business leaders, and community leaders are regularly invited for two-way exchange with faculty members, leaders, students, and parents.

☐ Student academic success is showcased in the school's most prominent display areas (trophy cases, hallways, and so on).

☐ The school recognizes student academic success with the same intensity with which the community recognizes athletic success.

☐ _____

☐ _____

☐ _____

☐ _____

☐ _____

☐ _____

A.16. Faculty Perceptions of Standards: Survey

Please respond to the following questions regarding your use of academic standards and your perception of standards. Your responses are anonymous, and no individually identifiable response will be published. Thank you for your participation.

Grade level(s) taught: _____ Subject(s) taught: _____

	Don't Know	Often	Sometimes	Rarely	Never
1. Daily lesson content is directly related to one or more state academic content standards.					
2. I refer to state standards in making decisions about classroom assessment and instruction.					
3. My evaluation of the academic performance of students is based on the quality of their work compared to the state standard of proficiency.					
4. I evaluate student work in collaboration with my colleagues at least once a month.					

(continued)

A.16. Faculty Perceptions of Standards: Survey *(continued)*

	Don't Know	Often	Sometimes	Rarely	Never
5. When I compare my evaluations of student work with my colleagues, 80 percent of our evaluations are the same.					
6. The great majority of my colleagues appear to base their lessons and assessments on the state academic content standards.					
7. In my conversation with parents regarding academic achievement, I regularly mention the state academic content standards.					

	Don't Know	Strongly Agree	Agree	Disagree	Strongly Disagree
8. More than 80 percent of my students are capable of creating assessments on the basis of state standards.					
9. More than 80 percent of my students are capable of evaluating.					
10. I prefer to use the normal curve in evaluating student work.					
11. If students receive a grade of C or higher in my class, they have met the requirements of the state academic content standards.					
12. If students receive a grade of B or higher in my class, they have met the requirements of the state academic content standards.					
13. If students receive a grade of A in my class, they have met the requirements of the state academic content standards.					

Short answer:

- Please identify any specific ways in which using academic standards has changed your approach to student assessment in the past year.

- Please identify any specific ways in which you need additional support for effective implementation of academic standards.

- What do you perceive as your colleagues' greatest need with respect to support for effective implementation of academic standards?

A.17. Power Standards Development Process

1. Identify all academic content standards for a specific grade level in a particular subject. Place them on a wall or other display so that the entire working group can easily read them and make appropriate notations.

2. Divide into three groups, with each group addressing one of these questions for each standard listed:

   Does the standard have *endurance*? That is, will the knowledge and skills to which this standard relates be used by students for several years after they use that standard in a single grade level?

   Does the standard have *leverage*? That is, will the knowledge and skills in this standard help students in other academic areas?

   Does the standard provide information that is essential for the next level of instruction? That is, do teachers in the next higher grade regard this standard as a *necessary* entry point for a student to enter that grade with success and confidence?

   Using markers in three colors, each group marks only those standards that meet its criterion.

3. Identify the standards that have all three colors marked, indicating that they have met all three criteria (endurance, leverage, and necessity) for the next grade, in this box:

4. Identify any additional standards that are essential but not listed in the original state standards document reviewed in step one. This may include standards in literacy, time management, organization, and behavior, as well as other standards that the working groups regard as essential.

A.18. Standards-Based Performance Assessment Development Checklist

☐ The assessment is clearly and directly related to specific state academic content standards.

☐ The assessment includes an engaging scenario that gains and holds student attention.

☐ The assessment includes a minimum of four tasks, with the entry-level task accessible to the vast majority of students, including inclusion students, in the classroom.

☐ For each task, there is a scoring guide (rubric) that clearly specifies performance levels.

☐ There is a sample of proficient or exemplary student work. It can be compared to the scoring guide so that an independent observer understands why it is proficient or exemplary.

☐ The specifications for proficient work are consistent with state expectations for student proficiency.

☐ The specifications for exemplary work are qualitatively different from proficient work, requiring extraordinary achievement by the student well beyond the proficient level of achievement.

☐ Sample student work can be scored by teachers who are unfamiliar with the assessment; there is an 80 percent or greater level of consistency between the scoring by the assessment creator and that done by outside teachers.

☐ The assessment shows evidence of revision on the basis of feedback from colleagues and students.

A.19. Classroom Checklist for Standards Implementation

☐ **Standards are highly visible in the classroom.** This need not imply every standard related to that grade level or subject, but it certainly must include the standards that are being addressed in the class during the current week. Students have a right to understand the expectations they are to meet, and teachers have a right to understand the parameters within which their instruction takes place. This serves not only to focus students and teachers but also as an antidote to administrators and policy makers who are sometimes tempted to suggest extras for the classroom. To put a fine point on it, school leaders must think twice before taking a good idea (such as character education) and transforming it into an additional curriculum in the school day. Teachers can reasonably ask, "Which standard on this wall shall I take down in order to make room for the new requirements?" The same is true for myriad curriculum requirements that, by themselves, seemed innocent but taken together form a mountain of time requirements for classroom instruction that inevitably compete with academic content standards. Examples commonly heard are the obvious ones of character education and drug, alcohol, and tobacco education, but also newly established mandatory curricula: sensitivity training, bully-proofing, diversity training, free enterprise education, sexual orientation tolerance training. There are a host of other items requiring curriculum documents, assemblies, and even assessments. When these ideas are implemented as part of a curriculum in critical thinking, social studies, or health education, that is one thing. If they have the practical impact of reducing the amount of reading and writing in a classroom and overall reducing the focus on achievement of academic standards, then leaders must confront the divergence between their principles (which are based on the value of fairness and the practice of standards-based education) and the reality of a fragmented day in which some students succeed, some fail, and teachers frantically bounce from one curriculum area to another like a pinball in a poorly leveled machine.

☐ **The standards are expressed in student-accessible language.** A few states, such as Illinois, have taken the time to express some of their standards in language that makes sense to students—and, for that matter, to parents not immersed in the jargon of standards. The work of most states, however, can be charitably described as the result of the effort of a very earnest committee. Membership in this committee typically excludes fourth graders, and as a result the wording of the standard not only eludes our students but also strikes their parents as obscure. The remedy for this problem is not to complain about standards, but to add value to the standards by restating them in language that is clear and accessible to all students. There is ample precedent for this. Teachers do not put the state criminal statutes on a poster at the front of the room, nor do they display the local board of education disciplinary code. Instead, they display the class rules, using language that students, parents, and teachers alike can understand. This should be the model for expressing standards and expectations for student academic proficiency.

☐ **Examples of proficient and exemplary student work are displayed throughout the classroom.** In some schools, this is called the "wall of fame," on which the work of present and former students is displayed. Some schools even use the trophy case for this purpose, making it clear to parents and visitors that student achievement is valued and that students in this school have already demonstrated success is possible. Some of these displays do not include student names; the purpose is not to elevate one student over another but rather to give a model to all students of what successful writing, mathematics, science, or social studies work looks like. Success in these schools is never a mystery. Displaying student work clearly links the standards to real student work. These displays have the added advantage of allowing school leaders to check that each classroom has the same level of quality expectation, and that expectations for student proficiency are always linked to the standard rather than to idiosyncratic judgment about a student.

☐ **For every assignment, the teacher publishes in advance the explicit expectations for proficient student work.** Although a full scoring guide may not always be necessary, it is absolutely essential that students enter every academic activity knowing in advance what success means. They need not guess, nor must they merely attempt to beat other students. They know precisely what is expected, whether through a rubric, checklist, or other document that clearly establishes the rules of the assignment.

☐ **Student evaluation is always done according to the standards and scoring guide, and never on the curve.** When I ask students, "How did you get that grade?" I frequently hear the honest reply, "I don't know." In a standards-based classroom, this is never the case. The rationale for grading is not the mysterious judgment of the teacher, but a reflection of a scoring guide that is based upon a clear set of standards.

☐ **The teacher can explain to any parent or other stake-holder the specific expectations of students for the year.** Parents must be able to ask, "What does my child need to know and be able to do in order to be successful this year?" They should receive an answer that is consistent and coherent. Although the initial impulse to reply "Work hard and follow directions" may be tempting, parents and students deserve more detail. In any activity outside of school, parents would expect a clear definition of success, and they deserve the same within the school. Leaders can profitably devote the first few faculty meetings of the year to role play in which the leader assumes the role of a parent and asks this question. Teachers and leaders can collaborate in crafting the best response to the query regarding what students must know and be able to do to succeed. The time to answer that question is at the beginning of the year, not when a controversy arises about a grade or curriculum decision.

☐ **The teacher has the flexibility to vary the length and quantity of curriculum content daily to ensure that students receive more time on the most essential subjects.** This criterion is counterintuitive to many teachers and leaders, particularly if they have assumed that implementing academic standards implies standardizing teaching practice. In fact, an integral part of successful standards implementation is greater flexibility for teachers. Because student needs vary from one classroom to the next, the greatest need is flexibility in timing and emphasis, provided that this does not lead to flexibility in expectations. Therefore, administrators should devote more attention to classroom assessment and teacher expectations, not to whether each teacher is delivering the same lesson at the same time on the same day.

☐ **Students can spontaneously explain what** *proficiency* **means for any assignment.** Larry Lezotte asks the question well when he inquires, "What are you learning about today, and how do you know if you are learning it?" If students are unsure or hesitant, it may be time to allow them to play a greater role in restating standards and creating scoring guides. My experience suggests that if students have the opportunity to create expectations, the requirements are clearer and more rigorous than if the job of articulating requirements is left exclusively in the hands of adults.

☐ **Commonly used standards, such as those for written expression, are reinforced in every subject.** In other words, spelling, capitalization, and grammar always count. When teaching mathematics, whether to elementary students or graduate students, I begin the semester by explaining: "Mathematics is about describing the universe using numbers, symbols, and words. We will use all three this semester, and all three are important enough that we will express them correctly." Symbols, including inequalities, exponential notation, periods, and commas, are important. Words and letters, whether in an algebraic equation or an English sentence, are important. The same emphasis on clarity of expression applies to science, social studies, physical education, and music. There is, in other words, no class in any school in which English expression is unimportant or in which thinking, reasoning, and communicating are extraneous.

☐ **The teacher has created at least one standards-based performance assessment in the past month.** Training teachers in standards and standards-based assessment is not enough. The real question is whether the training is being used in the classroom. With respect to the issue of determining whether standards are really in use, the question is not whether the teacher likes standards or had a good attitude about the last training session. The only relevant question is whether an assessment the teacher creates and uses in the classroom is related to state academic standards.

☐ **The teacher exchanges student work with a colleague for review and collaborative evaluation at least once every two weeks.** Collaboration is the hallmark of effective implementation of standards. In fact, standards have never been implemented by virtue of a colorful wall chart from the state department of education. Standards have only been implemented successfully when professional educators and school leaders agree, through intensive and consistent collaborative effort, on what the word *proficient* really means.

☐ **The teacher provides feedback to students and parents about the quality of student work compared to the standards, and not compared to that of other students.** School leaders are called on to deal with this criterion when aggrieved parents notice that their child received the same score as another child, and the other child had to submit the assignment several times to be deemed proficient. "That's not fair," the parents assert. "Our child got the problem right the first time, and that child only got the problem right after working hard, respecting teacher feedback, meeting the standard, and resubmitting the work. That just can't be fair!" Leaders must support teachers in two clear rejoinders to this complaint. First, in a standards-based school, teachers never compare the work of one student to that of another student. "I'll devote an entire hour to comparing your child's work to a standard," the teacher might say, "but I will not spend a single moment comparing your child's work to that of another child. That sort of discussion is out of bounds, and I won't do it." Second, the teacher might note that, "I am quite familiar with the academic standards of this state, and not a single one of them requires that our students complete proficiency quickly. In fact, not a single standard refers to speed, but all of them refer to the quality of work. Therefore, I evaluate student work on the basis of the standards and the quality of work, never in comparison of one student to another."

☐ **The teacher helps to build community consensus in the classroom and with other stakeholders for standards and high expectations of all students.** National polling data make clear that the teacher is a trusted purveyor of information, particularly about educational policy. Voters trust teachers more than they trust board members, state policy makers, or school administrators. Therefore, teachers bear particular responsibility for carrying the message of the fairness and effectiveness of academic standards. Effective leaders give teachers the tools, time, and opportunity to practice effective communication with the community at large. Role-playing dialogue with skeptical community stakeholders is an excellent practice for a faculty meeting or professional development seminar.

☐ **The teacher uses a variety of assessment techniques, including extended written response, in all disciplines.**

A.20. School Checklist for Standards Implementation

☐ Faculty meetings are routinely devoted to collaborative examination of real student work compared to academic standards.

☐ There are schoolwide assessments administered to every student in the same class (secondary) or grade (elementary) at periodic intervals.

☐ Professional development is based on an analysis of teacher familiarity with and application of essential skills in standards-based instruction (see checklist A-22).

☐ Student performance in key standards is posted monthly or quarterly, with the "percentage proficient or higher" tracked during the year.

☐ Eighty percent or more of the faculty agree on the standards-based scoring of an anonymous piece of student work.

☐ The principal personally participates in evaluating student work at least once a week.

☐ Students who do not meet academic standards receive immediate and decisive intervention, including mandatory tutoring and schedule adjustments.

☐ A review of the agenda and minutes of faculty meetings, grade-level meetings, and department meetings reveals an overwhelming focus (90 percent or more of agenda items and time) on academic achievement and collaborative scoring of student work.

☐ Faculty meetings are held jointly with other schools at least once a quarter to ensure that there are comparable expectations for student achievement.

☐ Teachers evaluate student achievement on the basis of performance compared to standards and not on the normal curve, any comparison to other students, or average performance during the grading period.

☐ The grading reporting system allows teachers to give a narrative explanation for student work, including alternative explanation for letter grades.

☐ Analysis of data—including test data, classroom assessments, and professional practices in teaching, curriculum, and leadership—are regularly reviewed. The building leader can readily articulate specific changes made since the previous semester that are directly related to this data analysis.

☐ The building leadership regularly identifies best practices, documenting in detail successful practice in teaching, curriculum, and leadership, and sharing it with all faculty members.

☐ The building leadership conducts a "weed the garden" exercise at least once a semester and can identify initiatives and activities that have been dropped in the past six months.

☐ The school analyzes data at the level of classroom and building to analyze the relationship between teaching, curriculum, and leadership indicators and student results. These results are analyzed on the Leadership and Learning Matrix; the most effective practices are shared with all faculty members.

☐ School goals are obvious, regularly measured, and understood by faculty and students. List school goals here and note evidence of regular measurement:

A.21. District Checklist for Standards Implementation

☐ The district curriculum clearly reflects state academic content standards and adds value to those standards through prioritization and focus.

☐ The district has gathered consensus from every building on the standards for each grade that are essential for the next level of instruction. The consensus power standards have been shared throughout the district.

☐ The district regularly identifies and shares best practices in standards-based teaching, assessment, and curriculum.

☐ The district regularly conducts a weed-the-garden exercise and can identify specific initiatives and activities that have been dropped in the past six months.

☐ The district monitors information requests and other requirements from the central office to classrooms and buildings and reports to the superintendent monthly the nature of those information requests and other requirements and their relationship to student achievement.

☐ The district accountability plan includes not only test scores but also building and classroom-based practices in teaching, curriculum, and leadership.

☐ The district regularly identifies the relationship between effective practice and student results using the Leadership and Learning Matrix.

☐ The board has established standards for its own conduct, including standards regarding communication with faculty members and information requests from buildings, classrooms, and central office departments.

A.22. Professional Development Self-Evaluation Scoring Guide

Instructions: Please evaluate your own proficiency in these essential areas. Your responses will be used for planning and approving professional development in the next year to ensure that we focus our resources and time in the most appropriate areas and also to make sure we respect and capitalize on the strengths in our own faculty.

	4: "I am willing to lead a professional development seminar on this subject."	3: "I routinely apply this in the classroom but am not ready to lead a professional development seminar about it."	2: "I am aware of this subject but do not routinely use it in the classroom."	1: "I am not familiar with this subject and do not use it in the classroom."
Academic content standards to guide instruction and learning				
Standards-based performance assessments				
Standards-based reporting to parents as supplement to report card				

	4: "I am willing to lead a professional development seminar on this subject."	3: "I routinely apply this in the classroom but am not ready to lead a professional development seminar about it."	2: "I am aware of this subject but do not routinely use it in the classroom."	1: "I am not familiar with this subject and do not use it in the classroom."
Scoring guide (rubric) for almost every assignment				
State standards restated in student-accessible language				
Collaborative scoring of real student work on the basis of comparing student work to academic standards				
Review of curriculum and textbooks to ensure focus on the most important standards				

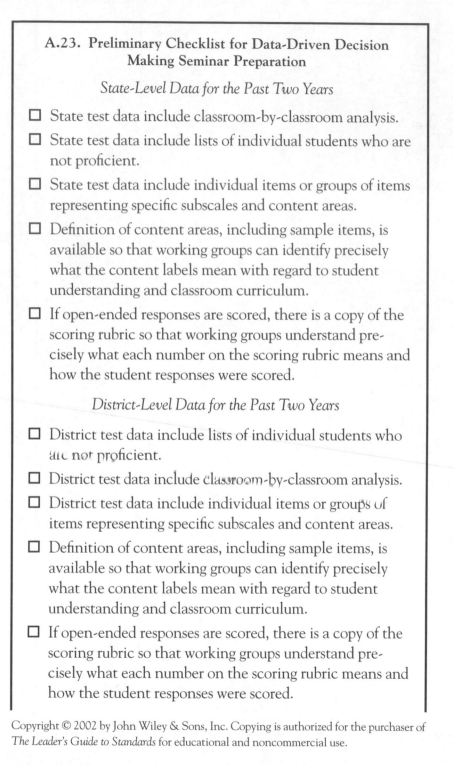

A.23. Preliminary Checklist for Data-Driven Decision Making Seminar Preparation

State-Level Data for the Past Two Years

☐ State test data include classroom-by-classroom analysis.

☐ State test data include lists of individual students who are not proficient.

☐ State test data include individual items or groups of items representing specific subscales and content areas.

☐ Definition of content areas, including sample items, is available so that working groups can identify precisely what the content labels mean with regard to student understanding and classroom curriculum.

☐ If open-ended responses are scored, there is a copy of the scoring rubric so that working groups understand precisely what each number on the scoring rubric means and how the student responses were scored.

District-Level Data for the Past Two Years

☐ District test data include lists of individual students who are not proficient.

☐ District test data include classroom-by-classroom analysis.

☐ District test data include individual items or groups of items representing specific subscales and content areas.

☐ Definition of content areas, including sample items, is available so that working groups can identify precisely what the content labels mean with regard to student understanding and classroom curriculum.

☐ If open-ended responses are scored, there is a copy of the scoring rubric so that working groups understand precisely what each number on the scoring rubric means and how the student responses were scored.

Teaching, Curriculum, and Leadership Practice

☐ Classroom-by-classroom analysis of specific teaching and curriculum practices is available, tracked quarterly or monthly.

☐ Leaders have specific indicators of leadership performance, tracked quarterly or monthly.

☐ Curriculum participation, interventions, and other program data are available classroom by classroom or by individual student.

☐ Other logistical and data requirements for the data-driven decision-making seminars:

A.24. Data-Driven Decision Making:
Sample Completed Action Plan

Content Area

Math

Subscales

Measurement, problem solving, and reasoning; communication, number, data, etc.

Goal

The percentage of students who will be at or above proficient in mathematics, as measured by the state math test, will increase from 42 percent last year to 60 percent next year, 80 percent the following year, and 100 percent the year after that.

Subgoal

The percentage of students who will be at or above proficient in mathematics problem solving will increase from 32 percent last year to 50 percent next year, 75 percent the following year, and 100 percent the year after that.

Strategies to Achieve Goal or Subgoal

- Monthly math problem-solving assessment for each grade level common throughout the district. Each month faculty and leaders will discuss results and make curriculum adjustments to provide additional emphasis where necessary
- Integration of specific math problem-solving skills, including graphing and measurement, into PE, art, social studies, science, technology, and music classes

- Celebration of 100 percent proficiency classrooms
- Documentation of successful teaching strategies associated with 100 percent proficiency
- Development of adaptations and accommodations for math problem-solving for IEP students
- Problem solving across curriculum
- Explain math process to reach solution in writing
- Teacher modeling of strategy

Best Strategy (Identified from List and Expanded)

Explain math process in writing through problem-of-the-week and scored with rubric to determine student proficiency for both math content and math communication

Results Indicator (How We Will Know That Strategy Worked)

Increase number of students achieving 3.0 or higher on bimonthly problem-solving assessments (rubric scale from 1.0 to 5.0, with halfway-in-between rubric score points)

Action Plan with Scheduled Events Relative to Goal

This includes what teachers will do, what teachers will use to assess, and when teachers will report results—this needs to be calendared for accountability and effectiveness

Action Plan Events (Dates to Be Added for Each Listed Event)

- Conduct staff development to explain goal
- Show examples of finished problem-solving products with scoring guides

- Schedule the classroom and school reporting assessment schedule
- Discuss goal with students, and introduce sample problem-solving write-ups and scoring guides to be used to assess math and communication
- Model process for students
- Lead students through guided practice
- Students practice problem solving independently
- Assess student work with scoring guides (math and communication)
- Conduct scheduled problem-solving assessment
- Score student papers; report and chart results at staff meeting
- Celebrate incremental movement
- Revisit strategy
- Talk and reflect on what worked and what didn't
- Make needed revisions; modify action plan if necessary
- Implement next phase of strategy in classrooms

A.25. Data-Driven Decision Making: "Treasure Hunt"

Purpose

To review the test, attendance, grade, and demographic data from your own school to gain insight about the strengths and weaknesses of your teaching and learning programs.

Rationale

School decision makers need a deliberate process to guide them through examining and analyzing data. Without this, they may be apt to substitute strongly held opinion for a fact-based conclusion that would be derived from reviewing the actual data.

Find the Data

- Use whatever graphic organizer works best for you to get an overall picture of your school's data.
- One suggestion: Make a simple graph or table to gather information by topics listed across the top (reading scores, math scores, writing scores, free or reduced-cost lunch, LEP [limited English proficiency] students, Title I, special ed, attendance, etc.)
- List down the side the categories you want to examine (by grade level, individual teacher, all students in school, gender, etc.)
- Hunt for the data and record it on your graph
- Disaggregate data when necessary

Data Organizer

School: _____ Categories: _____

Leadership team: _____

Data source(s): _____ Topics: _____

Date this form completed: _____

Enter Percentage of Students Proficient or Higher

Grade Levels or Subgroups	Content Year	Content Year	Content Year	Content Year	Content Year	Content Year

Instructions: From the data that you have available, complete this chart to get a snapshot of the data from your school.

Data Review Questions

Test Scores

1. What trends, strengths, and areas of concern do you notice in your test data?

2. What content areas show significantly lower or higher results than the others?

3. What percentage of students are meeting state and/or national standards? How has this changed from the previous year?

4. Do gaps in student performance appear to be present between groups according to gender, ethnicity, or socioeconomic status?

5. What specific strategies appear to be working? For example, math scores have improved because of the emphasis our school has placed on real-world application relevant to student use and on problem-solving skills.

6. What comparison can you make among content areas? For example, if there is a weakness in reading and writing, how does this affect other content areas?

Other Relevant Data

Attendance

- What patterns of absence (excused, unexcused) and tardiness appear to affect student performance (number, day of week or month)?

- What impact may classroom instructional methods have on attendance? Are a variety of instructional methods used to meet diverse learning styles? Is instruction linked to real-life applications and situations?

Retention

- What trends or patterns do you notice in the performance of students who have been retained?
- What implications may this have?

Dropout Rate

- What are the trends in the number and age of dropouts at the school level? At the district level?
- What reason do students give for dropping out of school?
- How effective have alternative programs for students been in improving attendance and achievement?

Student Discipline

- What types of discipline and discipline referral have shown a steady increase or decrease? What patterns appear to exist by grade, teacher, day of week, and so forth?
- What trends appear to exist in discipline referral for one group over another (male or female, race, low-income or not, regular education or special education, certain grade levels, and so on)? Why for those groups?
- What types of training have been provided to staff on how to prevent discipline problems or methods for handling discipline problems?
- What do the data indicate about follow-up or lack of follow-up on discipline referrals? For example, if students are assigned to detention, is there a system for ensuring that the student attends? If the student does not attend, what further action is taken? What process is in place for repeat offenders?

Student Well-Being: Health

- Review your school information on immunization, screening, and other related areas.
- What health-related concerns or school-site health problems have been identified?

Nutrition

- Review your school food services data for children eligible for free or reduced-cost meals.
- What trends in nutrition-related concerns have been identified? What follow-up strategies are needed to address these concerns?

Instructional Support Programs

Review information available from school support programs. This may include (but is not limited to) self-studies; surveys; peer review; and school, district, and state monitoring reports for specific school support programs.

- Does the design of the program support student achievement and the school's teaching and learning goals?
- What future program focus is needed to improve student achievement?
- What trends are present that need to be addressed at the school level? The district level?

Textbooks and Instructional Materials

- On the basis of your identified curriculum needs, are additional instructional resources and materials required to assist with classroom instruction and student achievement?

- Is current funding adequate?
- What percentage of staff use their own money to purchase needed classroom materials?

Technology

- What access do teachers, students, and support staff have for:

  Computer use
  The Internet
  Electronic mail
  Appropriate software related to subject areas
  Video networking

- How is technology being used to enhance instruction?
- How are technology resources being used to support assessment practices?
- What types of training or professional development have been offered to students, teachers, and staff to enhance the use of technology? Is ongoing support provided?

Staff: Professional Development

- Are professional development topics related to student performance?
- How do you monitor implementation of professional development activities to determine if they have a direct positive impact on student learning?
- How are teachers selected to participate in professional development activity? Are all teachers participating in special areas, or only a few? Why?
- Are teachers given the opportunity to learn from their colleagues at the school level? At the district level?

- What type of follow-up activity is offered after each professional development opportunity to ensure successful implementation of the concepts learned?
- Are instructional assistants receiving appropriate and adequate professional development to help students learn at a higher level and support classroom instruction?
- How many new teachers do you have or expect to have? What are the training implications? Is a mentor teacher assigned?

Staff Attendance

- What trends are noticed in staff absence? How does this affect student performance?
- What methods are used to ensure that adequate lesson plans are made available to substitute teachers?

Staff Credentials

- Are any teachers teaching out of field? Do any teachers not have proper certification or training for the position in which they are assigned?
- On the basis of school test data, how do discrepancies in teacher certification or credentials appear to have affected student achievement in these areas?

Use of Instructional Time

- How does your school use time to address academic achievement? What barriers exist?
- How might changes in the school calendar or the daily or weekly schedule assist in improving student achievement?

Parent and Community Involvement

- What types of activity do parents regularly attend at school? Why do parents say they choose a particular activity?

- What types of parent support groups exist in the school? How many parents or community members usually attend these meetings? Are there trends in attendance over several years?

- What types of communication are sent home? How often? What efforts are made to ensure that communication is provided in the parents' native language? Are efforts made to communicate in both positive and negative situations? Are two-way communication links in place?

- How do home-and-school relations appear to be affecting student performance?

- What methods are used to encourage parents to read to their children and support school learning goals?

- Identify the top employment opportunities and businesses in your area. What collaborative efforts currently exist between these businesses and your school in preparing students for application of skills and future employment? How can this linkage be further developed or improved? What impact are these linkages having on student improvement?

- What efforts are being made to engage and communicate with all stakeholders in your community?

A.26. Data-Driven Decision Making: Analyzing the Data

You've finished the Treasure Hunt. Now it's time to take a deep breath, stretch, and *reflect* on what you've learned about your school data. As you proceed through these activities, refer to your handouts, including the notes from the presentation, and to the Treasure Hunt, to record your observations. Ask questions at any time.

- Identify content areas where improvement was made.
- Identify content areas where improvement is still needed.
- Identify areas of greatest potential growth.
- Identify student groups needing the most assistance.
- Review other relevant data (student attendance, free and reduced-cost lunch, etc.).
- Record your observations.
- General statements such as "Math scores are low" or "Fifth and eighth grade math scores are lowest" may not be specific enough information.
- Better statements might be:

    "Math achievement of students taking the bus is disproportionately low."

    "Reading achievement of high-mobility students is low."

- Look at two-year trends to note growth (or lack of it) over time.
- Total scores alone give enough information; look at related subscale scores for more insight.
- Note "subscale differentiation"—where are the same students alternately strong and weak?

Reflection

Review the Treasure Hunt. Did you learn something new by charting the data? List three facts that are new to you or that stand out more clearly than before.

1. _____

2. _____

3. _____

Cause(s) for Celebration

What content area(s) showed improvement? Announce them, and celebrate with staff!

1. _____

2. _____

3. _____

Area(s) of Concern

What do your collective data show for each major subject matter area? How do this year's data compare to last year's data? Refer to content clusters (subscales) as necessary to identify specific areas of need.

Templates

Note: By *subscale* we mean the components of a major subject. For example, in English language arts tests, subscales might be inference, summarization, vocabulary, and spelling. In mathematics, subscales might be computation, problem solving, measurement, and geometry. In writing, subscales might be organization, conventions, and other dimensions of writing.

School: _____ Class: _____ Year: _____
Subscale Analysis

Content	Subscale
Highest	Lowest
1.	
2.	
3.	

School: _____ Class: _____ Year: _____
Subscale Analysis

Content	Subscale
Highest	Lowest
1.	
2.	
3.	

School: _____ Class: _____ Year: _____
Subscale Analysis

Content	Subscale
Highest	Lowest
1.	
2.	
3.	

A.27. Data-Driven Decision Making: Draft Needs Analysis

Identify the areas in which your school's academic achievement needs improvement the most. Draft some statements reflecting your prioritized needs for subject area and student group in the lines below.

Templates

Content area: _____

Grade level: _____
Needs for improvement
1.
2.
3.

Content area: _____

Grade level: _____
Needs for improvement
1.
2.
3.

Content area: _____

Grade level: _____
Needs for improvement
1.
2.
3.

Content area: _____

Grade level: _____

Needs for improvement
1.
2.
3.

Content area: _____

Grade level: _____

Needs for improvement
1.
2.
3.

Content area: _____

Grade level: _____

Needs for improvement
1.
2.
3.

Content area: _____

Grade level: _____

Needs for improvement
1.
2.
3.

A.28. Data-Driven Decision Making: Establishing New Goals or Revising Existing Goals

Revise Goals So They Are S-M-A-R-T

- Specific
- Measurable
- Achievable
- Relevant
- Timely

What Goals Must Contain

- Targeted subject area, grade level, and student population
- Criterion or criteria to be achieved
- Measurement instrument to be used
- Expected change

Establishing New Goals

- Identify your most important objectives for student achievement on the basis of priority challenges your school team identified in your needs analysis (A.27).
- If the desired result is improved student performance in a particular subject area (as measured by the state test and key district assessments), what are the specific goals that will achieve that result?

Revising Existing Goals

- Review the goals currently included in your school improvement plan. On the basis of your needs analysis, should your goals remain the same, or must they be revised? If you choose to revise these goals today on the basis of the needs analysis, what will you change?

Consider Writing Subgoals

- Subgoals increase specificity within a particular content area.

Goals That Are Based on Needs Analysis

1. _____
   _____

2. _____
   _____

3. _____
   _____

Review these goals and improve them:

- Integrate technology into the classroom.
- Establish a parent outreach program.
- The number of students who meet or exceed standard on end-of-year or end-of-course assessments will increase by 5 percent.
- Eighty-five percent of sixth grade students will score at or above the proficient level on nonfiction writing, as measured by the district writing assessment.
- Develop strategies that promote character.
- The school will implement an assessment instrument to measure student growth on the research paper project.
- Promote problem-solving and critical-thinking skills across the curriculum.
- Revise the science curriculum to promote discovery and hands-on involvement.
- Throughout the year, students will increase their reading and writing skills.
- Three-fourths of the ninth grade students will score proficient or better on the end-of-course assessment for algebra.
- All students will have maximum opportunity to participate and succeed.

A.29A. Data-Driven Decision Making: Strategies to Support Specific Goals

To identify the strategies associated with your specific goals, use the "fishbone" diagram in this form to identify the various causes associated with the performance area of the goal. Then highlight those causes that can be influenced with specific strategies in teaching, curriculum, and leadership.

"Fishbone" Diagram (Sample)

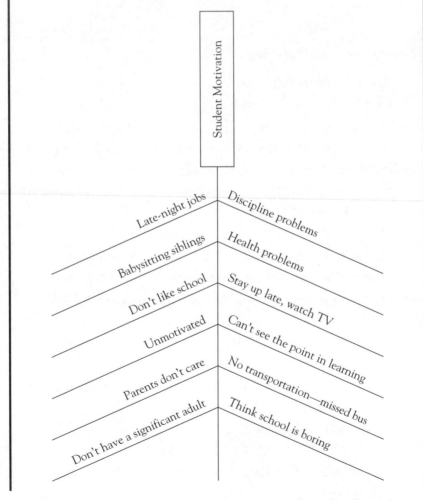

"Fishbone" Diagram

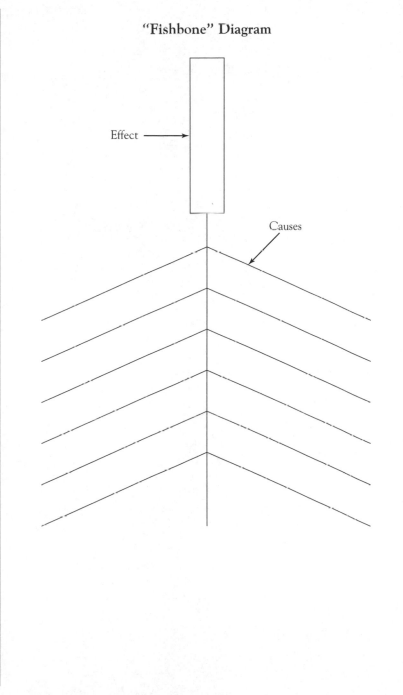

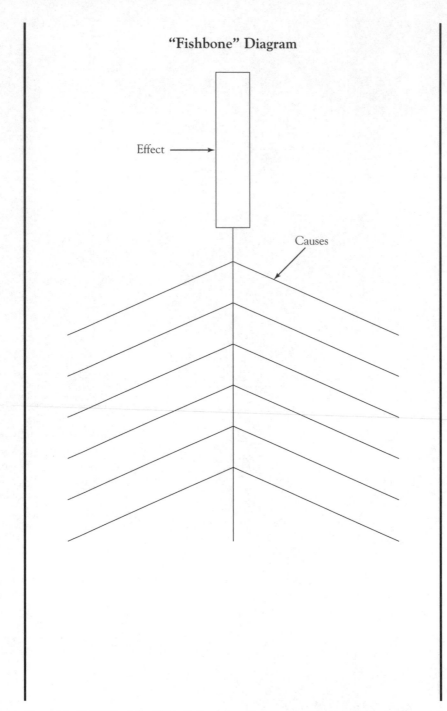

"Fishbone" Diagram

"Fishbone" Diagram

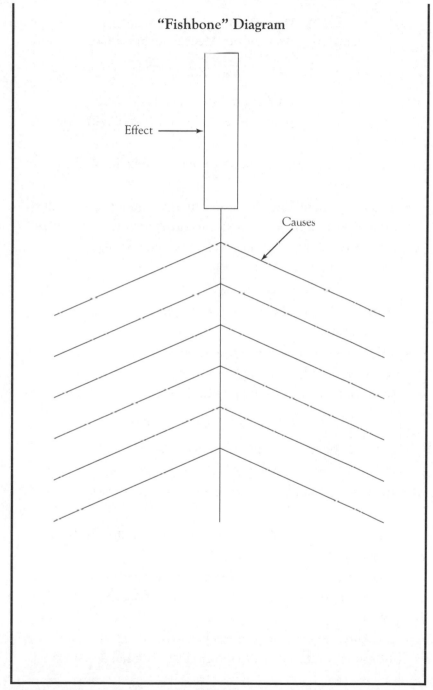

A.29B. Data-Driven Decision Making:
Identifying Strategies to Meet Prioritized Goals

Identifying Strategies

- For each goal, brainstorm the strategies that could be implemented to increase the likelihood of achieving the prioritized goal.
- Each strategy should be action-oriented, specific, and measurable.
- Strategies might include classroom assessment practice, classroom instruction, prioritizing the curriculum, resources, staff development opportunity, instructional flexibility, parental support, and program changes.
- List strategies in order of priority.
- Which previous strategies have been most successful in reaching student achievement goals?
- When developing a strategy to support the prioritized goal, consider also identifying practices or activities that can be stopped, to focus on implementing the most effective strategy.

Examples of Specific Strategies

- Increase the number of classrooms that successfully incorporate structured cooperative learning.
- Increase the number of teachers who use mastery learning techniques.
- Increase the amount of staff development that focuses on designing performance assessment.
- Increase the percentage of teachers who report that academic achievement is the most significant aspect of their school climate.
- Increase the percentage of teachers who use classroom assessment information to inform instructional decisions.

- Increase the percentage of teachers who use classroom assessment information to provide frequent feedback to their students regarding academic progress.
- Increase the number of grade levels or subject area curricula that have been prioritized.
- Increase the number of grade levels or subject areas that have complete curriculum class matrices to articulate the curriculum across grade levels and thereby eliminate areas of redundancy.
- Increase the number of writing performance assessments scored by building principal.
- Increase the number of strategies modeled during staff development opportunities that are incorporated into classroom practice.
- Increase the use of peer coaches for teachers in implementing new reading strategies.
- Increase implementation of best practices in math instruction at the classroom level.
- Increase the number of academic achievement charts posted in each building that include collecting classroom data monthly.
- Design and administer district quarterly assessments to assess proficiency on specific reading skills.
- Create and deliver workshops that afford structured instructional activity for parents to use at home with their children.
- Create and deliver a Parental Responsibility in Student Success workshop.
- Create and administer a district writing plan to assess student writing monthly, using a district scoring guide for writing.
- Create an opportunity for collegial scoring of student work and sharing classroom strategies that have been successful.
- Increase the number of classrooms that use monthly performance assessment.

- Increase the number of interdisciplinary writing assessments.
- Increase the percentage of art, music, and physical education classes that focus on writing, measurement, or problem solving.
- Increase the percentage of science, social studies, and math assessments that include requirements for student writing.

Identifying Successful Strategies

- What are the specific strategies that help achieve the prioritized goal?
- Brainstorm a list of potential strategies.
- Identify the one that seems most effective for achieving the goal.
- List other brainstormed strategies in descending order of potential effectiveness.

Goal:
Strategies:
1.
2.
3.
4.
5.
6.

Goal:

Strategies:

1.

2.

3.

4.

5.

6.

Goal:

Strategies:

1.

2.

3.

4.

5.

6.

A.30. Data-Driven Decision Making: Determining Results Indicators for Targeted Strategies

Determining Results Indicators

- What evidence (results indicators) can we gather regularly throughout the year to determine if the new strategies are proving effective in improving student performance?
- Each strategy includes one or more results indicators.
- Results indicators identify:

    Whether the strategy is actually being implemented

    If the strategy is having the intended effect on student learning and improved performance

Now, determine a results indicator for each of your targeted strategies.

Targeted strategy for:		
	Content:	*Subscale:*
Results indicator:		

Targeted strategy for:		
	Content:	*Subscale:*
Results indicator:		

Targeted strategy for:

| | Content: | Subscale: |

Results indicator:

Targeted strategy for:

| | Content: | Subscale: |

Results indicator:

Targeted strategy for:

| | Content: | Subscale: |

Results indicator:

Targeted strategy for:

| | Content: | Subscale: |

Results indicator:

A.31. Data-Driven Decision Making: Sample Action Steps and Schedule

Targeted Goal: Increase the percentage of students proficient or higher on state math tests.

Strategies (What Adults Will Do)	Results Indicator (Measurement Tool)	Persons Responsible, Resources, Start and End Dates
Integrate math problem solving in all subject areas	Percentage of instructional units in physical education, art, technology, social studies, science, and music and explicitly including instruction and assessment in math problem-solving. The results are posted monthly on the school data wall.	Building principal—September through June

Targeted Goal: Increase the percentage of students proficient or higher in reading comprehension.

Strategies (What Adults Will Do)	Results Indicator (Measurement Tool)	Persons Responsible, Resources, Start and End Dates
Weekly practice in summarizing nonfiction text in every class. Practice includes a "15+5" exercise in which students read material related to the class for fifteen minutes and then write a summary of the main idea and supporting details for five minutes. Teachers spot-check student proficiency.	Percentage of students proficient or higher on monthly reading comprehension assessment in which students must read a grade-level nonfiction reading selection in science or social studies, and then accurately summarize the main idea and supporting details of the reading passage. Results posted September through June.	Principal and all classroom teachers.

Targeted Goal		
Strategies (What Adults Will Do)	Results Indicator (Measurement Tool)	Persons Responsible, Resources, Start and End Dates

Targeted Goal		
Strategies (What Adults Will Do)	Results Indicator (Measurement Tool)	Persons Responsible, Resources, Start and End Dates

Targeted Goal		
Strategies (What Adults Will Do)	Results Indicator (Measurement Tool)	Persons Responsible, Resources, Start and End Dates

Targeted Goal		
Strategies (What Adults Will Do)	Results Indicator (Measurement Tool)	Persons Responsible, Resources, Start and End Dates

Action Plan to Meet Prioritized Goal

School:	Team members:

Goal:

Strategy:

Results indicator:

Person Responsible	Starting Date	Ending Date	Estimated Cost	Funding Source

Monitoring Implementation of Action Plan

School:	Person responsible:	Date:	Report to be completed by:

Goal:

Targeted strategy:

Has this strategy been implemented?	Has this activity had impact?
_____ Not implemented _____ Partially implemented _____ Implemented fully Reasons implementation was incomplete or did not occur:	_____ Yes _____ No If yes, quantify the impact: _____ Reasons expected impact did or did not occur:
Evidence of actual impact on instructional practice or student learning:	Suggested adjustments or recommendations:
Reflections:	

A.32. Master Task List

Instructions: Use this form to start your time management system. Using as many pages as you need, list every task that is now pending for you. Because you are using a single comprehensive system, include all tasks related to family obligations, professional requirements, community service, and others from any list that you keep. The start of your journey to effective time management is use of a single list for all tasks. Prioritize each task using these codes:

A = Must be done by you and only you

B = Should be done by you, but will give way to A-level tasks

C = Request to be done by you, but can be delayed or delegated to others

Name: _____ Date: _____

Page _____ of _____ pages

Task	Priority (A, B, C)	Date Originated

A.33. Daily Prioritized Task List

Note: Create a new prioritized task list every day. Throughout the day, add to it any new requests for your time. If you have more than six A priorities for today, then you must either defer some of the A-level tasks or change some to B-level priority.

Name: _____   Date: _____

Page _____ of _____ pages

Task	Priority (A, B, C)	Date Originated

A.34. Project Task List

Instructions: Projects must be broken down into manageable tasks. Any task that takes more than the time allowed for a single uninterrupted work session must be broken down into several tasks. In general, if a task takes more than three hours to complete, it is not a task but a project.

Project name: _____ Start date: _____

Task	Person Responsible	Start Date	Deadline

References

Anderson, G. "Achieving Excellence and Equity in Education: An Integrated Approach to Improving Student Achievement." Houston: APQC Education Initiative, 2001.

Barth, R. S. *Improving Schools from Within: Teacher, Parents, and Principals Can Make the Difference*. San Francisco: Jossey-Bass, 1990.

Benfari, R. C. *Understanding and Changing Your Management Style*. San Francisco: Jossey-Bass, 1999.

Buckingham, M., and Coffman, C. *First, Break All the Rules: What the World's Greatest Managers Do Differently*. New York: Simon & Schuster, 1999.

Buckingham, M., and Coffman, C. *Now, Discover Your Strengths*. New York: Simon & Schuster, 2001.

Capella, E., and Weinstein, R. S. "Turning Around Reading Achievement: Predictors of High School Students' Academic Resilience." *Journal of Educational Psychology*, 2001, 93(4), 758–771.

Christensen, D. "Building State Assessment from the Classroom up." *School Administrator*, 2001, 58(11), 27–31.

Collins, J. *Good to Great: Why Some Companies Make the Leap . . . and Others Don't*. New York: HarperBusiness, 2001.

Csikszentmihalyi, M. *Flow: The Psychology of Optimal Experience*. New York: HarperCollins:, 1990.

Danielson, C. *Teaching Evaluation*. Alexandria, Va.: Association for Supervision and Curriculum Development, 2002.

Darling-Hammond, L., and Sykes, G. (eds.) *Teaching as the Learning Profession: Handbook of Policy and Practice*. San Francisco: Jossey-Bass, 1999.

Education Commission of the States. "State Governance Structures Legislation, 2002." Apr. 12, 2002. (www.ecs.org/clearinghouse/33/28/3328.doc)

Elmore, R. "Building a New Structure for School Leadership" (monograph). Washington, D.C.: Albert Shanker Institute, 2000.

Friedman, L. (ed.). *Argument: The Complete Oral Argument Before the Supreme Court in Brown v. Board of Education of Topeka, 1952–55*. New York: Chelsea House, 1969.

Garvin, D. A. *Learning in Action: A Guide to Putting the Learning Organization to Work*. Boston: Harvard Business School Press, 2000.

Gemberling, K. W., Smith, C. W., and Villani, J. S. *The Key Work of School Boards Guidebook*. Alexandria, Va.: National School Boards Association, 2000.

General Accounting Office. "Report to the Secretary of Education: Title I, Education Needs to Monitor State's Scoring of Assessments." Washington, D.C.: General Accounting Office, Apr. 2002.

Goleman, D. *Working with Emotional Intelligence*. New York: Bantam, 1998.

Goleman, D. *Primal Leadership*. Boston: Harvard Business School Press, 2002.

Guskey, T. *Evaluating Professional Development*. Thousand Oaks, Calif.: Corwin, 2000.

Guskey, T., and Bailey, J. *Grading and Reporting for Student Achievement*. Thousand Oaks, Calif.: Corwin, 1999.

Hammer, M. *The Agenda: What Every Business Must Do to Dominate the Decade*. New York: Crown Business, 2001.

Haycock, K. "Good Teaching Matters: How Well-Qualified Teachers Can Close the Gap." *Thinking K–16*, Summer 1998, pp. 1–16.

Haycock, K., and others (eds.). *Dispelling the Myth: High Poverty Schools Exceeding Expectations*. Washington, D.C.: Education Trust, 1999.

Heifetz, R. A., and Linsky, M. *Leadership on the Line: Staying Alive Through the Dangers of Leading*. Boston: Harvard Business School Press, 2002.

Herrnstein, R. J., and Murray, C. *The Bell Curve: Intelligence and Class Structure in American Life*. New York: Free Press, 1994.

Hill, P. T., and Harvey, J. R. "Superintendents' 'Coach Speak.'" *Education Week*, 2002, *21*(30), 34, 48.

Hirsch, E. D., Jr. *The Schools We Need and Why We Don't Have Them*. New York: Doubleday, 1996.

Holloway, J. H. "Setting Standards for the School Superintendent." *Educational Leadership*, 2001, *58*(5).

Holloway, L. "Increasingly, the Principal Is a Newcomer." New York Times, Oct. 2, 2001. (http://query.nytimes.com/search/restricted/articleres=FB0A15F939590C718CDDA90994D9404482)

Kaplan, R. S., and Norton, D. P. *The Strategy-Focused Organization: How Balanced Scorecard Companies Thrive in the New Business Environment*. Boston: Harvard Business School Press, 2001.

Kohn, A. *The Schools Our Children Deserve: Moving Beyond Traditional Classrooms and "Tougher Standards."* Boston: Houghton-Mifflin, 1999.

Lawrence, C. E. *The Marginal Teacher: A Step-by-Step Guide for Fair Procedures for Identification and Dismissal* (2nd ed.). Thousand Oaks, Calif.: Corwin, 2001.

Leeman, N. *The Big Test: The Secret History of the American Meritocracy*. New York: Farrar, Strauss and Giroux, 1999.

Marzano, R. J., Kendall, J. S., and Cicchinelli, L. F. What Americans Believe Students Should Know: A Survey of U.S. Adults. Aurora, Colorado: Mid-continent Regional Education Laboratory, 1998.

National Staff Development Council. Standards for Staff Development. (Rev. ed.) Oxford, Ohio: National Staff Development Council, 2001.

Ohanian, S. One Size Fits Few: The Folly of Educational Standards. Portsmouth, N.H.: Heinemann, 1999.

Peters, T. J., and Waterman, R. H., Jr. In Search of Excellence: Lessons from America's Best-Run Companies. New York: Random House, 1982.

Pfeffer, J., and Sutton, R. I. The Knowing-Doing Gap: How Smart Companies Turn Knowledge Into Action. Boston: Harvard Business School Press, 2000.

Popham, W. J. Testing! Testing! What Every Parent Should Know About School Tests. Boston: Allyn and Bacon, 2000.

Putnam, R. D. Bowling Alone: The Collapse and Revival of American Community. New York: Simon & Schuster, 2000.

Ravitch, D. Left Back: A Century of Failed School Reforms. New York: Simon & Schuster, 2000.

Ravitch, D. "Real Test of Exams Is What Parents Say." Sacramento Bee, Feb. 20, 2001, p. B7.

Reeves, D. B. Accountability in Action: A Blueprint for Learning Organizations. Denver: Advanced Learning Press, 2000a.

Reeves, D. B. "Standards Are Not Enough: Essential Transformations for Successful Schools." NASSP Bulletin, 2000b, 84(620), 5–13.

Reeves, D. B. Crusade in the Classroom: How George W. Bush's Education Reforms Will Affect Your Children, Our Schools. New York: Simon & Schuster, 2001a.

Reeves, D. B. "If You Hate Standards, Learn to Love the Bell Curve." Education Week, June 11, 2001b, p. 48.

Reeves, D. B. Twenty-Minute Learning Connection: A Practical Guide for Parents Who Want to Help Their Children Succeed in School. New York: Simon & Schuster, 2001c.

Reeves, D. B. The Daily Disciplines of Leadership. San Francisco: Jossey-Bass, 2002a.

Reeves, D. B. Holistic Accountability: Serving Students, Schools, and Community. Thousand Oaks, Calif.: Corwin, 2002b.

Reeves, D. B. Making Standards Work: How to Implement Standards-Based Performance Assessments in the Classroom, School, and District. (3rd ed.) Denver: Advanced Learning Press, 2002c.

Schmoker, M. Results: The Key to Continuous Improvement. Alexandria, Va.: Association for Supervision and Curriculum Development, 1996.

Schmoker, M. The Results Fieldbook: Practical Strategies from Dramatically Improved Schools. Alexandria, Va.: Association for Supervision and Curriculum Development, 2001.

Senge, P. M. *The Fifth Discipline: The Art and Practice of the Learning Organization.* New York: Doubleday, 1990.

Senge, P. M., and others. *The Dance of Change: The Challenges to Sustaining Momentum in Learning Organizations.* New York: Doubleday, 1999.

Sergiovanni, T. *The Lifeworld of Leadership: Creating Culture, Community, and Personal Meaning in Our Schools.* San Francisco: Jossey-Bass, 2000.

Sorcher, M., and Brant, J. "Are You Picking the Right Leaders?" *Harvard Business Review,* Feb. 2002, pp. 78–85.

Stricherz, M. "Groups Pushing for Measures to Attract, Retain Principals." *Education Week,* July 11, 2001. (www.edweek.org/ew/ewstory.cfm?slug= 42principals.h20&keywords=Principal%20Shortage)

Tichy, N. M. *The Leadership Engine: How Winning Companies Build Leaders at Every Level.* New York: HarperCollins, 1997.

Walters, L. S. "Putting Cooperative Learning to the Test." Harvard Education Letter, 2000, *16*(3).

Wiggins, G. *Assessing Student Performance.* San Francisco: Jossey-Bass, 1995.

Wiggins, G. *Educative Assessment.* San Francisco: Jossey-Bass, 1997.

Wong, H., and Wong, R. *The First Days of School: How to Be an Effective Teacher.* Mountain View, Calif.: Harry K. Wong, 2001.

Ybarra, S. *DataWorks Assessment Newsletter,* 2000, *2*(2), 1.

Index